LIONESS

Beth Mead is a professional footballer playing for Arsenal WFC and the England Women's team. She was the top goal-scorer in the UEFA Women's Euro 2022, which saw England crowned champions - their first international trophy since the 1966 men's FIFA World Cup. She was also named Player of the Tournament, won England Women's Player of the Year and was nominated for the 2022 Ballon d'Or Féminin. Beth also won the BBC Sports Personality of the Year Award and the BBC Women's Footballer of the Year 2022. In February 2022 she launched the Beth Mead Scholarship with Teesside University to support students who have the potential to become professional female footballers.

LIONESS

My Journey to Glory

Beth Mead

SEVEN DIALS

First published in Great Britain in hardback in 2022,
this paperback edition published in 2024 by Seven Dials,
an imprint of The Orion Publishing Group Ltd
Carmelite House, 50 Victoria Embankment
London EC4Y 0DZ

An Hachette UK Company

3 5 7 9 10 8 6 4 2

A CIP catalogue record for this book is
available from the British Library.

ISBN (Mass Market Paperback) 978 1 2996 1168 8
ISBN (eBook) 978 1 3996 1169 5
ISBN (Audio) 978 1 3996 1170 1

Typeset by Born Group
Printed and bound in Great Britain by Clays Ltd, Elcograf S.p.A.

www.orionbooks.co.uk

To Mum, Dad and Ben

Who'd have thought?
I couldn't have done any of this without you

Contents

FOREWORD

For Beth Mead and the Lionesses, lifting a European trophy at Wembley wasn't a dream come true – because they never thought it would be possible.

They come from a generation of girls that had to search for football, a generation that was stopped from playing with boys at a certain age, and which was bullied and told girls shouldn't play football. But they ended up achieving something that was beyond any of their wildest dreams, giving us all memories that will last for ever.

I'll never get tired of saying, 'England women, European champions!'

I get goosebumps thinking about that Women's Euros final at Wembley and all of England's games and goals in the lead-up to that special and important moment.

Without Beth, England wouldn't have been in that final. From the first game to the last, she was ruthless and dangerous.

I loved it all, from that first moment at Old Trafford when Beth chipped her Arsenal teammate Manuela Zinsberger in front of 70,000 people, to the semi-final, when her goal broke the tense deadlock in Sheffield, easing everyone's nerves, especially those of us in the pundits' booth! She's one of those players where you feel like something is always going to happen – she's going to try something; she's going to make a difference. I love working with players with that ability – the ability to change and influence a game in a few moments. Beth has always had that skill, whether she's out wide or drifting into the box; during that tournament, you always felt that if we got the ball to Beth, something was going to happen.

There was a fire within Beth at the Euros, and it spread through the entire team.

Belief is so important in football. I always needed coaches and teammates who believed in me, who trusted me. Since Beth got that belief from Arsenal manager Jonas Eidevall and England's head coach Sarina Wiegman, she's been unstoppable.

There was a moment I knew Beth had gone up a gear – it was at the Emirates Stadium in September 2021. I'd watched Beth play plenty of times before, but that game felt different. Arsenal had a new manager and new players, a few of whom were pushing Beth for a place in the starting line-up. She was coming off the back of a frustrating summer where she'd fallen out of the England squad and missed out on the Tokyo Olympic Games. There was a lot of pressure on her, but she didn't let it faze her, and in the opening weekend of the Women's Super League season, Beth blew Chelsea apart.

She scored two incredible goals against the league champions and Champions League finalists like it was a pre-season friendly. The ease with which she slipped the ball past Ann-Katrin Berger, who was at that point one of the best goalkeepers in the world, was incredible. Beth had so much confidence and looked like a completely different player to the one who had been at Arsenal for four years. I remember thinking – we need to see this version of Beth more consistently.

I was impressed and excited that day, being an Arsenal and England fan, but I was also just so pleased for her. I sent her a message straight after that game and let her know just how good she had been and she replied, 'Thanks legend.' Little did she know, she was on the way to becoming a legend herself.

On the pitch, Beth has swagger and attitude that the opposition fear, but off the pitch, she's a sweet, warm and calm person. There have been plenty of times when things haven't gone her way, from injury to team selection, but Beth has remained determined. Attackers need a certain level of arrogance; you'll try something and it won't come off but you have to try it again – Beth has that in abundance. That belief is core to the player and person she is.

Beth's determination comes from what she had to go through as a young girl playing football. Like so many of the Lionesses, she grew up playing with boys and had to travel far and wide to play. Her mum had to work an extra job to cover the cost of petrol, and when she moved from playing in a village team to Middlesbrough Girls' Centre of Excellence, she struggled to make the step up and admitted to crying every week because it was so tough. With the support of her parents and coaches, Beth began to fly, and when times are tough, she draws on those moments and lets them drive her. Even though she's known for her goal-scoring ability, it's her work rate that has always impressed me. She is one of the best pressers in the WSL and that's what has really elevated her game over the last few years.

What Beth delivered in 2021 and 2022 is almost unheard of. I can think of only a few players who have come close to doing what she did: Wayne Rooney, who headed into Euro 2004 on top of the world and lit up the tournament until sadly getting injured in the quarter-final against Portugal, maybe Gazza at the 1990 World Cup, and Kelly Smith, who scored thirty goals in thirty-four games for Arsenal in their quadruple-winning season.

It takes someone special to consistently deliver at such a level for ten months.

Beth was a runaway train last season, too – nothing could get in her way. Just before the end of the campaign, as Arsenal pushed Chelsea all the way to the last day, I sent Beth a message, a few days after Arsenal had demolished Aston Villa 7–0 and Beth had scored, and told her, 'A goal every game, that's your level now. I will make the noise if you do the work.' I didn't need to remind her because she knew 2022 would be the year her game rose to another level and the whole world was going to stand up and take notice.

I'm so proud of Beth as a person and a player. To do what she did on arguably the biggest stage in a highly pressured home tournament; I can't help but smile when I think about it. Not only the Golden Boot winner but also the Player of the Tournament – achieving that individually whilst part of a group that achieved something remarkable. It's special. I can't wait to see what she's going to do next because there's absolutely no limit to her ability. She has proved she can be the best in the world and given us memories that will last a lifetime.

Ian Wright
Former Arsenal and England forward
September 2022

PROLOGUE

My stomach heaves and twists with nerves. I jiggle my legs, hammer my fingers against the countertop, pace the front room. I want to lock my phone away. I feel jittery. Caged.

I'd been out the previous evening for my birthday, to the Snug Bar in St Albans. I'd turned twenty-six and all of my Arsenal teammates had turned up to surprise me. We'd had a great night, but in the back of my mind, I'd felt a little restless and uneasy, and I had for a few days.

The Team GB squad for that summer's Tokyo Olympics would be announced any day. I fear, being honest with myself, that my chances are on the slim side.

For a few months now, I've felt like my face hasn't fit at England. Importantly for Team GB, I've felt like my face hasn't fit with Hege Riise, who is the England interim boss following the departure of Phil Neville and also the head coach for the Olympics.

Hege was considered one of the best footballers of her generation and won a gold medal herself for Norway at the 2000 Summer Olympics in Sydney. That made her one of the very small number of women to have won the Olympics, the World Cup and the Euros. Two decades on, my Olympic dreams are in her hands.

Hege had dropped me for her first England squad, for a game against Northern Ireland in February. In the media, she had said that the scouting report into me hadn't been good enough. A few days after the squad announcement, she called me back in as a late replacement.

I knew how to handle the ups and downs of a football career, but I hated that training camp. I was played out of position in practice games, didn't play in the match, was never given a chance to prove myself – and I don't think they wanted to let me. I felt like a spare part, like they didn't want me, and it weighed heavily on my shoulders as I returned to Arsenal. My confidence was seeping away.

It doesn't bode well for the Olympics, I think, churning it all over in my mind months later, but I have to remain hopeful. I have daydreamed about playing beneath those five interlocking rings for as long as I can remember. It would mean so much to be an Olympian.

My phone shudders across the table and lights up with Jordan Nobbs's name. It's 10am. How can it only be 10am? Jordan is my Arsenal teammate and has been one of my closest confidantes ever since we met as teenagers playing for Sunderland almost ten years earlier. Like me, she's hoping to make her first Olympics – even more so after missing the 2019 World Cup with an ACL injury.

'I've just got a call from Hege,' she starts. I stop pacing. My racing thoughts snap to a halt. 'She told me I'm not going to the Olympics. I'm not even a reserve.'

Shit, I think. If I get a phonecall from Hege today, that's it. My Olympic dream will be over before it's even started.

After commiserating with Jordan, I spend the next few hours feeling more restless than I've ever felt before. My nerves are taut, shredded to within an inch of their life. I stalk the front room. I make endless cups of tea and coffee and leave them to go cold. I cycle through TV channels with glazed eyes, barely registering anything. What I do know is I really, really don't want to look at my phone.

It's close to 5pm when I get the call. *Hege Riise.* My heart plunges.

'I'm just ringing to let you know that you're not going to the Olympics,' she says. She's brisk, brief, to the point. 'Let my assistant know if you'd like a one-to-one conversation about why you're not going.'

I feel raw, flayed. Tears race down my cheeks. The call with Hege the next day does little to improve my mood and I'm left with the feeling that she's making excuses. She tells me that I'm too aggressive, and it hits me like a sucker punch. I've always been told that I play my best football when I'm angry and when I've got a point to prove. It stings. It's like who I am as a player is being ripped apart.

The squad is announced the next day. I still think I deserve a place.

I don't like the person I become over the next few weeks. I feel bitter and full of darkness. I'm in a lonely place. I feel like the Olympics have been taken from me. I struggle to process the situation. I want to totally shut out the world. Months later, I'll look back and wonder if I was depressed.

I love all of those players, but because of how I've left things with Hege, I don't want her to do well.

That's not who I am. I struggle with those thoughts. And I struggle with becoming this darker, moodier version of myself who feels so far removed from who I've always been. I hate that this is how I feel. But I can't deny these feelings.

I lose count of the number of times I return from training with Arsenal to find that Team GB have won. I feel blasé, indifferent, and that's how I ghost through much of the month. On 30 July, I leave for training with Team GB leading Australia 2–1 in the semi-finals and get home to find that Australia have come from behind to win 4–3. *They've been knocked out and come away with nothing.* The torture, the what-ifs, the agonising over the difference I think I could have made, is finally all over. Then I feel awful, and guilty, and the cycle starts all over again. Is this how I'm meant to be feeling? What does this make me?

I return for pre-season with Arsenal with the anger and injustice still bristling inside me – but changed. Over the summer, I'd felt depressed; now I'm determined to prove everyone wrong.

My teammates can tell that I'm in my own head when I bludgeon my way through the running drills.

Shit to all this, I think. I start as I mean to go on. Be better. Be balanced. You're good at what you do. You're good at football, and you wouldn't be here, playing for one of the best teams in the country, in England's only professional women's football league, otherwise. You need to get over it all. You're twenty-six and you're being this childish?

Our new manager, Jonas Eidevall, arrives a little while later. He's an intense man. When he speaks, he looks right into your eyes, his gaze boring into yours. I find it intimidating initially, but I don't shirk his eye contact. In fact, I feel a comfort with him immediately because we are on the same wavelength.

About most things.

'I want you to come to the next level,' he says one day. 'You have the ability to be one of the best wingers in the world. You can be a Ballon d'Or nominee.'

I splutter, roll my eyes. *Thanks,* I think, *but really?* His words don't feel prophetic. I don't know what he sees.

But back then, I don't know what's around the corner. I don't know of the news to come that will shatter my world. I don't know of the moments on the pitch that will help me put it back together again. I don't know that I'm soon to experience more glory and more despair in eleven months than in any other year of my life. And I don't know how deeply, how suddenly, it will change not only the way I see the world, but the entire future of women's football.

I

Disrupting the Class

Botham's tea room on Skinner Street is Whitby's best bakery. Tucked away just a few streets from Whitby Beach and the West Pier, it's been part of the town for more than one hundred and fifty years and has been passed down through five generations of the Botham family.

After the Euros, on a trip back home before another England camp, Botham's was the first place my family and I visited. After sharing a Stottie – a ten-inch soft bread bun that you split between four, traditional to the north of England and stuffed with our fillings of choice – I had a Chocolate Japonaise. That's two almond and hazelnut macaroon meringue biscuits, sandwiched together with buttercream and covered in chocolate sprinkles. They're only available during certain parts of the year, as are the strawberry tarts. My other favourite is the traffic light, a shortbread biscuit with red, amber and green buttercream running through it.

Botham's is special to me because it played a role in getting my parents together. My dad, Richard Mead, worked in the Botham's branch in Baxtergate. Once Whitby's main shopping area, it is further inland than the Skinner Street shop. There was a nightclub nearby and Dad would begin his shift in Botham's at 2am, the same time my mum, June, would be leaving the nightclub with all her friends. My parents had met at a party a few years earlier but Mum hadn't been all that interested in Dad. They were both still teenagers then. In the weeks and months that followed, Dad would watch and wave through Botham's shop window until he plucked up the courage to ask her out at a dance in 1986. The Wilson Arms was an inn in Whitby that held a disco every Saturday night and was, my parents say, the place to be. They married on 30 September 1989, two days after Mum's birthday.

I'm very much inspired by my parents, their journey together and the love they still share. To this day, they're still like little children. I know I've been very lucky to grow up with two parents who have not only always been present, but remain very much in love with their families and each other. I truly cherish that. I know not everyone's so lucky.

I was born on 9 May 1995 in Whitby and lived in Runswick, a cliffside village in the Scarborough borough of North Yorkshire, seven miles north of Whitby. Our house on Nettledale Close gave way to a cul-de-sac but, by following the main road, we could be at the sea in a couple of minutes.

Runswick is half a mile from Hinderwell, the village further inland that we'll move to when I turn eleven. Both villages, and those around them, are the kind of places people tend to describe as having more sheep than people. Runswick has a population of just over two thousand people and Hinderwell's is a few hundred less. My first football matches were often backdropped by fields filled with sheep, and my first school, Oakridge Community Primary School, almost slips into the fields, hills and heather of the North Yorkshire Moors. The area has changed since then, largely due to the 2001 outbreak of foot and mouth that saw farmers across the country having to slaughter their animals to try and stop the disease from spreading. Many locals lost their businesses. Barely any farmers in those villages keep sheep now.

Hinderwell, in particular, is a small village. You can walk from one side to the other in just a few minutes, and the community is close as a result. My godmother's house is a few doors down from where my parents live now. My grandmother on Mum's side – Grandma Dotty, who we all call Ninny – lives around the corner.

By all accounts, I was an easy baby. I would never take a warm bottle, which saved my parents some work, and I'd sit in my cot happily feeding myself. When I'd finished, I'd throw the bottle on the floor. Mum and Dad would hear the thud, come into my room to check on me and find me sleeping soundly. Maybe all that was an early sign of my strong will and independent streak, and Dad says I took some tiring out before they could even think about putting me to bed. That's why Dad, starting when I was two, would kick a football to me every night in the hallway. I'd kick it back. Left foot, right foot. Left foot, right foot. Over and over and over until my eyelids began to close and my head started to droop, then Dad scooped me up to take me to bed. I wonder, looking back, if Mum hated us wrecking the house, because I can remember the door shaking and rattling when the ball smacked against it – just as, twenty-five years later, the goal netting will balloon and bulge for me for England.

Mum was grateful for my strength the day we were surrounded by swans on a family holiday to Windermere. She had steered me down to the shoreline in my pushchair to show me the boats when the swans began to make their way up the pebbled beach. As they closed in on us, Mum panicked and dashed backwards. One particularly vicious one stepped into the space she'd left and was inches away from my pushchair. Mum covered her eyes in panic. When she opened them, she saw a swan writhing and quacking with my hand closed around its neck. Mum was screaming for help, too afraid to move, while I made friends with the local wildlife. This incident became a family joke for many years. 'Fancy leaving your daughter to fend for herself,' we'd say to Mum.

When I was three, Mum fell pregnant with my brother. Around this time, I developed an imaginary friend. His name was Wesley. To this day, none of us know where that name came from, but I took looking after Wesley very seriously. Mum and Dad simply had to set a place at the table for him, else I'd get really upset. If one of them sat in the wrong place, I'd sit bolt upright in panic, shrieking, 'You're sitting on Wesley!' Whenever we left the house, I made Mum put his seatbelt on for him and bring a book for him to read and toys for him to play with. But the day Ben was born, Wesley disappeared. I never mentioned him again. I had a new man in my life.

Ben and I never argued or fell out, even though I loved to wind him up. Mum has a picture of us both from a family wedding and it's a favourite because it sums up our relationship to a tee. Sadly, it's faded now, but you can still make us out: me in a bridesmaid's dress and him in a page-boy outfit. Ben had chicken pox that day, and if the photo is anything to go by, I was the epitome of sympathy. I grip his wrist tightly, smirking slyly. Ben is crying. I've no idea what I wanted him to do, but I was always dragging him places and ordering him about. Ben was far quieter and probably acquiesced for an easy life.

The most traumatic moment of Ben's early life came during the Christmas our parents bought him a remote-controlled robot. It should have been right up his street, but he was terrified of it. This, of course, thrilled me. I'd put it on the floor and watch it stomp from one end of the living room to the other while Ben wept on the sofa, his feet tucked against his chest, refusing to leave the couch.

Mum and Dad didn't believe in grounding kids – what was the point of trapping either of us in our rooms when we needed to be socialised? – but they raised us well. Dad was a touch softer and, for that reason, I was more of a daddy's girl growing up. I knew he was the lenient one and that I'd be able to wangle my way out of things far more easily than I would with Mum. Mum was, and still is, a higher-level teaching assistant at St Joseph's School in Loftus and was probably wise to all the tricks that kids like me tried to pull. Dad worked on the machines team at the Boulby potash mine for most of my childhood.

Mum says now that I was a nightmare of a kid. I prefer to think that I kept her on her toes. I was so strong-willed and liked to blaze my own trail. This started fairly early with a trip to B&Q, and a story so mortifying that I cannot believe she continues to tell it to people . . .

My parents were redecorating the bathroom. They probably went to B&Q filled with excitement at the prospect of looking at tiles and paint samples. They were also potty-training me. I can't imagine the terror that gripped June Mead when she heard the words: 'Mummy! I've finished!' and turned around to find me bent over, bum in the air ready for her to wipe, and a present left for her in the show toilet.

Shopping with me didn't get much easier as I grew older. I loved to vanish, but Mum and Dad never had to look too far to find me. They would hear a giggle and a rustle, then see me hiding beneath the clothes rack. While Mum was picking out my school uniform, I'd slide the different size cubes from the hooks of the coathangers and either swap them around or slip them in my pocket. I'd rattle out of the shopping centre and Mum would stand there incredulously as I tipped my haul into her hand.

'Why do you even need all these?' she'd gasp.

In those early days in Runswick, Dad used to tell me that I had glass ankles. He'd be milling about the house then come outside to find I'd fallen off the kerb and was lying in the cul-de-sac waiting for someone to rescue me. I was always fine, but it's funny that, after my big move to Arsenal in 2017, I had to do a month of rehab before I could get going because I had . . . an ankle injury. Maybe some things never change.

I'd always been the kind of kid to jump in first and worry if it was a good idea later. I ruined one family caravan holiday by sticking my big toe through the grilles of a disposable barbecue just because my dad told me it was too hot to touch. The toe ballooned right away into weeping blisters and I spent the rest of the holiday waddling around in flip flops. We went on scores of caravan holidays, hopping between the Haven holiday parks in Yorkshire. Mum still has my certificate from Primrose Valley in Filey for joining in with the activities in the Tiger Club, the kids' club run by the mascot Rory the Tiger.

When I was five, Mum enrolled me in ballet classes because she thought they would help with my coordination. Once a week, she would take me to St Hilda's Farm, a gable-fronted detached house that has since been converted into a boutique hotel but which used to be home to Mrs Francis and her family. They lived on one floor but had turned the other into a dance studio. What had been the front room had a wall of mirrors at one end and a ballet bar at the other. The next room was the parents' waiting area, where my mum probably spent most of her time wondering why she bothered.

I was bored out of my mind. I didn't understand what we were doing, and I didn't really want to. The terminology – arabesque, relevé, second position – flew way over my head, and I quickly went from future prima ballerina to destructive force. I would faff around in the back row, totally ignoring the ballet mistress, who would drag me out by my wrist and take me to Mum.

'She's disrupting the class, again,' she would say. 'The girls aren't concentrating because Beth's distracting them all.'

'I paid £3.50 for this class!' Mum would reply. 'Get her back in there!'

Mum persisted, even though she knew I hated it. I hated the leotard. I hated the tutu. I hated my ballet shoes. Most of all, I hated that it was all so slow. There just wasn't enough going on to keep me focused and entertained. In the end, Mum had to bribe me to take my ballet exam. I can't have been so bad, though, because at some point they put me on the stage for a dance recital at Whitby Pavilion, a theatre that sits right on the edge of the cliffs near the beach. Mum's friend still has the photo of my classmates and me gathered backstage, me at the front in a red and white dress.

I loved animals. Always have: I had toy farms with horses and dogs and a tiny cuddly Andrex puppy that I used to sleep with every night and which is still at my parents' house. My favourite toys were my Animal Hospital figures and rescue vehicles. You would run the animals under warm water and cuts would appear on their paws. You could treat them with the medical kit, which came with tiny bottles, stethoscopes and little plasters.

And then there were real animals. Our first neighbours in Runswick would let me wander down to play with their Labradors, and I spent hours rolling on the floor with them, having one-sided conversations as they snuggled into me and licked my face. I once went out the front door without telling Mum and for a frantic fifteen minutes she tore up and down the street in panic, screaming my name, until she found me cuddling the dogs in that back conservatory. The one thing I wanted more than anything was a dog.

Mum initially tried to meet me halfway and bought me a black rabbit. I called him Beethoven, after the St Bernard in the American family comedy films. That made her take the point.

'Look, Beth,' she said. 'If you complete this ballet exam, I'll get you a dog.'

I paid attention then. For the next few weeks, I was a model pupil – and, to the school's surprise, I passed. Mum still has my examination certificate in a folder at home; printed on white card, it has the Royal Academy of Dancing crest, below which it says: 'Bethany Mead, pre-primary assessment, November 2000'. The report inside says I'm a 'well-poised little dancer' who showed 'some pleasing work' but needed to focus on pointing my feet. I was, however, 'swift of foot in the runs' and 'expressive', which makes sense.

I wasn't sure if Mum would uphold her end of the bargain, but she had actually been eager all along for Ben and me to grow up around animals so that we understood what it meant to care for something. Mum took me to Gran's house later that afternoon. I squealed when I saw a Border Collie puppy skipping about the furniture. She was all black with little white socks. One sock was pulled all the way up one leg   a quirk I fell in love with immediately. Mum helped me carry the puppy into the kitchen and we washed her in the sink, as Mum explained that the dog was called Jess and had come from a farm in Ugthorpe, one of the neighbouring villages. Jess was one of the last dogs left of the litter.

'She's the cutest thing,' I said.

'She's yours,' Mum smiled.

It was the best feeling ever. I stopped ballet – as Mum knew I would – and we took Jess home that night. Mum made up a dog bed in the back conservatory and looked at me sternly.

'She will howl all night,' Mum warned. 'No matter what happens, you must not go down to see her. She needs to get used to being on her own.'

I didn't go to see Jess. Instead, I lay in bed rigid with excitement. The moment the sun came up, I raced downstairs, and Jess and I quickly became best friends. Her first act of love was to take care of my pink Barbie pyjamas. I'd never liked them, and I let Jess's needle-like puppy teeth chew and tear my sleeves to shreds so that I didn't have to wear them anymore. Mum would go into my room each morning to find my bed empty and chuckle away, knowing that I'd let Jess into the house and was making mischief with her. Dad built a kennel for her outside, but Jess never used it. She would sleep instead on the corner of the decking, and we'd go outside in winter to find her hidden beneath a few inches of snow and still sleeping happily.

As I got older, I'd take Jess to the field near our house or play with her in our back garden and flick up the ball for her to knock back to me. We'd try and get a rally going. I'd never had to teach that to Jess, but growing up in the Mead household meant that she'd been around footballs all her life. Picking up some skill was inevitable.

Mum continued to try to find some way for me to burn off my energy. That was her polite way of telling me that I was doing her head in. Someone had told her that there was a Saturday morning football club in Hinderwell and, when I turned six, she took me along. It's an unremarkable field:

a cricket and football pitch, both balding and pockmarked with molehills. Phillip Nedley, a local man, was running the community football session that day.

'Go on,' Mum said, ushering me over to the boys. 'This will do you good.'

'Will she be OK?' Phil asked. He pushed his glasses further up his warm, friendly face. 'She's welcome to come, but most of the players are boys and they can be a bit . . . rough.'

'She'll be fine,' Mum said immediately. 'Just throw her in. She'll get on with it. Don't worry.'

Phil's sessions were all about enjoyment. They were light on drills but we played dozens of games. At that age, we'd all just chase one ball like sheep, and I loved every minute. I loved the freedom and speed of the game, and I was lucky that I was a skilful kid who instinctively used both feet. I read the game well, too; it felt like I was always a step ahead of the other kids and on a different wavelength. I'd see things they wouldn't.

At the end of that first session, a flustered Phil approached Mum.

'I need to apologise,' he said. 'She's rougher than most of the boys. I was really surprised. You needn't worry about her because she's very good. She's like a little terrier.'

I persisted with Phil every Saturday morning. Once Mum realised I was sticking at this one – that this hobby wasn't about to go the same way as ballet and we wouldn't end up with a whole zoo of animals from me trying and rejecting various activities – she went to buy me my first pair of football boots. She went to a car boot sale in Hutton-le-Hole, a village about twenty miles inland from Runswick, and discovered them there: blue Umbro boots with a red tongue. They cost a grand total of 50p, and, as we picnicked by the stream, I ran up and down the field with my ball to test them out, Jess following behind me. Dad still keeps them at home, along with Ben's first boots, in a carrier bag with the old Morrisons logo. That's how long he's had them.

Dad had always been a Manchester United fan. The kids he'd gone to school with had all supported Leeds, Liverpool or Middlesbrough. He wanted to be different so picked United. My growing interest in football meant that the time was right for his love of them to rub off onto me. My first kit was one of the iconic Vodafone ones from 2002–04 and my favourite player was, of course, David Beckham. Like me, he was number seven. I had a Manchester United cake for my eighth birthday: one of those printed ones you'd get at the supermarket, with pictures of the players on the icing and a Manchester United ribbon around the base. We went to Old Trafford a handful of times when I was growing up to watch United under Sir Alex Ferguson and I remember being surprised at how much taller the players were compared to how they looked on TV. Fans have such an expectation for players to support the team we play for, but the reality is we grew up supporting someone else, so they tend to be who we still support. Everyone knows by now that I love and care for Arsenal and that's how I play my football.

One year in, Dad came to pick me up from the Saturday session to find Phil waiting for him. 'She's got a lot of footballing talent,' Phil said. 'She's too good to be coming here. She needs to go further afield. You need to take her to Middlesbrough.'

Dad drove me to the Herlingshaw Centre, a sports complex run by Middlesbrough Football Club's Foundation, to join up with Middlesbrough's Academy. It was a fun girls' programme that anyone could join in with, but it would take us forty-five minutes to get there from our house because there are no dual carriageways until you get to Middlesbrough. Our area comprises mainly single country roads. Dad would drive me in his blue Citroen AX – Ben refers to it as a 'lunchbox on wheels' – and I'd rewind his cassette tapes for him as he drove. It was always old bands like Madness, Queen, the Clash and Meatloaf.

We would pass a derelict house near an apple orchard and there was an abandoned red ball on the roof. Every trip, Dad or I would point and call: 'Red ball!' The windows were bricked up but someone had stuck a sticker of a person across the front to give the illusion of life. As we came out of the apple orchard, we would nearly always see deer flitting about the field on the left. The red ball disappeared a few years into my time at Middlesbrough's Centre of Excellence – the more competitive development programme that girls had to trial for, and that I joined aged nine – and it unnerved us both. Dad still takes the same route to work and he says that he thinks of the ball each time he drives that way.

Middlesbrough's Academy was a far cry from the bare pitch back at Runswick. Boro had an indoor 3G pitch, overlooked by a mezzanine balcony from which the parents could watch us train. What they saw each week was some kind of skills contest. Girls would be pulling off tricks on demand. I've never been that kind of player, and I'm still not – I'm far more instinctive. As I moved on the pitch, ideas just came naturally to me. I didn't think twice or question anything. Back then, at under 10s level, I felt like an actor: stand in this spot, read those lines, do it on cue and do it again so we have all the angles covered. It was a staged performance. Football had never felt like that to me before.

It didn't help that there were cliques in the squad. The girls had all come from the same part of Middlesbrough and they were comfortable – not only in each other's company, but in their own skin. I was the classic little village girl and I felt like an outsider.

I'd be fine when I had the ball at my feet, but as soon as the drills stopped, I felt unsettled. Groups of girls would talk among themselves and I'd feel awkward, unwelcome. I'd wish I had a little group to make me feel more settled, but I didn't. My stomach would drop, my top lip would tremble, I'd look frantically for Dad on the balcony and that would be it. I'd run off and he'd come racing down the stairs to meet his sobbing daughter in the corridor, my tiny body heaving with panic.

'What's wrong?' he'd ask. He knew me inside out and was sure I'd be fine once I got going.

'I'm not enjoying it,' I'd weep. 'I don't feel like I belong here.'

'You're all right,' he'd reassure me. 'You'll get used to it. You just need to go and play.' He knew I'd be ready to go once those feelings were out my system. I wouldn't keep running in and out after that.

That was the way for a long time. Football was my way of communicating with people and expressing myself. Only once I'd got going with a ball could I start to come out of my shell socially, and be the outgoing Beth my family and friends knew at home.

A few months into my time at Middlesbrough, Dad met a local man called Dave Scott. Dave ran his own football team in Middlesbrough. There were a handful of girls in the squad and he wanted to try and find more so that they could create a girls' team. Those girls were two or three years older than me, but Dave had been watching me from the balcony at Middlesbrough's Academy and knew I'd be fine.

'Your little girl seems pretty good,' Dave said to Dad, handing over his number. 'See if she wants to play for California Boys.'

Dad's jaw dropped. 'California Boys? California?'

'No, no – that's the name of my road,' Dave replied. 'It's not as glamorous as it sounds.'

It had been two months but I still didn't feel settled at the Academy. That's what prompted Dad to call Dave. I was ready to give California a try.

Until the morning actually came. Dad drove me to what was known locally as the Rec, a set of council-owned pitches just a stone's throw from where I trained with Middlesbrough. From the window of the back seat, I watched the swinging ponytails of a handful of girls and refused to get out of the car.

Dad was steeled for battle. I was only eight, and I didn't know anybody. As the Middlesbrough experience had demonstrated, I was a tough kid to pull from my comfort zone. And as the ballet experience had demonstrated, I was stubborn.

'I don't want to go and play with the girls,' I protested. I was a little scarred after my experience at Middlesbrough. In my eight-year-old mind, girls weren't particularly forthcoming.

We continued like this for some time, Dad trying to coax me out of my comfort zone. I was used to playing with boys, not girls. When I saw a cluster of them playing further down the pitch, taking part in a separate drill, I accepted that joining in with them might be a good first step.

Dad approached the boys' coach, Wayne McGuinness, and explained the situation.

'I mean, if she wants to . . .' Wayne replied. I think he and Dave were a little perplexed, or thought that this quirk of mine would just be a first step to make me more comfortable before I joined up with the girls. Maybe the boys were apprehensive when I joined in, but I wasn't. I loved it. Football felt like home again. I stayed playing with California Boys.

Over the next few years, California came to symbolise, to me, what football is all about. We would spray-paint our hair green and white to match our hooped kits. One of the mums would raid the local cash and carry or the sweets aisle at the supermarket and put together paper bags of pick 'n' mix for us to have after the game for 50p. My mum would buy all the pictures from our annual photoshoot or any games the photographer attended and those prints are still up in the kitchen at home. I had to join the boys' team to play at primary school and rarely came across any girls in football beyond those who had joined the team because I had. It sucked that not more girls felt able to play, but as a kid I just loved football and I was comfortable enough playing with the boys.

My favourite time of year was when it came to buying new football boots. It was a full day out. We'd trawl all of the sports shops – JJB, Pro Direct, Sports Soccer – and I'd pick out the ones I liked and wait in suspense to see if they had them in my size. I loved my Puma Kings and Adidas Predators, but my favourites were my Astro turf trainers – my black and neon green Diadoras – which I even wore when I was a flower girl at an auntie's wedding. That hadn't been the plan, but I'd taken an instant dislike to the pink ballet slippers I was supposed to wear. I was not a fan. I told Mum that they were giving me blisters, that I couldn't possibly keep them on all day. It may have been a ruse.

'Mum! Mum!' I said. 'Can you go home and get me my Diadoras?'

She did, and I wore them under my dress, beneath white tulle that floated around my ankles. The arrival of my trainers gave me such a second wind that Mum came out of the venue later that night to find me swinging off the monkey bars in the playground of the Runswick Bay Hotel, the white dress flaring behind me, my Diadora-clad feet sailing through the air.

The boys at California respected me from the beginning, but this wasn't the case throughout the league. I would often take to the pitch to the sound of tutting.

Parents would laugh. 'Look at this little girl,' they'd point, filled with cynicism.

And their kids would copy them. 'Ha! There's a girl on the team!'

Blah, blah, blah.

Dad had warned me about those kinds of comments and those kinds of people. We'd have conversations about it in the car on the way to matches.

'You know how people can be, Beth,' he'd say. 'There are good and bad people in the world. People might laugh because girls aren't always accepted in football, especially in the boys' game.'

'I don't understand that, Dad,' I'd reply. 'I'm just playing football. I'm doing the same as the boys.'

That's how black and white my thinking was. It wasn't an issue for me.

'We all think the same, and your teammates do too,' Dad continued. 'You don't need to react to anything anyone says. Don't let it upset you. You just play football and that will say more than enough.'

I often didn't hear them. When I played, it was like the world outside disappeared. Oh, I thought, on the rare occasions a comment broke through. Maybe that's the norm. Dad always made me aware that sexist comments could happen at any point.

To this day, I still receive so many comments for being a woman who plays football. Some things don't change, and my attitude hasn't either – I'll always let my football do the talking.

We once played a tournament in Hunmanby, a large village in Scarborough, against teams from West Riding. Some of these teams had tall boys playing for them, up to twice my size – kids develop at such different rates. I was always one of the youngest on the team.

Not that it bothered me. The same day I'd heard those parents sniggering, a loose ball spilled towards me on the edge of my area. I made eye contact with the biggest boy on the pitch. *I'll beat him to this*, I thought, as I ate up the yards. *I've got this*.

Dad told me afterwards that he had just heard screaming. Filled with panic, he bolted towards me – only to see me spring back up and the boy squirming on the floor as I looked down at him and ran off, still chasing the loose ball. That remains one of Dad's favourite memories.

After those games, the respect always switched. The boys and their parents would speak to my dad after, either apologising or expressing their admiration for his daughter. I don't remember Dad ever letting it get to him; I don't think he ever rose to it because, like me, he knew my skills would do the talking. In any case, he was never the kind of parent to get involved in arguing with the others. He was happy to leave it to me to show them what I could do.

I was known in the area simply as the girl who played football. When Oakridge played another local school, Ruswarp, we won easily and I ran rings around the boys.

Our family friend, Lorraine Pound, used to work at Ruswarp and caught up with the headteacher afterwards.

'How did you get on?' Lorraine asked.

'Slaughtered us,' he replied. 'Absolutely slaughtered us.'

'Was there a girl there?' Lorraine continued.

'Yes. She was the one who did the slaughtering.'

I was never afraid to assert myself. This came to a head one caravan holiday when Dad and I were playing on one of the pitches. I was ten or eleven. Some boys joined in and we had a small-sided game, which was all going swimmingly until one of the boys cheated. The ball had gone out – it was my throw-in – and he had played on as though nothing had happened. I don't condone what I did next, and to this day I'm still not sure where I could have learned this from, but I swore at him.

Instantly, Dad sprinted the full length of the pitch and grabbed me by my wrist. He dragged me, kicking and screaming, back to the caravan and I stewed alone in my room for the next few hours, feeling wounded. That evening, Dad and I walked the length and breadth of the park to track down the children and their parents. When we eventually found them in the clubhouse, Dad asked me to apologise.

'I'm not having this,' I said. 'He cheated!' I told the boy and his mum as much, which went down about as well as you'd expect.

I began playing for Middlesbrough Girls' Centre of Excellence when I was nine. Dozens of coaches were telling me that I was too good for the local leagues and should try out for Middlesbrough, the place to be locally. I felt ready to, and won a place in the under 10s team after impressing at an open trial. Meanwhile, California had recruited enough girls to make a separate team, and I started playing with them as well the year after.

For two years, I played for California Girls and Middlesbrough Girls' Centre of Excellence. I'd train with Middlesbrough twice during the week, but we never had regular fixtures until the under 14s. That allowed me to train with Cali every Saturday morning and play a game on Sunday.

California Boys and, later, California Girls, travelled all across the north to play tournaments – the girls' team won our very first one – and invariably we'd reach the finals. That meant these became full day jobs, so my whole family would come. Grandma would prepare a picnic and I'd play seven or eight games in one day while refuelling on ice-cream and jam sandwiches. I don't know how we did it, considering what we were eating.

Ben was amazing during this period. I was in the limelight with football even then, and it dominated our parents' lives. Maybe Ben felt as though he was in the shadows, but I can't say enough about how incredible he was. During those picnics and tournaments, he'd sit on the blanket with his toys and never utter a word of complaint. He'd drink the games in, and he's the same all these years on. When he comes to my matches now, I can feel how proud he is.

We've never fought with each other, but whenever I come home he always jokes that 'the favourite child is back' and that everything will be done for me.

'Ben? Can you do the pots?' Mum will ask.

'Why can't Beth do them?'

'Well, she's a guest now. She's not here often. You do it.'

That's often how it goes. For the 2021/22 season, the Professional Footballers' Association commissioned an artist, David Roman, to paint each of the winners of the Fans' Player of the Month Award. Mine is on the wall in the kitchen, right above the kettle. It's a black and white portrait of me dribbling the ball. Whenever I'm home, Ben will turn the kettle round so that the painting will vanish behind the steam. It has no effect beyond infuriating Mum and Dad, but that sums up our relationship to a tee. As does his habit of taking all the best things from my old room without telling me. He's got a touch lamp and a mattress from me. But our bond is one in a million and I wouldn't change Ben for the world.

California Girls felt like family, too, especially when Dad took on a coaching role for the girls' team.

He will probably tell you I used to be a little shit, running around and totally ignoring him.

'Right!' he'd shout. 'Do a lap of the pitch! You'll get no preferential treatment from me. You'll do what everybody else is doing.' I'd giggle the whole way round. He put me in goal once and I picked the ball up in my goalmouth, beat every player and scored. I didn't set much store by some of his instructions.

2

The Mead Show

When I reached the under 12s age group, the FA stopped young players from being registered for both a local club like California Girls and a centre of excellence like Middlesbrough.

As much as I loved California, I was used to the Centre of Excellence by now and it brought together the best players in the county. That was the right place for my technical development, easily. We travelled everywhere, either on tours – a southern one in Brighton saw us play Fulham and Charlton – or in regular fixtures against all the other centres of excellence. Sheffield had Bethany England, now at Chelsea and one of my England teammates, as well as Jess Sigsworth, who would go on to play for Manchester United and Leicester. Leeds United had Leah Galton, another future Manchester United star. The fact that I'm still meeting them now, in the WSL, means that I've been playing against them for seventeen years.

Jordan Nobbs was in the age group above me at the Centre of Excellence. I still vividly remember the day we played her under 14s team in a practice game, mainly because I kicked Jordan and she went straight down. In my head, I thought I'd killed her. Jordan was the player to be. She was England's prodigy child.

I've just injured her, I told myself, unable to look at Jordan on the floor. I looked about me in panic, my mind and heart racing. *I've. Just. Injured. Jordan. Nobbs.*

She was fine. I will add that I wasn't the reason she moved to Sunderland a few years later when they came calling for her.

I had a fitting send-off from California Girls, when, at the umpteenth attempt, we finally won the Norton Stockton Ancients competition, a tournament we'd tried and failed to win for as long as I could remember. By that point I was also far more comfortable at Middlesbrough thanks to the tours, which were my favourite things. We'd stay up late in our rooms watching scary movies and laughing all night. It was my first real taste of team bonding, and I became closer to the girls instead of playing with them for a couple of hours, then going home. I'd grown out of leaving the sessions in tears by then.

The only time Dad did let me sit out was one freezing morning in Hurworth, a village in Darlington. I was playing for Boro's under 10s on the indoor pitch; our under 12s team were playing Sunderland outside. That day, the under 12s coach had wanted me to join them. Sunderland produced the best teams in the country and it was unheard of for Middlesbrough to beat them. They needed all the help they could get. The cold gnawed at my fingers and, within just a few minutes, the ball smacked me full on in the face. I flopped straight down and that was it. I didn't want to play for the under 12s that day.

'It didn't half wallop you,' Dad conceded.

As I grew older and the petrol needed to ferry me to football training began to swallow up most of her wages, Mum took on extra jobs. She waited tables in a pub in Runswick, worked in a chip shop and started cleaning cottages. She did all those jobs at once, her shifts spread out over the week. We could cover 300 miles a week going to and from matches.

The move from California Girls to Middlesbrough was one of my easier transitions, but I've never been good at handling change. And I wasn't thrilled at the prospect of moving from Oakridge to Caedmon School, which was a twenty-minute drive from our new house in Hinderwell, when I left primary school. I was one of only three pupils going from Oakridge and I was paralysed by the prospect. Until I got to know people, I was cripplingly shy and I worried they wouldn't like me. Mum couldn't see why I thought this way about myself.

I came home after the first day and told Mum that there was no way I would ever go back to Caedmon. I wasn't sure what the alternative would be, but I was adamant that Caedmon wasn't part of the equation. That night, Mum walked me across the cliffs and for the next couple of hours, she tried to get to the bottom of what was making me so unhappy. I couldn't explain it. She offered suggestions but I couldn't pinpoint why I was so uneasy. It wouldn't be the last time I'd struggle with change – or struggle to put those kinds of feelings into words.

I was lucky that one of my best friends from primary school, Alex Shaw, made the move with me. I felt able to confide in her and switch off when I was with her, and I was grateful for the slice of familiarity she gave me when we were placed in the same form. I made friends with a girl called Poppy Howell, who owned horses, and we'd ride them through the fields every weekend. Poppy's mum was a chef at a neighbouring school and made us cookies or brownies to tuck into after school.

PE was where I began to find my feet. I loved Mrs Fellows, the teacher. She brought me out of my shell and helped me find the confidence to be more sociable.

I was a cheeky, mischievous kid, but I was good-natured with it, and never strayed over the boundary into being genuinely troublesome. I hated the idea of Mum seeing a detention or negative comment in my planner, so that fear reined me back if I ever came close to crossing a line. I was more of a plotter, trying to get everyone else to do bad things, but I was too much of a goody-two-shoes to ever cause real bother. Academically, though, I hated everything about school. Maths was always my worst subject and I felt like it would never click, which made for a nerve-wracking GCSE results day. I completed every exercise on the revision website MyMaths and went to every after-school session. Mum and I both cried with joy when I opened my envelope and saw I'd got a C. Generally, though, parents' evening was a double-edged sword for Mum, who often heard how I had 'the ability to be good' at various subjects but let myself down by 'talking too much'.

Caedmon's houses took their names from famous Whitby boats. My house, Resolution, was named after HMS *Resolution*, which was commanded by Captain Cook during his second and third voyages to the Pacific and was built in Whitby. Mum had been in Resolution, too. I loved that I was in the same house as Mum and was continuing the Mead legacy. That's why it was easily the best house.

I was always a house sport leader, and my school tie was full of badges for all the sports I represented the school in. I even became a prefect at one point, a power I'll confess I did abuse a little. Pupils were only allowed to use certain doors – we were never allowed in the one closest to the canteen. There was always a mad dash to get there before a prefect came along to turn you away. I was the one who would let my best friends through but nobody else.

Once a year there would be a form football competition. On the rainiest day I can remember – as sleet slashed and whipped at our red knees and fingers – our Year 7 team played a team one or two years older than us. On the Astro turf, one boy banged into me from behind and I fell forward, my face breaking my fall. I grazed all the skin off my forehead and that was me done for the day. I was never thought of as weird or strange for playing sports at Caedmon, by the boys or the girls. I know I'm lucky in that – not everyone has the same secondary school experience. My parents and teachers encouraged me to be competitive. No one was affronted or intimidated by how much I wanted to win.

I kept one of my football trophies on the desk in my bedroom at Runswick and wrapped medals around the base and the handles until the whole thing got too heavy to lift. It would sit in front of my dolphin curtains, which were my favourite thing in my room apart from my Pokemon cards, which I would hide in my clothes drawers so that my brother couldn't steal them. I also loved collecting Match Attax football cards. Mum and Dad would scatter them about my room for me to find and tell me that the elves had hidden them for me.

'Look!' I'd say to Mum, rushing out to show her the packets I'd found under my pillow.

'There's another one here,' Dad would shout, pulling some from under the duvet.

'I can't believe I've missed the elves again!' I'd say.

When we moved to Hinderwell, I swapped my dolphin curtains for a huge painting of the Playboy bunny logo that Mum and her cousin stencilled onto my bedroom wall. It was the big thing at secondary school, along with Charlie body spray. I used to wear a Playboy bag to school, I think I was more into animals than the fashion side. My bedroom walls are white now, but you can still see the outline where the bunny's ears used to be.

Sport was gradually helping me to feel more comfortable in my own skin. Back at home, I was as happy-go-lucky as ever, the same fearless kid who wanted to ride all the biggest rollercoasters at Flamingo Land, our favourite theme park. I even used to wear platform trainers and my hair in a ballet bun to cheat the height restrictions.

Another favourite place to visit was Beacon Farm, an ice-cream parlour, campsite and tea room ten minutes from Whitby Beach. Mum and family friend Lorraine often took Ben and me, plus Lorraine's kids Tom and Jess, there in the school holidays. Ben and Tom were similar – both quiet and unlikely to cause any chaos – and I got on like a house on fire with Jess, although she was very well behaved and never did anything wrong. I spent my life trying to coax Jess into mischief, to no avail.

My favourite memory of Beacon Farm was when I was six. Mum and Lorraine were sat on a bench, watching us dash from the bouncy castle to the playground to the gates leading to the animal pens.

'Oh my God,' Lorraine gasped. 'Look at Beth.'

Mum turned to find me in the basin of the fountain, my mouth wide open, drinking the stagnant green water spurting from the stone lions' mouths. Aptly, there were three of them, arranged in a triangle. I'm not sure if Mum reacted – she was used to me – but Lorraine joked for years that the water must have given me magic powers.

I was equally strong-willed when Mum and Lorraine took us all to York Maze. It's the largest maze in Britain and one of the biggest in the world, the size of eight football pitches. But the walls are made of maize; they're flimsier than the hedges you'll usually find. You can easily cut through them and cheat.

Mum and Lorraine sat at the café while I acted as the ring-leader and marched Ben, Tom and Jess off down the path.

We emerged a few hours later.

'Mum,' Jess began. 'I've lost my phone in the maze.'

'That's not an ideal place to lose it, Jess,' Lorraine said, 'but see if you can find it on the paths you've been on.'

'Well, we haven't been on the *paths* . . .' Jess mumbled. 'Beth took us exploring.'

Caedmon School sits on one side of the River Esk and its rival school, Eskdale School, is over the bridge. Both schools filter into Whitby College, and I made friends with an Eskdale pupil, Steph Knight, who would sit next to me on the bus when we travelled to district athletics competitions. When we played rounders against Eskdale, I'd be bigging her up to my teammates, and she'd be doing the same for me. When either of us stepped up to bat, we'd be ordering our teammates to step further back.

When Ben moved up to Caedmon, he made the cross-country team. He wasn't as sporty as I was. He'd try to play football but wasn't so good, and I could never understand why this skinny kid with little knobbly knees didn't get stuck in like I did. When Ben and I used to kick the ball back and forth from opposite ends of the driveway, he'd make me stand closest to the road because I was always better at stopping the ball than he was. So running cross-country was a big deal for him. We were all very proud.

The day of Ben's cross-country meet, I'd trained at the Centre of Excellence in the morning and the race was close by in the afternoon.

'Beth,' said Julie Mastrolonardo, the teacher in charge. 'One of the girls has pulled out. Do you fancy joining in?'

I loved football, but I was never a fan of just running. I couldn't see the point, but after a while my arm was twisted. I finished in the top sixteen. 'Well done,' the race marshall said to me, 'you've qualified to trial for the county.' Poor Ben, the reason we were there in the first place, didn't.

'I don't want to go,' I said grumpily to Mum afterwards. 'I didn't even want to run!'

'It's your own fault!' she replied. 'You were the one who ran the race!'

One sport Ben was quite good at was cricket. I played with him at junior level for the local village team, and he went on to join the senior team. When one fielder was a no-show, I joined in for the day and sat on the boundary, catching two balls from my brother's bowling. The story ended up making the local paper, under the headline 'The Mead Show'.

Generally, I was happy to try any sport and hockey was another favourite. I was playing occasionally for the county and was asked to go to York to trial. Dad drove me there with a battered hockey stick I'd borrowed from school, my football kit and my old trainers, while the other girls talked among themselves, swinging their new sticks and hockey skirts. I stood on my own with Dad and watched them from afar. This was exactly the kind of clique-driven environment I hated, and I worried a lot about what people thought about me. I often had decent football boots, but I never took them to school in case people thought I was showing off. I only ever took my old ones. My parents couldn't understand that anxiety.

My passion for hockey didn't even come close to rivalling the way I felt about football. Put simply, football was my true love, but I don't think I ever said out loud that I wanted to be a footballer because it simply wasn't a career for women at that time. I knew there was an England women's team and I knew the players, but there were hardly ever matches shown on TV for me to watch. I always wanted to play football, but it wasn't realistic to aim to be a full-time professional footballer. I thought that I might like to be a PE teacher, or a police officer. Either of those would keep me on my toes, and I'd have to be fit. But a footballer? That wasn't possible.

3

Caps and Call-ups

I'm twelve when I get my first chance to trial for England.

Craig Nicholson, the Centre of Excellence technical director at Middlesbrough, has put forward his strongest players for a two-day talent identification camp at the University of Hull. I've never been to anything like this before and I'm riddled with nerves. My stomach is in freefall. On the two-hour car journey, I fret about how this trial will bring together the best players from our area. I won't be able to run rings around them all like I do in our Centre of Excellence games. I'll get stuck in, but I've always felt I'm not the kind of player who can stand out in a trial. I'm not the one people look at and just go: 'Wow!' I feel as though there's a nest of snakes writhing away in the pit of my stomach. I'm not sure I can do this.

I feel pressure throughout the drills to look good and be perfect all the time, but I know I haven't been able to express myself as a footballer. On the final day of the trial, we play small-sided games, and I feel instant relief. That sense is only magnified when I score my first goal.

In those matches, I immediately feel free, happy. I feel so light. I feel a sense of belonging, as though this is where I'm meant to be. I still remember those feelings all these years later. As soon as the starting whistle goes on a football pitch, it's like nothing else is there. Nothing else is around me. I don't have a care in the world. I'm lucky that football is like that for me. As arduous and nerve-wracking as the earlier drills were, this is where I come alive. I score four goals and dare to think that I might just have done enough.

On the drive back home, Dad pulls over to take a call from Craig and puts him on loudspeaker so that I can hear. 'England have called me,' Craig says, and I can sense the smile in his voice. 'They kept saying: "Why didn't we know anything about Beth Mead?"'

It's difficult to explain how desperately I wanted to play for England. The Arsenal and England forward Kelly Smith was my hero, so much so that I'd been speechless when I'd actually met her. Dad had driven us to Tadcaster so that I could watch her play for Arsenal against Leeds United. Even though Tadcaster is an hour from our house, the traffic conspired against us and we arrived late. We learned from those in the crowd that Kelly had scored twice before coming off, and from where Dad and I were standing we could make her out, leaning against the railings on the side of the pitch watching the game.

'Go and ask for an autograph,' Dad encouraged me.

'No,' I muttered, staring at the floor. 'I don't want to.' I was far too nervous to even think about going to see England's best player. I couldn't believe she was actually there, in person.

In the end, I plucked up the courage to get Kelly's autograph, and I met Karen Carney after the game, too. I was practically shaking when I walked up to them, and I wish I had photos of us together. The England captain Leah Williamson has a picture of herself as a ten-year-old England mascot standing beside Kelly Smith. Kelly had signed it 'Dream Big!!!' – and that picture has become iconic because of all Leah has since achieved. I'm not sure what I used for Kelly's autograph; it could have been a matchday programme. I know Kelly now – she presented me with my Player of the Season trophy at Arsenal in 2022 and we chatted like we were old friends – but I doubt she remembers that shaky little kid who was too in awe to talk to her.

Another treasured possession is my photograph of the England left back Rachel Unitt. Rachel had played in five major tournaments and one of Mum's old schoolfriends had sourced a signed picture of her to send to me. Matt Hewison worked for Scarborough Borough Council as a sport development officer and he wrote a letter to Mum to compliment her on my football skills. 'I was very impressed with Beth's football ability last Thursday at Caedmon during the Whitby Gazette World Cup, so much that I thought I would send her this,' he wrote. It meant so much to me to get something from an England player. That was what I wanted to be.

That said, my emotions were mixed when the letter from England dropped on the doormat. I was thrilled, of course. But, being me, my brain still jumped to what it would mean: leaving my comfort zone. Mum and Dad wouldn't be there by my side.

'You've got a letter!' Mum and Dad called. Printed on FA headed notepaper, it read: 'It is with pleasure that I write to inform you that your daughter has been selected or placed on standby for the upcoming England Women's under 15 training camp.' It was signed by Hope Powell, not only the England senior team manager at that time but the one tasked with running almost the entire women's football section of the FA.

I looked blasé, probably because I'm not very good at my showing emotions. I'm the same when it comes to opening birthday and Christmas presents. My family still complain that I never look happy even when I'm thrilled inside. But Mum and Dad had enough pride for all of us. Some of the parents at the California teams would tell Dad that I was good enough to play for England one day and he'd say they needed to dream on. He's never been a pushy parent, but I know that he was stunned that his daughter was about to be involved with the England set-up.

We went out for a family meal to one of the local pubs, and I was inundated with good luck and congratulations cards from family and friends. My parents still have those, along with all my letters from England.

Over the next few days, Dad began my preparations for the England camp. He called my teachers at Caedmon to tell them I would need to take some time off. Not all of them were happy about it, but they agreed. Over the next few years, I received piles of worksheets, textbooks and revision planners to take away to England camps with me, and, when I was at home, Mum would sit down with Ben and me every night to make sure that I got everything done. My headteacher at Caedmon, Mr Hewitt, wrote a letter to Dad to congratulate me on my selection: 'This is an excellent opportunity for Bethany,' he wrote. 'However, she may feel the facilities at Caedmon School no longer come up to scratch on her return. Please take this letter as approval of your request for Bethany to take time off.'

As the camp drew closer, though, I came to a difficult realisation: I didn't want to go. I really, really didn't want to go. I started to feel sick with dread. The nerves sat heavily in my stomach.

The night before, I crawled into Mum and Dad's bedroom and slept curled up on the edge of their bed, like a cat. For the next six years, this would happen before every England camp. Mum would come to dread this, come to recognise it as a sign that sending me off in the morning would be even more traumatic than it was last time. She would come to wait for the creak of the door and the pad of my feet on the carpet and her heart would sink.

'I don't want to go,' I'd begin the next morning.

'Don't worry,' Mum would say. 'Just get your breakfast.'

This is how we lived: breaking each day into tiny, tiny parts so that I didn't have to face up to the enormity of being apart from my family for a grand total of two days.

'I don't want to go.'

I'd pace the hallway. I'd tell Mum that I felt sick. She'd tell me that I'd be fine. I'd tell her that I wouldn't be. I had agreed to go on that first four-hour drive down to Lilleshall with my Middlesbrough teammate Ellie Christon; when I heard her dad Michael's car pull up outside, my stomach plunged. I lingered on the stairs by the door, feeling as though a trap door was about to open up beneath my feet.

'She'll be fine,' Mum told Michael, as I hovered in the doorway. 'She'll tell you she's sick, but she's not.'

From the back seat, I took one last look at my house, Mum's face indistinct and out of focus. Mum told me years later that this is her strongest memory of my first England camp: me waving silently from the backseat, eyes brimming with tears. It broke her heart, but she knew that, on the pitch, I'd be fine, that I wouldn't let this homesickness hold me back. The sight of Mum and Ben shrinking from the back window as we drove away broke me every time.

At Lilleshall, we slept in dingy underground dormitories, in beds on wheels. The rooms had an aged, fusty smell. My first roommate was Bethany England and, at night, I stayed awake listening to the rise and fall of her breath as I wept silently. I lay awake for hours, wishing I could just go home. I'm not sure if I ever went to sleep.

Day two was all about testing, which was another source of anxiety. When that first camp was over, I was just grateful to be going home. I put my player report in my bag. 'Quiet at times during training and classroom sessions,' read one section. 'Try to be more vocal, even if you are one of the younger players within the squad!'

One camp was at Warwick University, another at Loughborough. At Warwick, we ate in the canteen with the students, who towered over us. I felt in the way and out of place. What did they think of these England kids wandering in and out?

I found some of the England coaches too stern and struggled to open up to them. Lots of the drills were robotic and I didn't even feel comfortable when actually playing football, which Mum had banked on being a lifeline for me. The whole thing felt overwhelming and I was desperately uncomfortable in my own skin the entire time.

When I was picked to play in Poland, I felt so poorly when I got there that the England coaches sent me straight home. It was anxiety, but the physical symptoms – stomach ache, headache, nausea – could have been anything, so they erred on the side of caution in case I infected the team. The problem was that Mum and Dad had booked flights to Poland. They were disappointed – not in me, but in my coaches. Mum wished they'd known me well enough to realise it was just psychological.

Mum and Dad thought I would warm to the idea of going to England camps, but I continued to struggle. Every time, we repeated the same cycle: I felt sick for days, slept on the end of my parents' bed, told Mum I was too ill to go when the day finally came. England sent cars – Mercedes, BMWs – to

Hinderwell to collect me and I was filled with dread when I saw them from the window.

Ben would take my case outside and speak to the drivers while I plucked up the courage to follow him out.

'I wish I could go,' he'd tell me. 'I wish I could travel and have that experience.'

I wish you could go instead of me, I'd think.

Sometimes, the stress of going made me physically poorly. I hurt my back at one camp bending to pick up my case. I agonised over it afterwards, analysing it to death. Did I really hurt myself, physically? Or was it just in my brain? Maybe I'd worked myself up so much that my body started to reject everything. I was no longer playing for enjoyment. *This could end up breaking me,* I thought. *I can't keep doing this.*

One night at home, I told my parents that it was over. That I was not going away with England anymore. To prove the point, I stuffed my football kit in the bin.

'I hate it there,' I said, for what felt like the umpteenth time. 'You don't understand. You're at home with each other. I feel shit.'

Neither of them reacted.

'I'm not going to another England camp,' I repeated. 'I can't do it.'

'Fine,' said Dad.

'We're not going to force you to do anything,' Mum added. 'If you really feel that way, fine.'

I just wanted my England career to be over, so that I would never have to go away again. I knew deep down, though, that I was only punishing myself, and my resolution to quit England didn't last very long. I was back in the kitchen within a couple of hours, retrieving the shorts and socks I'd thrown out earlier.

I needed to get out of my own head, and, even though it took years, it happened eventually. There was no lightbulb moment – I kept struggling all the way up to the under 19s – but, as I moved into the older squads, we were handed a little more responsibility. We were no longer treated like robots, with timesheets to record our every move as though we were at school. That frustrated me all the way through the age groups and I relished the chance to be treated like an actual human being, and an adult, rather than a little kid.

I told myself to stop overthinking everything and reminded myself that, as much as everything around football caused me pain sometimes, I was fundamentally doing something I loved. I wish I'd learned to get rid of those worries and fears at a younger age. I wish I'd taken a breath to really enjoy growing up with England and drink in what was such a transformative stage of my life. But I suppose I just needed that time, and needed to be patient with myself. I needed to learn how to embrace England camps, and to see being a part of the England squad for the huge achievement that it is.

'Haven't you changed!' our Arsenal goalkeeper coach Leanne Hall said to me the other day. 'Remember all the crying you did at England? Look at you now! Nowt phases you.' Leanne's from Yorkshire too. We understand each other well and I've known her since I was twelve because she was a coach on those early England camps. I often call her Auntie Leanne. And she's right about me changing. Losing some of those anxieties allowed my true, cheeky and fun-loving personality to shine through. So many England coaches over the years never saw that side to me because I kept it hidden beneath layers of worry and homesickness.

I'm lucky that I had enough talent for my England coaches to bear with my off-field problems. Despite everything, my ability shone through. Andy Cook, one of my coaches from Middlesbrough's Centre of Excellence, says now that my talent bought me time when it came to the national team. The coaches were willing to give me more chances because they could see something in me – I'd earned the benefit of the doubt. They hoped that as I got older, my anxieties would leave my system.

It's a tough balance for coaches to strike. Everyone has had a different upbringing and we all have difficulties. Coaches should be understanding of that, but they do need to push players beyond their comfort zones. If they – and my parents – hadn't done so with me, would I be playing for England now? I doubt it. But I don't think you should write someone off because of how they feel. Mum and Dad knew that homesickness was all that would stop me from reaching the top level.

I played my first game for England against Germany, for the under 15s, when I was 14. Our family holiday in Turkey ended just a few days before the match. When we landed in Newcastle, Mum and Ben headed for the bus home; Dad and I had to go to a different terminal to fly straight to London, where the England players were meeting before flying out to Germany. When our flight from Turkey was delayed, it gave me hope that I could go home with Mum and Ben after all.

Of course, I was crying when the time came to leave them. My family's motto for dealing with me at this point was 'say bye and walk away', because they knew I was guaranteed to get upset. This time it was extra hard because we'd just been on such a lovely holiday, even though I'd taken a suitcase packed with football gear out to Turkey with me and felt it staring at me all week. Now I was being pulled away to be on my own again.

In the end, it barely felt worth it. I look happy and cheeky in the photos before the game – so thrilled to be making my England debut – but I've tried hard to forget what happened in the match. Put simply: we got battered. It was very nearly double figures.

My second trip abroad with England was a pair of friendly matches against the Netherlands in Zwolle. Mum and Dad travelled over on the ferry to see me start both games, scoring England's third goal in a 3–3 draw and our only goal in a 1–1 draw the following day. This made the Friday, 2 April 2010 edition of the *Whitby Gazette*. Dad framed my shirt from that game, making a border out of photographs and teamsheets. Who was on the opposing team that day, also making her debut? Someone called Vivianne Miedema. You might just be reading more about her later.

4

It's a Big Girl's Game

As I place my hands flat on my mattress and heave myself upright, I can't move my neck. I tense my shoulders and try to turn my head, but my neck muscles remain rigid and stiff. Middlesbrough's Centre of Excellence are supposed to be playing Sunderland today, but I'm not sure if I'll be able to.

'I must have slept badly,' I tell Mum, as she watches me eat breakfast. My neck still isn't loosening. On the coach up from Middlesbrough, one of the mums tries to massage my neck as I sit hunched over on the bus. She rubs and tugs all the way up the A19, to no avail. I'm not fit to start the match.

From the sidelines, I spend the first half shrugging my shoulders and wobbling my neck to try and relax it. It finally works. At half time, I feel well enough to come on. In fifteen minutes, I've scored a hat-trick. I finish the game with four goals. Sunderland go from leading the game comfortably to being on the wrong end of a 7–6 Middlesbrough win.

As soon as the game finishes, Mick Mulhern – Sunderland's first team manager and the director of the Girls' Centre of Excellence – approaches Dad. As Mick shakes my hand, my first thought is that he has a funny accent, a strong Geordie one, and a cheeky face. What he says next changes my life.

Mick tells us that he wants to sign me as soon as I turn sixteen that May.

'We've heard about you,' Mick says, 'so I wanted to come up today to see you play. You need to come up to Sunderland. You'll score loads of goals for us.'

It's just amazing to be wanted by a women's team. I still had the rest of the season to play with the Middlesbrough Centre of Excellence so I'd never thought about how quickly the future would come to me – or that this kind of opportunity might be waiting on the horizon. For a long time, Sunderland has had a reputation of being one of the best places in the country for developing talented female footballers. They've also effectively acted as a pipeline for the England team. Jill Scott? Produced by Sunderland. Steph Houghton? Produced by Sunderland. Carly Telford? Produced by Sunderland. Ditto Lucy Bronze, Lucy Staniforth and Demi Stokes. A few years earlier, Jordan had also moved to Sunderland and everyone at the Centre of Excellence had been excited for her.

Now they wanted me.

At that time, Sunderland Ladies – as they were known back then – operated independently of the wider Sunderland AFC structure. The women's team had been financed by the men's team for a while in the early 2000s, but that stopped amid financial troubles in 2004 and the women's team wouldn't be formally reintegrated into the rest of the club until 2013. That meant that the set-up I'd be entering into, for the 2011/12 season, was run mainly by volunteers. Parents would sell raffle tickets along with teas and coffees. The team were always organising fundraising events and searching for sponsorship deals. Mick was actually a full-time police officer. Sunderland would often lose the players they produced to richer clubs, but, being sixteen, they wouldn't have to pay a transfer fee for me. My registration with Middlesbrough would simply expire at the end of that season and then I would sign new forms with Sunderland.

Sunderland's offer meant that I had to make the biggest decision of my life. That year, the FA changed the age bandings from even numbers – like under 10s and under 12s – to odd-numbered bandings. Middlesbrough's centre of excellence now extended up to under 17s, meaning that I could stay another year if I wanted to. I was tempted. The Centre of Excellence had become, by now, my comfort zone. I was regularly scoring sixty to seventy goals a season, and five or six goals a game. I don't think you ever get bored of scoring goals, especially when each game brings so many. That I was so young meant that, on the one hand, I felt like there was no urgency to move on, but when I was honest with myself I knew that it was too easy for me. I wasn't developing. Dad's worry was that it didn't challenge me enough. Would I see anything new by staying another year?

Dad wasn't the only one who felt that way. One of my coaches at Middlesbrough, Andy Cook, had said the same. I'd known Andy since I was thirteen and he was my head coach at under 16s level. He and the other Middlesbrough coaches had often likened me to Thierry Henry because of the way I wrapped my foot around the ball. I was a number nine, and would drift out left, collect the ball in the channels and run at defenders, cutting inside and skipping through the backline because I had such good close control.

One summer evening, Dad and I stood at the side of one of the outdoor pitches at the Herlingshaw Centre and, as the sun set on the horizon, we let Andy know of Sunderland's interest.

'That's fantastic,' Andy said. 'You should go and enjoy it.'

'Really?' I asked.

'Why is that even a question?' said Andy. 'You've got to go now because it's the right time. Everything fits. You're ready.'

Mick travelled to Stockton to meet us. We met in the Morrisons café at the Teesside Park shopping centre. I stayed silent for most of the meeting, listening to Mick and Dad talk about their plans for me, my potential. It felt slightly surreal, but I didn't feel ready to start inserting myself into the conversation even though it was about me and how I would fit into Mick's team. He would play me as a number nine, latching on to the balls coming over the top from Rachael Laws and Rachael Furness, and he could see me becoming a prolific striker for Sunderland, one of the best women's teams in the country.

Mick would say later that he was struck by how shy I was, and how I didn't have a great deal of faith in my own ability. Dad wanted assurances that I would start every game – promises that Mick wouldn't give because then I'd have nothing to work for.

'What I will say,' Mick began, 'is that I will give you the number nine shirt. The rest is down to you.'

'I don't know,' I told Dad afterwards.

Several coaches at the Centre of Excellence wanted me to stay. I knew, deep down, that it was for Middlesbrough's benefit more than it was mine, but being a big fish in a small pond was a far more comfortable prospect for me than seeing if I'd sink or swim in the elite leagues.

I was leaning heavily towards staying at Middlesbrough; Dad and Mum pushed for me to move to Sunderland. For the next week, the decision – Sunderland or Middlesbrough? – was all we talked about. I felt trapped. Whenever Dad brought up Sunderland, I snapped at him.

'You're not going to force me to do something I don't want to do!' I shouted as I seized my football kit and stuffed it in the bin. Again.

'Why are you throwing this opportunity away when you're so good?' Dad asked, pleading with me. That's always been the way with my parents. They believed in my ability far more than I did and they knew that, once I'd got the emotions out of my system, I was good enough to cut it at Sunderland. That lack of self-belief, and my desperation to stay in the shallow end, would always come up in my end-of-season assessments at Middlesbrough. I was very good at sabotaging myself because I'd get worked up into such a state over change or the prospect of leaving home.

Andy's words ring in my head. 'The only person who will stop Beth from achieving anything is herself.'

Dad duly rescued the kit from the bin. Mum washed it. And Mick met us in the Morrisons café for a second time.

What I liked about Mick was that he was persistent but not pushy. He could sense that I wasn't good at leaving my comfort zone, so gave me the time to process the enormity of all these discussions. He offered me the chance to train with the women's team to give me a taste of life in senior football, reminding me that I was under no obligation to go. The choice, he said, was all mine.

'Go and train with them, at least,' Dad said. 'You need to see if you like it.'

I stared uneasily out the window on the drive to Sunderland's Academy of Light, second-guessing myself. Usually, Sunderland train on a 3G pitch in Gateshead in the evenings – being at the Academy of Light is rare at this point – and, as we arrived in the North East, Mum asked me if I was looking forward to the session. I mumbled something about playing against grown women and how I wasn't sure if I'd be able to handle it. My knees knocked together as we parked at the back of the training ground.

Steph Bannon was the first to take me under her wing, encouraging me to go on over and get involved. Once the ball was at my feet, that old trick of the light happened: the world dropped away and my worries vanished. I became that little girl at Hinderwell, at California Boys. Only this time I'm in Sunderland, with the big girls, in a senior football team.

'You kicked up a storm all the way up here,' Dad said, 'yet you love it.'

My decision was made.

Dad and I thanked Andy for his contribution. 'You always believed in her ability and made sure that she was being pushed in the right direction,' Dad says to him, and he's right. Andy was one of the handful of coaches who had encouraged me to take the leap to Sunderland. He had always been the kind of coach who, at youth level, would put the players' development above the interests of the Centre. I know that Andy took some bullets internally for those conversations with me – a few people were unhappy with him for his role in letting me leave – but I will always be grateful for his honesty and integrity when it came to my career.

My shyness was a big reason why Mick hyped me up to my teammates before I joined them. He knew that I could be timid off the field but that I had it in me to hit the ground running. The squad took me under their wing immediately and looked after me because I was one of the youngest players there. I was lucky that they trusted me right away.

A few weeks later, I travelled to the pre-season tournament in Manchester in a car with Steph Bannon and Abbie Holmes. We stayed in a dormitory at Keele University. In one of our first games, we played Liverpool, and a challenge from an opposition player was so crunching that it sent me sailing through the air, landing with an audible thump. Nearly all of my teammates ran up and confronted the woman who clattered me, while the other few rushed over to check that I was OK. It was a huge early moment for me; I realised quickly that I was going to really enjoy being part of this team. They had my back, even if they'd only known me a few weeks. I scored in most of the games in that tournament and felt settled. I had landed on my feet, and it was a huge relief.

Around this time, another player's parent was angry that I'd started ahead of their daughter and called Mick saying as much. Mick never questioned his belief in me, even for that short period where some people might have second-guessed his decision to play a teenager they'd never heard of. He could see beyond my age and I shouldn't have been surprised given all the players he'd developed years before I came along.

Mick was happiest when I got the ball outside the box and ran at defenders, but said that I had work to do with my back to goal. He coached me in how to get away from defenders. My pressing needed work, too, because I was playing with something Mick called 'half aggression', when I half closed a defender down but didn't go the whole way. My finishing was one of the few things that needed little work. He told me I was a natural goalscorer, that I had an innate ability to steal half a yard on defenders and then find the power to finish.

I took on a part-time job at the Fox and Hounds, a country pub in Staithes just a few minutes from home, to fund playing at Sunderland. I began as a potwasher, then graduated to waiting tables in my white shirt and black pants. I dashed in and out of the restaurant, doing exactly as I was told. I'm not clumsy by any means, but my biggest fear was spilling something on someone. All the staff in the kitchen were big football fans and between serving customers we would talk about what I was up to with Sunderland. The locals from back in Hinderwell supported me too and held a coffee morning at the Methodist Chapel, raising over a thousand pounds to help fund my early career.

When I turned eighteen, I started serving behind the bar, something I'd always wanted to do. I enjoyed pulling pints, particularly for the regulars, who quickly came to like the eighteen-year-old girl with so much energy and confidence. My Saturday shifts would finish at 11pm, and then I'd be darting across the country to play for Sunderland the next day. Sunday was double time behind the bar, so I'd work Friday, Saturday and Sunday during the off-season. It was full-on, but I loved those days working behind the bar. There are still some photos of me in the pub now. I spent one of my early wage packets on a pair of football boots costing £100, something I'd never have been able to do otherwise.

My first season at Sunderland was a success. In the FA Women's Premier League, I scored twenty-three goals in as many games, winning the Golden Boot en route to winning the league. We also won the FA Women's Premier League Cup for the first time, and I was named Sunderland Player of the Year. The following season followed the same pattern: I scored thirty times in twenty-eight matches, again winning the Golden Boot and the FA Women's Premier League and I was named Sunderland Player of the Year. Those were happy days. Every win turned our six-hour coach trips home into parties. I was learning constantly, and I always had the girls' support.

Later that year, I completed my A-levels: BTEC sport, BTEC science and History. I failed the latter but knew even before results day that I'd passed the other two because they were based on coursework and I knew I'd got distinctions. I won a place to study Sports Science at Northumbria University, ninety minutes from Hinderwell but just half an hour from Sunderland's Academy of Light. Northumbria had offered me a sports scholarship that would cover my tuition and living costs, and I'd signed up for a year's lease on a flat with one of my Sunderland teammates.

Mum and Dad wanted me to go into halls, but I'd wanted to concentrate on football. I thought halls would be one constant party, and I didn't want to live with strangers getting drunk all the time when I was supposed to be an athlete. Looking back now, I was just being a bit of a snob, but I didn't know any better then. When one of my Sunderland teammates, Becky Salicki, said that she was looking for a flatmate to live with her while she completed her final year at university, I thought that would be a better fit. But she was wrapped up in her own life. I was on my own a lot more than I'd expected to be.

My room in the flat was tiny and dingy, with little space for anything beyond a bed. I sat there that first night talking to myself. Is this where I'm meant to be? There you go again, Beth. This is what you do.

I was really unhappy at Northumbria University. I'd been called up to play for England during Fresher's Week, which meant when I returned to lessons, everyone else had already met each other and I felt like I didn't know anybody. I went to one of the induction classes but I didn't enjoy it. I stared at the rows of silent students, none of them making conversation.

Lessons hadn't even properly started when I called Mum. 'I can't do it,' I say. 'I don't want to do this. It's not like football. I don't like the course. It just doesn't feel right.'

Dad came across to see me, waiting on campus while I went to a lecture. On the walk back to my flat, I blurted out how I was feeling.

'I don't want to stay here.'

Dad tried to help me get to the bottom of these feelings. How could I want to leave after just one class, he wanted to know. But Dad also knew how stubborn I could be, and he knew that I'd got it into my head that Northumbria wasn't right, so it never would be.

Our conversation was a passionate and heated one. Dad decided to leave me to cool off. I went back to my flat and looked into other courses, and found one in Sports Development and Psychology at Teesside University. I called them. I'm lucky that the world of women's football is a small one and they wanted to have me. The course leader outlined what I'd be studying over the next three years and my intuition immediately told me that Teesside was where I needed to be. I withdrew from my course at Northumbria and enrolled on a different one an hour away, all without telling Mum and Dad.

The first they heard of it was when I turned up on their doorstep at Hinderwell. I'd packed my bags and called Alex Shaw, my best friend from school, to take me home, where I told my parents I'd be commuting to Teesside and Sunderland. We only trained at Sunderland during the evening back then; I thought I could study during the day without football taking away from the degree, which would likely open more career paths for me than football. I paid subs to play at Sunderland until 2015, when we received a small wage to help cover travel costs. I didn't think a full-time career in football was really possible.

Mum and Dad, though, were guarantors for the flat in Northumbria, and had to pay for this for the rest of the year. It was a big inconvenience for them, but my view was that I needed to do what was best for me and it was better to come away with a degree than drop out even further down the line at Northumbria. I paid them back by being the perfect student at Teesside. I stayed on top of my work and had all my assignments in two weeks early. It's the least I can do, I thought, as I set off on another 130-mile round trip from Hinderwell to the North East.

In 2014, the FA established the Women's Super League 2 as the second tier of women's football, replacing the Premier League. The WSL had been formed in 2011, and the FA's plan was to change the WSL from one tier of eight teams to two leagues totalling eighteen teams. This meant that clubs were invited to apply to the expanded WSL. One new licence was up for grabs for WSL 1.

Sunderland had missed out on one of the eight WSL places when the league had started three years earlier. Sixteen clubs had applied for eighteen places, so there was disappointment across the country at that time as the likes of Leicester City, Newcastle United and Nottingham Forest were rejected.

This time, Manchester City, Coventry, Leicester and Barnet, as well as the existing WSL 1 clubs, were competing with us to join the league for the 2014 season. The FA would part-fund WSL teams with a sum of £70,000 per club, but clubs had to demonstrate in their applications how they would match the FA's contribution.

We were crushed when we learnt that Sunderland's bid was unsuccessful and the final place in WSL 1 had gone to Manchester City. We moved to WSL 2, and were hurting. We had wanted to play the top teams, the likes of Arsenal, Chelsea, Liverpool and Everton. We felt ready. We knew we were good enough. Mostly, I was disappointed for my older teammates who had deserved a chance to play on the main stage after all they'd given to the club over the years.

We vowed to get there regardless, and we did. That season, we won promotion to the WSL on our own terms. We felt as if we were coming home, returning to where we truly belonged. It felt like we were sticking two fingers up at those who hadn't given us a chance last season.

In the days after our promotion, I took a call from Pedro Martínez Losa. He was the manager of Arsenal, then the most successful women's club in English football.

'We'd love to have you at Arsenal,' Pedro says.

I was stunned. It shouldn't have been a total surprise – in September 2014, I'd appeared on the BBC Sport website under the headline 'Is Sunderland striker Beth Mead a future England star?' I'd explained that I knew that a number of WSL were interested in me but that I'd wanted to see out the season with Sunderland. My dream, though, was to become a professional footballer. The game had accelerated rapidly in the previous few seasons and the players at Manchester City were training full time, with access to all the facilities at the Etihad. Arsenal and Chelsea were similarly committed to their women's teams.

There are no two ways about it: Arsenal were an unbelievable team. Only the best played for them. But as I listened to Pedro, I was laced with doubt, as well as the overriding sense that this wasn't the right time for me. I'd won promotion with Sunderland barely a few days earlier. I'd never played in WSL 1. Could I compete, both in the league and for a starting place, against Champions League winners? Against players flying to senior World Cups and European Championships? Against the kinds of players whose autographs I'd collected as a kid? I just wasn't sure, and I didn't have an agent to mull things over with. I knew that Arsenal were far better resourced than Sunderland, but what did that matter if I didn't play? If I went backwards?

For once, I was on the same page as Mum and Dad. 'Maybe you need more experience and playing time,' they advised.

'Those are my thoughts,' I replied, though I spent the next few days agonising over the decision. What if I couldn't replicate my Sunderland form in the WSL? What if the magic that's powered my early success finally runs out? Maybe Arsenal won't be interested in me in twelve months' time – what if they find somebody else? I didn't sleep easily for the few days before I finally called Arsenal with the news.

'The timing isn't right for me now,' I told Pedro, 'but I hope you persist with me. I appreciate you wanting me.' He was gracious about it and kind, although maybe he would have been less so if he knew I was to score against them twice that season.

That same summer, Sunderland had big news for us. Margaret 'Mags' Byrne, Sunderland's chief executive officer, met us at the Academy of Light after training to tell us that the women's team would be turning professional. Sunderland AFC was ready to recognise our importance to the club and would be employing a head of women's football, with a view to signing every player on a full-time contract in the next few years. It wasn't possible to do that right away – we needed to gather sponsorship, grow the fanbase for the women's side – but there would be money to allow about ten players to be fully professional immediately.

The reaction in the room was mixed. Many of us were thrilled – turning professional was all we'd ever wanted to do. Others were a little more subdued and anxious. What would our wages be? How long would our contracts run for? Many of the girls had careers, lives and families in the North East. They wouldn't want to give up secure jobs to try and make a career in football on a one-year contract. All they'd ever known was juggling football with studying or a full-time job and then training most evenings. I had the utmost respect for their determination to do both, but being a professional footballer was my dream. It's scary to think that, if I'd been born ten years earlier, it might not have worked out for me.

Mick was among those to step down. He didn't want to give up his career in the police force, and he left Sunderland having won seven league titles.

My existing contract at Sunderland was due to expire the following season. Mum and I were called to a meeting at Black Cats House, the club's offices right on the edge of the Stadium of Light, with Mags.

I was shitting myself. You don't mess with Mags. She's a badass bitch. She'll eventually leave Sunderland and become my agent, and I'll discover then that she's nothing like how I feared her to be when she was the CEO and the big boss. But I didn't know that before our initial meeting.

I gazed up at the line of grey windows. I'd never been involved in any kind of contract negotiations before. Neither had Mum. What should I expect? What kind of wage was reasonable to ask for? I had no clue. All I knew is that I loved playing football.

'We need to think about what you want,' Mum said, much more practical about the whole situation than I was. 'This is your chance. The most important thing is some kind of living allowance. Maybe you could get somewhere to live, instead of having to do all this travelling.'

We came up with a figure: £5,000 more than I was currently earning. As we waited in the corridor, we heard the click-click of heels from around the corner. Mum still says that this is one of her strongest memories of the day: Mags's Louboutins.

'We'd like to sign you for four years,' Mags said instantly. The initial figure was double my current contract. 'How do you feel about that?'

Internally, I was doing cartwheels. On the outside, Mum and I stayed silent. I didn't know much about negotiating, but what I did know was that you're never meant to act pleasantly surprised. Mum looked at me from the corner of her eye.

'Yes, well,' began Mum, probably thinking exactly the same as I was, 'but what about living costs?'

'We can sort that,' Mags said. She added on a few thousand.

Mum and I left the meeting and stared at each other in shock. We couldn't believe what had just happened. I'd just signed my first professional contract, for four years. It was a dream I thought would never come true, not because of a lack of trying on my part but because none of us knew if women footballers would ever be able to earn any kind of wage. That it was now my reality was simply incredible. And Mum still managed to squeeze a little bit more from Sunderland. Typical Yorkshire.

I'd learn later that Mum had been more panicked than she'd let on before the meeting – she couldn't believe that my football had reached the point where we were dealing with five-figure sums and that she had to act as my agent – but the contract allowed me to buy a house in Newcastle when I graduated. That's reassuring for any parent.

Being a professional footballer, and learning the ropes in WSL 1, made my final year of university more frantic than the first two. I didn't have time for any resits so I needed to get this right on the first try. I trained with the full-time players each morning for Sunderland, completed my work in the afternoon and then trained again every evening when the rest of the girls came in. The university sent my work across the online portal and my coursemates brought me worksheets and let me know when my deadlines were. I wrote my dissertation on the barriers in women's football and I got a First, achieving a 2:1 overall. I'm still so pleased with my grade because I've never been naturally academic. I've had to work for every good mark I've ever had and it means even more because my dissertation was on something I really care about.

Being around the Academy of Light in the morning meant that I ended up spending time with the men's team. We sat on adjacent tables; as a Manchester United fan, it was funny eating breakfast behind John O'Shea and Wes Brown.

But Jermain Defoe was the one who really took me under his wing. Every morning, he waited for me with a green tea.

'This is why I'm still playing,' he'd say, giving it to me. He was in his mid-thirties back then, on the brink of forcing his way back into the England team, and was always stressing to me the importance of looking after my body. Over our omelettes, we would talk about our lives as strikers. He invited me to come and do a shooting session with him – although sadly we never managed to fit that in because of our schedules – and he kept track of all our results. I was so surprised by his respect for the women's game at a time when it wasn't even on most people's radars. He has always been such a huge supporter of mine and we're still in touch now.

Even though we were now professional athletes, we would still go out after every win. As the victories stacked up, a 3–0 win over Birmingham, a 2–1 win over Bristol, a 4–0 win over Chelsea, we became superstitious.

'Girls,' we'd say to each other on the bus home from the south as we played music loudly and relished the fact that, halfway through the season, it was impossible for us to be relegated, 'we might have to keep partying if it's bringing us this much luck!'

In April 2016, I capped off my first season in WSL 1 with a night at the Grosvenor House Hotel in London, where Steph Houghton presented me with the PFA Women's Young Player of the Year trophy. I beat my future Arsenal teammates Danielle Carter and Nikita Parris, as well as Keira Walsh and Hannah Blundell. I was only twenty and it was one of my first big award ceremonies. The whole night was surreal, far more formal and fancier than any events I'd been to before. Mum and Ben came with me to enjoy the meal and free wine, and we spotted Premier League footballers and legends of the game sat at nearby tables. After I won, Ben got a photo with my trophy in front of the winners' backdrop to use as his Facebook profile picture, adding: 'Got a nice photo with my award.' Totally normal.

5
Life and Death

Sunderland training usually finishes at 9.30pm. It takes me an hour and a quarter to get back home to Hinderwell. I've done this journey more times than I can count. I've never had any issues. Until this night. Friday, 16 July 2015.

At 11pm, Mum calls in a panic. 'Where are you, Beth?' she asks. 'Are you safe?'

'I've been diverted onto the A19,' I say. I usually take the bottom road home, the coast road. That route is dominated by dual carriageways; it's busier, well lit. Sections of the dual carriageway run into local villages and, to put it one way, civilisation.

The moors route, the A19, doesn't have any streetlights. The hills all roll into each other and the roads rise and dip sharply with the contours of the landscape. There are no crash barriers. Trees or dry-stone walls flank the road on either side. It's lonely. And it's pitch black.

I judder across a cattle grid, my headlights the only illumination for miles. The road rises to a blind summit about to drop steeply into another cattle grid. I climb in the dark.

Something darts towards me. Human? Deer? I jerk the steering wheel and swerve wildly, seeing the retreating form of a deer bounding into the distance from the corner of my eye.

I rock forward as my rear end hits the grass. The car spins. The bushes seem to expand before me until the rear driver side smacks against a road sign.

The car flips.

I can't see anything. I'm thrown about the seat as though in a tumble dryer. I have no idea what is happening. I close my eyes as my body jerks in one direction and then another. I wait for the car to stop.

It takes me a few moments to gather my thoughts and realise I'm upside down. Immediately, a timer is set in my head. I have to get out. I hate small spaces. Can I smell petrol? How long do I have? What if I pass out? Panic pulses through me. My phone dangles in mid-air from the AUX cable plugged into the USB port below the dashboard. I snatch it free, unclick my seatbelt and fly downwards, smacking against the roof. The door has creaked ajar. I fold myself in half and force my body through the crack, rolling into the gorse bushes the car has landed in. The needles scratch and claw at my arms and legs as I push against the branches, heaving myself to the road. I try and steady my breathing, my heart lifting as I see twin lights bobbing in the darkness and coming towards me.

I wave my arms in the air. The driver pulls over.

'My car's in there,' I say. 'I've just flipped it.'

He steps out and I show him the silhouette of my white Seat Ibiza, its boot jutting out from the bushes.

My car begins to beep. I'm seized with a new wave of terror. I sniff the air for petrol, terrified the car will explode.

'Dad,' I say down the phone as the other driver paces beside me. 'I've just flipped the car. I need you to come. I was avoiding a deer.'

I'm suspended in shock, shaking and glassy-eyed. The ordeal only sinks in once I make it home, and I cry – heaving, juddering sobs. The doctor calls from the village to check on me. The only mark on me is a line of bruises where the seatbelt saved my life.

The car is recovered the next day. From the road, I watch the recovery van haul my car from the bushes and count the dents. The bonnet has crumpled into a concertina. The roof and rear driver side have folded in on themselves. One of the back windows is smashed. A branch has forced its way into the gap I escaped through.

The car had flipped three times. If that road sign had hit the front windscreen instead of the rear one, it would have sliced my face off. At best, I'd have been knocked out cold. If another car had been coming over the top, my parents could have been planning my funeral. I'm a very lucky girl.

This rings in my head over the next few days. I'm too young – just twenty – to be fazed by what happened. As ever, all I want is to play football.

We play Chelsea two days later. The staff at Sunderland give me a full medical, examining the stripe of bruises across my chest. I'm thankful my injuries are superficial, but they still ask me to tell them how I feel after the warm-up. I know within the first few minutes that I will be fine.

I give Sunderland the best game of the season. I come on at half-time and shoot across the box and into the far corner for my first goal. When the ball falls towards me a few minutes later, Chelsea's Niamh Fahey gives chase. I'm filled with a focus like I've never known. Fahey claws at me, but I win the ball and slot it effortlessly into the bottom corner. My final goal requires little to no effort on my part, the ball bouncing back off the far post from a corner and in off my knee for my hat-trick. A goal from Abby Holmes, arriving ten minutes later, sees us beat Chelsea 4–0. That Chelsea team contained Katie

Chapman, Eniola Aluko, Gilly Flaherty, Millie Bright, Drew Spence, Ji So-yun and Hedvig Lindahl. It is an enormous win.

It sums up the effortlessness of my form at Sunderland at that time. Everything felt right, instinctive, easy. Even a car crash couldn't deter me.

'Bloody hell, you were in an accident two days ago,' my parents say, shaking their heads in disbelief. 'This sums you up.'

I am safe, but in the months following, we lose somebody else: Jess, my Border Collie.

For the previous sixteen years, Jess had been my best friend. In demeanour, she was still a puppy. In reality, her arthritic legs had given up. She could no longer walk. We knew that it was time.

Granddad Alan, Mum's stepdad, had been close to Jess, too. Every morning, he would collect her at 6.30 and take her to the beach at Runswick Bay. Among the sand, they would find Whitby jet, a black gemstone that can be polished to turn the colour of liquid oil. People collect it to make jewellery and Whitby has dozens of stores specialising in this. Granddad said that people were always asking him whether Jess was a jet-finding dog. I'm not even sure if that's a thing, but she brought enough of it home.

Ben, Granddad and I took Jess to the vets to say our final goodbye. In reception, Granddad said he couldn't go in. It was down to Ben and me, and we stroked our lovely dog's head as lovingly as we could while the vet explained that Jess wouldn't feel any pain. The injection would just put her to sleep.

Jess stared up at us as we talked to her and told her that everything would be OK. I thought of those days when Jess would sleep outside in the winter and we'd wake up in the morning to find her hidden beneath a blanket of snow. I thought of the Barbie pyjamas she destroyed for me. I thought of the afternoons playing football on the field outside my grandma Ninny's house. As I stroked Jess's ears, I thought of how much I would miss her and hope she knows I'm grateful for every moment we shared.

Finally, she closed her eyes. Ben and I cried, silently. 'This is the hardest thing I've ever had to do,' I told him. 'She's been a member of our family for so long. She's been the best thing ever.' Pulling myself together, I left the room as my former next-door neighbour, now a vet, appeared and ushered me back in. She wept with us. Like me, she had known and grown up with Jess. Together, we cried for the next half an hour.

6

Happy in Who I Am

I probably should have realised that I was gay a little bit sooner than I did.

I was obsessed with the singer Cheryl, known at the time as Cheryl Cole. I was a big Girls Aloud fan, but Cheryl was special to me. Back then, I thought she was just someone I looked up to, someone to be interested in outside of football. I liked her music, her clothes, her whole vibe.

Was it a crush? Was it my sexual awakening? Was it just a phase? It's hard to know. Lots of teenage girls admired Cheryl. They loved her style, her looks, everything about her. Maybe her popularity muddied my true feelings for her. Looking back now, I can see that I might have liked her *in that way*, but I didn't think too deeply about it at the time.

As a teenager, I dated a lot of boys, but I never felt committed to a real relationship with any of them. That might have been because I always classed boys as my mates. I'd grown up with them and played football with them. As a kid, my favourite thing to do was to gather up every boy in the village and take them to the industrial park down the cul-de-sac, where we'd painted crossbars across the garage doors. My gran on my mum's side, who we all call Ninny, lives across from a tiny football pitch that was another favourite haunt. The old, rusty goal is still there now. She called me just the other day to show me that they've now added a net, which is a luxury we never had. The goal backed onto the playground, so every time we scored, we'd have to jump over the fence and chase the ball beneath the swings and slides.

Ninny would be watching all this unfold from her living-room window. 'Not ever does one girl come and see what you're doing,' Ninny would say. 'It's always a boy wanting to play football with you.'

That line summed up how I felt about boys, but that didn't automatically make me gay. I never had any feelings towards girls until I met Rachael Laws, my Sunderland teammate. Even then, it took me four years to really like her. At first, neither of us even knew we were gay.

Rachael and I became especially close after my accident. I'd been without a car since the Seat Ibiza rolled to its doom on the North York Moors and I couldn't travel to training and games. I started staying over at Rachael's house in Newcastle and we bonded on those car journeys all over the country. Jess Glynne had just broken into the mainstream at that point and we'd sing those songs as we drove up to the Metro Centre on our days off. We'd wander around the shops, always eating at Wagamama, and explore Newcastle together. Each time, saying goodbye became a little harder. I wanted to spend all my time with her. I didn't want to just see her for the day and for that to be it, for that to be all we were to each other.

I'd never felt those feelings for a girl before, but I was comfortable with them, and comfortable with Rachael. I wanted to kiss her.

Our first kiss was clichéd – at her house while watching romantic movies. We'd been in that situation together dozens of times before and nothing had ever happened. But that time, it was almost like we could feel the tension.

We turned to each other, and it happened. And it felt normal. It didn't feel weird. It just felt like everything had clicked. I wouldn't say it was a lightbulb moment for me because I never viewed our relationship as a moment of realisation that made me go: 'I'm gay.' In my eyes, I was just with someone I really, really cared about, and everything felt right. I wanted to be with Rachael. She made me happy. I'd never felt a connection like that with anyone before.

I can't remember which one of us took the initiative and asked the other to be her girlfriend. I'm not sure if we needed to. I had this conversation with Vivianne Miedema at Arsenal just the other day. What do people do now when they like someone? Do they need to ask the question? Is that old-fashioned? Are you seeing someone or *seeing* someone? And when does *seeing someone* become *with someone*? I'm twenty-seven and I'm still confused. I think that first relationship with Rachael was so chilled that we just gently slid into a relationship.

'Is this a thing with us now?' one of us might have asked.

'Yes.'

I was never ashamed of being attracted to women. I had openly gay teammates at Sunderland and they were among the few people who knew about me and Rachael. It felt normal for me, but we didn't tell our families we were dating for two years, mostly because Rachael wasn't ready to come out. I'd bought a house in Sunderland in January 2016, but when my family came to visit, Rachael wouldn't be there. We would sit together on the couch in the evenings, cuddling and holding hands, then one of us would hide out of shot when our families Skyped and FaceTimed us. We didn't want to keep secrets, but Rachael was my first female partner and I was hers. There is no handbook to tell you how to deal with that. We moved through our relationship in the way that felt best for us at the time.

I did, though, find it difficult to say it all out loud. I didn't say the words 'I'm gay' for a long time. Part of the reason was because I didn't need to. I was happy in who I was. But telling other people is sometimes another matter.

There weren't many openly gay or bisexual people in Hinderwell. I didn't know of any while I was at school. Who could I relate to? Some people in our village would have never met a gay person before. None of my friends back home were openly gay or bisexual. I knew they loved me, but I couldn't predict how they would react. Would they look at me differently? Would they be upset and offended that I hadn't told them earlier? What would they think?

I'd always used my trips back home to catch up with the girls at their houses over a takeaway. That was the scene for my coming out to them. I hadn't planned to tell them that day; I hadn't had weeks of agonising over when I would do it. It was far more instinctive but I felt compelled in that moment because all I wanted was for my coming out to be low-key. I didn't want to have to make a big announcement. Girly chit-chat with a pizza suited me fine.

The girls teed me up perfectly.

'What's going on in your life, Beth?'

'Actually, I'm seeing a girl.'

'I've kissed a girl before,' one of them replied, and we burst out laughing. In that second, it became normal. It made everything light-hearted.

'What's going on with you, Alex?'

'I'm seeing this boy and, to be honest, I'm not feeling it . . .'

That's how we continued, the conversation as normal as could be. My friends have always been down to earth anyway – they find it hilarious that I have 'fans' when, to them, I'm just the same old Beth from school – and they've met all of my partners and loved them. I guess they're more accepting of my sexuality because they're of the generation where homosexuality started to be viewed as normal. Many of them went away for university and saw outside the bubble of our little village.

Maybe that's why Ben took it so well. 'That's fine,' was his reply. We spoke as we always did. Nothing changed, and that was one of my biggest fears – that he would treat me differently, that I'd lose him. I feared for him, too. I didn't want anyone to tease him: 'Ha! Your sister's gay!' They never did, and Ben wouldn't have let it get to him even if they had. Luckily, people continued to see me as 'Beth Mead the footballer' rather than 'Beth Mead the lesbian'. There's no label on who I am. I'm just the same human being.

I wanted to write about my sexuality in this book because being gay or bisexual is fine in the women's game. It's accepted as totally normal and we don't even have to talk about it. We don't have to do big interviews or put out open letters announcing that we're gay. We're just being us.

Those were among my thoughts in May 2022 when Blackpool's Jake Daniels became the UK's first male professional footballer to come out publicly as gay since Justin Fashanu in 1990. He showed so much bravery and courage, but he shouldn't have had to. The culture in the men's game demands that of him. I never had to announce my relationships to fans. I just posted photos with my girlfriends on Instagram without a second thought.

I would love to help bridge the gap between men's and women's football when it comes to the perception and acceptance of homosexuality. That will have a big impact on wider society. It's only right that we keep changing attitudes.

Ultimately, you can't help who you fall in love with. I want to spend the rest of my life with someone I love. We all do. That's what I want for my parents and my children. It's what I want for everyone. I wanted my family and friends to accept who I was – who I am – and my relationship with the person I'd fallen in love with. I want everyone to be able to be true to themselves and to feel comfortable in their own skin.

Love is about being happy with the person you're with. That's all that matters. Gender and sex certainly don't.

7

250 Miles from Home

The entire Sunderland team has been called to a meeting in the Academy of Light press conference room. That's the first sign that this is serious. We never have meetings there. We're just a month away from the start of the new season, an interim edition of the WSL called the Spring Series. The league had always been a summer one, March to September, but in 2017 it will move to a winter league, following the men's football calendar. The Spring Series will run from February to May 2017 to bridge the gap. We're as ready to go as we always are. At least, we were before they brought us in here.

Sonia Kulkarni, the general manager of the women's team, joins us in the room and her face is drawn. My heart heaves. Whatever we are about to hear is bad news. Sonia is as heart-broken as we're about to be.

I can't remember, writing this five years later, who actually told us the news. I think it was one of the Sunderland board members. What is clear as day in my mind is the devastation, anger and uncertainty that ripples through the room when we are told that the club can no longer fund our full-time model. We will revert to a fully part-time model with near-immediate effect. Players will have to find other jobs and go back to training in the evenings. We don't know if we will still train at the Academy of Light. I don't know what will happen to my contract, which is still two years from expiring.

Why? Because the men's team is about to be relegated. The club need to cut costs. Mags has left the club by this point and is working as an agent. I'm one of her clients, but she was the spearhead for women's football internally at Sunderland. With her gone, it feels like the women's team has lost its protection.

It didn't matter how well we had done. We'd finished seventh in the league in the 2016 season just gone, and fourth the season before. We'd been seven points behind Arsenal; only they, Chelsea and Manchester City had won more matches than we had. I'd been the top scorer in the WSL that season with twelve goals, five ahead of my nearest competition. We'd exceeded expectations. But none of it mattered. Not now. Had it even mattered at all, if this was the end result? Just to be punished for something that the men were about to do?

Rachel Furness is one of the first to break the silence. 'How are you going to keep Beth Mead?'

Why are you worried about me? I think. *Why aren't you asking about your own future?*

'She's technically contracted,' the board member says, 'but it's going to be tough. We need that money now.'

It sucks. What will happen to the girls now? Those who still want a career in football will have to move quickly, starting all over again. Do they want to conceivably move to the other end of the country? Will anyone want them? I know that other clubs will be interested in me – I'd had Arsenal come in for me a year ago – but what about everyone else? What about those local girls who have already built their whole life in the North East but want to play football at a club that cares about its women players? Where will they go?

The next few weeks are frantic and panicked for those players as they try to work out what's next for their football careers. Suddenly they all face uncertain futures.

I learned from Mags that Sunderland was now willing to listen to offers for me. They were happy to sell me to make some money for the club. Maybe hearing that would make some players feel unwanted or rejected, but I was just filled with frustration at the injustice of it all. The men hadn't done well, so the women's team had to suffer? It was just shit.

Mags told me that she had been inundated with offers. It was funny to hear her talking like this. When Arsenal had approached me a year ago, she had been adamant that I wasn't for sale, that what they were offering didn't come close enough to my value to Sunderland. Now, she was my shopfront, fielding calls from clubs and managers.

One interested party was Emma Hayes, the new Chelsea manager. I spoke to her on the phone but was immediately intimidated by how strict she sounded. She told me that she didn't think I was fit enough, that I could do a lot more to improve on my game. She was right, of course, and it was the kind of thing I would hear scores of times over the next few years, but I was young and already feeling unsteady after the news from Sunderland. Her words weren't easy for me to hear in that moment, when I just wanted to be in demand. I wasn't sure their playing style was right for me at that time, either. That was the only call I had with Emma, and, in the end, Chelsea never made a formal offer for me.

Meanwhile, Arsenal had come back. They were still interested, and Sunderland gave me permission to speak to them.

I think back to one of my favourite memories of the Middlesbrough Centre of Excellence. I was thirteen and we were on one of our annual tours, all of us packed on the bus, our parents in tow, for a weekend of games against other centres of excellence. Those tours always ended with the Women's FA Cup final, and, that year, we were at Derby's Pride Park to watch Arsenal beat Sunderland 2–1. It's one of my strongest memories of watching women's football as a child, and one of the first games I saw in the flesh. I remember watching Lucy Bronze, who would only have been seventeen then, playing for Sunderland. And of course Kim Little sealing the win for Arsenal in injury time. But what I remember most clearly is the crowd. There were 23,291 there that day. The FA Cup finals always had such huge attendances.

But the memory now felt strange to me: Arsenal 2 Sunderland 1. The two clubs I had to choose between. The two clubs that meant so much to me. Sunderland had developed me, taught me so much. Arsenal were the club I'd looked up to for so long. The Kelly Smith connection played heavily on my mind. I wanted to play where she played.

I travelled down on the train with Mum to meet Mags in London. She took us to Arsenal's training ground at London Colney in Hertfordshire, where we met Clare Wheatley, Arsenal's head of women's football, for a tour of the facilities. There were ten full-size pitches, one of which matched the pitch at the Emirates, training and rehabilitation areas, physiotherapy and massage rooms, hydrotherapy pools, a squash and basketball court, a sauna, a steam room, a restaurant, a weight room, a classroom, a TV studio, a player performance centre, offices for the scouting teams, academy staff and data analysis team, a spa and a cryochamber. The gym was being rebuilt as part of a multimillion-pound refurbishment, but it meant that, in the meantime, we'd be training in a far smaller facility that wasn't too far from what I'd been used to at Sunderland. But it was obvious that Arsenal had a plan, that they cared about their women's team. I'd just come from a team that had been kicked to the kerb because the men had underperformed. I didn't even know if Sunderland Women would be training at the Academy of Light next season. It was a scary prospect. Where would we go?

'It's fabulous,' Mum said of Arsenal, totally awestruck. The facilities were out of this world. We went around St Albans, the Hertfordshire town where all the Arsenal Women players live. It was beautiful, with rural parts just like in Hinderwell. It seemed homely, and different to what I'd expected. In my head, I was moving to London; I'd be right in the middle of the city centre, amongst all the hustle and bustle. I'd never fit in with that life. But St Albans was different. It felt comfortable. When Clare drove me past the house I'd be moving into with some of my Arsenal teammates, I could actually imagine myself living there.

That evening, we went to see the musical *Wicked*. Largely, I felt good about all of this. But a part of me didn't want to go. As the evening wore on, Mum could sense my mounting unease. I know that might sound silly as there was nothing to dislike about anything we'd seen – except it was 250 miles from my parents' house.

Turning Arsenal down the first time had been difficult because they were my dream club. Who had Karen Carney, one of those footballers I'd been so nervous about meeting that day in Tadcaster, played for? Arsenal. They had led the way in the women's game for decades and I knew that signing for them would give me an experience unlike anything I'd ever had before. But it had been too early for me then; I wasn't sure I was ready to compete with the top players.

Things were different now. I knew I could hold my own in the WSL.

Moving to Arsenal was the only option for me if I wanted to continue in football. It was absolutely the right thing to do. I knew this. My parents knew this. The whole world knew this. But I was dragging my heels, trying to come up with any excuse to stay. I loved Sunderland. I loved the girls there. I was with Rachael, and I didn't want to leave her behind.

It was the same kind of battle I'd had with my parents 200 times before. Me yearning to stay in my comfort zone, and them knowing that a better life – the one in which I fulfilled the potential that I sometimes feel imprisoned as much as freed by – awaited me if only I was willing to take the leap. I agonised over this for days, but, truthfully, it wasn't even a contest. In January 2017, I signed.

One of my final training sessions at Sunderland took place in the Barn, the indoor 3G pitch at the Academy of Light.

'Could you just stay a minute?' I asked the girls at the end of the session. They did, and, though I was nervous about speaking in front of the girls, I knew I had to tell them. It would've killed me if they'd found out the news from somebody else.

'I love this team and the club,' I said, 'but you know what's happened. I want to develop, and I've decided to move to Arsenal.'

Some of the girls were visibly taken aback. Rachael and Steph were the only ones who had known that I'd been to look around at Arsenal. 'We don't blame you,' they'd said. 'What's happened is shit. Do what you have to do.' The girls reacted amazingly. They were so happy for me. The senior players, who had been like sisters to me, laughed: 'You've gone past us now!' Arsenal had beaten us 7–0 a few weeks earlier. 'Don't do that to us,' they warned.

I spent my final night up north with Rachael in Newcastle, packing up my flat. On the drive down to London, I cried for two hours.

I signed for Arsenal while still carrying an injury I'd picked up during the winter break with England's under 23s. I'd ruptured my ankle ligaments while being tackled in a training session. My grand unveiling at Arsenal involved me hobbling around as I posed with the shirt. Arsenal promised to look after me – they wouldn't have signed me otherwise – but I was still laced with panic. I wasn't as mobile as I would've liked to be, so anything that involved kicking a football was off limits. There's no video of me zinging one top bins, and I really dislike the pictures they took of me. My apprehension about moving is written all over my face.

This was the biggest step of my career. I wasn't at home anymore. London is huge. Its population is 5,713 times bigger than Hinderwell's. It felt so sprawling and impersonal, and there were times when I felt out of place. I'm a village girl at heart.

Worse was that Arsenal trained in the morning and were done by 1pm, and then our schedules were blank for the rest of the day. I knew nobody. I lived with Jordan Nobbs, Katie McCabe and Jemma Rose. They were forthcoming, but they had their own lives and their own friends. They had places to be and it felt like they were always off doing something else. I didn't want them to baby me. But I'm also very good at saying I'm OK when I should be asking for help and support. I should've told them how lonely I felt. Instead, I kept everything bottled up.

And my ankle meant that I didn't have football to give me an escape. After meeting the girls on my first day, they went out to train on the pitch and I went to the gym for my rehab work. In those first few weeks, I felt like I was always waiting. Waiting to get better. Waiting for them to come back in so that I could socialise with them again. Waiting to join them on the pitch.

All this pain, these worries, were constant. The feelings were with me all the time. I spent hours in my room, distraught and upset, trying to work out if I'd made the right decision. There was no way for me to switch off. I felt sad every waking minute. There was no rest.

Clare Wheatley keeps her office at the training ground. Her door is literally always open, and I knew that I had to go and see her.

'Can I talk to you?' I asked one day, hanging in the doorway.

'What do you need?' Clare replied, looking up from her computer.

My voice wobbled. Breaths darted in and out of my lungs. I might be good at hiding my emotions, but never at holding them in once I've made the decision to open up.

I think my eyes said the words before I did. 'I don't know if I want to be here anymore – at Arsenal.'

I was adamant that I wanted to go. I was struggling. I was finding it too hard. This just wasn't the place for me. But Clare had dealt with this before. She told me that it was normal, that she'd had more girls than I can imagine saying the same things to her as I was.

'What can I do to help you?' Clare asked. 'What do you need?'

Clare agreed to meet me for coffee during the afternoons to break up my week, but I continued to spiral. It wasn't long before I was ready to leave. I was in a really, really low place. Every day, I dreamed about packing it all in and moving home. I worked myself into a frenzy until there was nothing to do but call Mum. I rang her while she was at work. It didn't matter to me what time it was: I just knew that I needed to hear from her, right then, before I fell to pieces. I had to hear her voice. I needed its comfort, its familiarity, its reassurance.

Mum was in the classroom. She caught the eye of the teacher. 'Can you cover me?' she asked, and disappeared into the store cupboard at the back of the room to take my call and talk me down. 'I'll ring you in a couple of hours,' she said. 'Can you just get to that point? Do your training, come home and I'll ring you again then.' Every break, every lunchtime, she called, just like she said she would. 'Just think about the tea you're making. Just think about the coffee you're drinking. Don't think about what will happen tomorrow.' When she got the chance, she came down to London and stayed with me, stuffing the freezer with her homemade shepherd's pie and lasagne.

I missed Mum more than I ever thought possible. She has always been my comfort blanket. When she came to visit, she hid envelopes and notes in my pillowcase so that I would find them after she left. She brought me a pebble from the beach at Runswick Bay, decorated by a local artist. *One step at a time*, it read. She wanted the rock to say this to me when she couldn't.

Mags had regular calls with Clare to help with my home-sickness, and asked Clare to speak to Mum.

'Do you know she's really struggling?' Mum said. Arsenal hadn't realised the true extent of the problem, but that was probably my fault for keeping everything hidden. Clare promised Mum that she would take Jordan to one side and ask her, on the low, to keep an eye out for me. That made a huge difference and I started going out for coffee with the girls. Rachel Furness moved from Sunderland to Reading and she came up to sit with me some evenings. But the biggest change was having the ball back at my feet. My ankle was healed. Back on the pitch, I felt alive again.

Those experiences, as awful as they were, are the reasons why I'm now always so protective of our new signings. I always offer to take them for a coffee in the afternoon or go out somewhere to socialise after training. Although training finishes later these days than it used to – maybe two or three o'clock – the rest of the day still leaves us with lots of time to fill. If you have nothing to do and no one to be with, those hours can be really painful. I always vow to make an extra effort because I used to be that person: alone, in a new city, unsure of where I stood and if I'd ever feel OK again. We've all been there, but some people forget how it feels. I never will. I don't want anybody else to ever feel as low as I did.

Returning to training in February gave me an instant lift. I wanted to prove myself. *Pedro must believe in my ability to want me two years in a row,* I told myself, and I hit the ground running. Back on the football pitch, everything made sense to me. It was my outlet, as it always has been, and it took the edge off my anxiety.

I made my debut in a 10–0 FA Cup win over part-time Spurs on 19 March. I'd not played football for so long; the excitement as I crossed the white line was indescribable. I felt like I'd returned home and I was ready to show everyone exactly what I'm about. When the ball was slipped to me, I launched it as hard as I could, and I swelled with joy when I saw the net balloon. I threw my arms out wide, bathing in the relief. This *is the start of my Arsenal career,* I told myself, as I spotted Mum and Dad in the crowd. I've worn the Arsenal shirt now. I'm going to create my own memories now.

I felt lighter and I moved more easily, carried myself differently. It was almost as if the last few weeks had never happened. In a five v five in training, I lobbed the goalkeeper, Sari van Veenendaal. Daniëlle van de Donk turned to me, her eyebrows raised in pleasant surprise.

'You're actually all right, you, aren't you?'

I laughed, feigning offence, with no idea that Daan and I would begin dating in late 2017. We hit things off fairly quickly because we both have similar, cheeky personalities, and she was among the first people to make me feel welcomed into the team. She invited me over for dinner at her house and cooked for me with her Arsenal housemates. I appreciated her reaching out to me because my housemates had their own schedules and, in those early days, I was often left twiddling my thumbs. What Daan and I had grew into something else and we were together for four years, but things just didn't work out once she moved to France to play for Lyon.

Back then, I was just happy that my introduction was going well. My Arsenal teammates would have heard me spoken about as a key player at Sunderland, but you never truly know someone until they're your teammate.

I was having the kind of sessions where everything came off for me. My body and mind felt united as one. Every shot I hit was clean, and I became braver, more daring. Things were going great. So great that I went too hard. The ball dropped into the box and set me up for a one-on-one against goalkeeper Anna Moorhouse. I made eye contact with her, vowing to beat her and conveying as much with my gaze. I was powered on pure adrenaline. *I'm going to get there*, I told her. I broke into my run, but Anna was quicker. I was so committed that I flew over the top of her. The ground rushed up to meet me.

The next thing I was aware of was a screaming pain searing through my shoulder. My arm dangled limply to one side.

'What's happened?' I heard someone call. 'I just heard a snap.'

I couldn't process who said it, or the scene unfolding around me. I was utterly consumed by the pain scorching around my neck and shoulder, by the throbbing of my head where it smacked the ground. I think I cried; through blurred vision, I saw a flurry of limbs trying to soothe me, heard hushed voices telling me to keep calm.

I was carried away on a buggy, sucking on an analgesic. This, obviously, sent me loopy. I refused to leave the training facility to get an X-ray until I'd waved goodbye to all the girls. Our doctor, shaking his head in disbelief, carried me into the gym to see them. My teammates were so concerned about me that they practically wet themselves with laughter. It might not have been any good for me, but at least it put their minds at ease to see me, in my drug-induced fug, totally away with the fairies.

The news came back: a broken collarbone. I'd never had bad luck with injuries, never broken so much as a bone. Yet in the few months since signing for Arsenal, I'd spent three months out with ruptured ankle ligaments and, one month into my comeback from that, then faced six weeks out with a broken collarbone. To this day, I still have six pins in my collarbone.

The timing was difficult because I'd just started genuinely enjoying life at Arsenal. I was getting to know people, making new friends. I'd also broken up with Rachael because being long-distance just didn't feel right for us. I was the one who ended things, which always makes walking away easier, but it still added to the upheaval of those months. Now the doctors were telling me to go home. 'There's nothing physically you can do right now, and we know you've struggled with loneliness before,' they said. 'Go and be with your family.'

It made sense. I returned to London for my surgery a few days later feeling refreshed and better placed to cope emotionally with sitting on the sidelines for the foreseeable. The surgery went well and, after ten days, I was allowed to run. The range of motion in my shoulder was just as it had been, but I wasn't allowed any contact for another six weeks. Six weeks of running, after all the time I'd already endured away from football, hardly thrilled me.

Joining me in the rehab room was Alex Scott. Having been diagnosed with osteoarthritis in her twenties, by the end of her career Alex would have to receive regular steroid and joint injections just to be able to play on Sundays. At the side of the pitch, we ran together. Run, stop, turn. Run, stop, turn. Run, stop, turn. Rinse and repeat, for half an hour. All the while, we could see our teammates running through drills: dancing through cones with the ball at their feet, smashing into each other as they chased the same ball, bringing the ball down on their chest to volley it into the top corner. My stomach clenched with sadness that I wasn't allowed to do the same.

Alex sensed this. 'One day, you'll remember this,' she said. 'When I'm shouting at you to run that little bit harder and give that little bit extra, you'll know why. It will all be worth it.' She was correct on that score, and I felt lifted that someone understood what I was going through.

I was back in full training when Pedro signed someone called Vivianne Miedema from Bayern Munich. Viv had turned professional at just fourteen years of age, playing in the Eredivisie, the top Dutch women's league. In that debut season, she scored ten times in seventeen games. In the 2012/13 season, playing in a cross-border league in the Netherlands and Belgium called the BeNe League, she scored twenty-seven times in twenty-six games. The season after, she scored forty-one goals in twenty-six games. She would have just been seventeen then. No wonder nearly forty different clubs tried to sign her when she moved to Bayern Munich in 2014. She kept up her goalscoring form there for two seasons. She had been the top scorer in the Champions League the season before she came to Arsenal.

I didn't know any of this because I didn't know the German league. What I did know was that she was a number nine, just like me. I was fresh talent at Arsenal, but, clearly, I wasn't enough. *Am I inadequate? How can they sign Viv just a few months after me?* Whatever I'd done, she had done already.

Pedro came up with a new role for me.

'I'd like to try you on the wing,' he said one day.

I was baffled, and, if I'm honest, a little reluctant. A winger? Why?

'I've been a number nine all my career,' I responded grumpily. 'This is all I know. Now I'm having to start afresh? At twenty-one? Really?'

'You have a great right foot,' he said. 'You strike the ball well. You have good vision. You have all the qualities a winger needs.'

I joke about it with Viv to this day.

'Of course *you* came in,' I say. 'Vivianne Miedema. Then I get chucked out.'

Viv will just give me a wry smile. 'Well, I probably was better.'

Now, it's obvious to me that twenty-one was still very young. That I just needed to stop being childish, to listen to someone who saw something in me that I didn't. If I could go back in time, I'd tell that younger me to grasp that opportunity with both hands. Here's someone offering you a chance to play and a route back into the team. Stop being a little brat. But my first few months at Arsenal had been marred by so many bumps and bruises; I felt I'd only just got going for it all to be taken away from me.

But this was what I needed to do if I was to stay at Arsenal, I realised quickly. I'd overcome too much to give up now.

So, despite my reservations, I jumped wholeheartedly into my new role. With the analysis staff, I broke down videos of the Arsenal men's team. I observed their positions off the ball, their movements when the team were in and out of possession. Pedro coached me from the sidelines, and I found that it came to me more instinctively than I'd anticipated. It felt natural. I loved the freedom, and I quickly discovered new parts to my game that I never knew were there. I understood what a number nine wanted and needed because in that position I'd always wanted things played to me a certain way.

On the eve of the new season, I was filled with hunger. The final few weeks before the 2017/18 season began to feel like climbing to the top of the rollercoaster. I was ready to throw my arms high and plunge right in.

8

Spiralling

One month into the new season, Arsenal and Pedro part ways. The season has only just begun and we are already looking for a new manager.

Many Arsenal fans have never known a start as bad as this one. We are sixth in the WSL – the league had just ten teams that year – and among our early results are a 3–0 defeat by Turbine Potsdam in the Champions League and a 5–2 turnover by Manchester City. Viv and I watched the first half of the game from the bench, but City stepped up into another gear and we were chasing shadows even after we came on.

We feel hopeless. It's difficult to describe what it's like to be in that kind of rut; living it is even harder. Frustration colours everything. You try everything in your power to make yourself better, and that's one of the biggest misconceptions fans often have towards a team enduring a bad run. Just because everything is falling apart doesn't mean that we don't care, that we stop trying. But on the field, we're spiralling.

It's a vicious circle. None of us have anything against Pedro personally, but the playing style feels stale and unsuited to too many players in the squad. It's difficult to execute a system that, deep down, the girls feel uncomfortable in. On the pitch, we're sluggish, ponderous, hesitant. Sometimes, player and manager need to meet each other in the middle, but we cannot get it right. We sit in scores of meetings trying to figure everything out, but none of us can snap our fingers and pinpoint the problem. There's no handbook on how to do it, no doctor to diagnose the issue. Maybe we're scared to confront each other and be honest about how we feel. Perhaps, as a team, we don't say to each other all the things we need to. It's painful to not have all the answers.

It doesn't take a body language expert to see that we are anxious and uncomfortable on the ball, that our minds are cluttered. If you're happy, you can feel untouchable on the pitch. Mistakes don't bother you. This is the reverse. The more things go wrong, the more you second-guess yourself and trick yourself into doing things you never normally would.

This is the case even when nobody is watching; I come away from training countless times knowing that the session wasn't what we needed if we wanted to win that weekend. So many drills broke down halfway through. We tried so many combinations and systems that never felt quite right. How can you have confidence on the pitch if your rehearsal goes so badly? This is especially noticeable on our matchday minus one training sessions, the final ones before our games at the weekend. You should leave those feeling on top of the world. We never do. The girls leave training frustrated, unable to buy into ideas that didn't work in practice.

I don't have anything against Pedro personally. I don't think any of the girls do. All I know is that I play my best when I feel like that little six-year-old girl running around on the pitch with the boys again. But that mindset feels a million miles away. We're not a happy team.

At the end of October, Clare approaches us to gather our views on Pedro. She comes up to Leah Williamson and me as we walk into training, but we're reluctant to say anything. I'm twenty-one and new to the team; Leah is even younger than I am. We feel too green, too inexperienced, to offer much beyond that we feel the style is tired and we're not playing our best football. We leave it at that. We don't throw Pedro under the bus, even if the senior players are more direct in their views.

Our final meeting with Pedro is deeply awkward. We sit on the sofas in the Hub, the tiny meeting area in the part of the training ground reserved for the women's team, as Pedro comes to the front to address the group. He is quite bitter, and his speech essentially amounts to 'the club has got rid of me'. There is no warm feeling, no well wishes, and I don't really know how to process it all. I've never seen a manager be sacked before; I've no idea if this is the norm.

'Right,' Clare says, 'I think we should go now.' She brings the conversation to an end before Pedro can say something he regrets. We rise to shake Pedro's hand. I hug him before he turns and leaves.

A month passes before we hear news about the next head coach. We hear that an Australian guy is coming in. Arsenal player Kim Little knows Joe Montemurro having played under him at Melbourne City and speaks highly of him. When he finally does arrive, we learn that he is half-Italian, and so relaxed that he's almost horizontal. And I love him immediately.

From day one, Joe has a warmth to him and is deeply personable. Every day, he walks around the training ground with a tiny espresso cup and checks in on each of us. He takes us out as a team to his favourite restaurant in St Albans, La Cosa Nostra, a family run Italian place in a converted end-of-terrace house. He is best friends with the staff there and speaks to them in Italian, all while we look slightly bemused and joke that he is probably bitching about us all.

His accent causes me no end of fun, and, in an early team meeting, he catches me sniggering away.

'What's funny?' he smiles, bemused.

'You sound like the seagulls from *Finding Nemo*,' I tell him. I offer up an impression of the seagulls arguing over the fish on the pier. 'Mine! Mine! Mine!' I've probably given him some kind of complex about saying the word 'my', but he chuckles along with me.

Joe's tactical knowledge is supreme and he is clear in what he wants from us. He is a possession-based manager who wants us to control and dominate the ball. He presents us with six style rules that we must fall back on if the game risks running away from us. The idea is that these principles will catch us when we're looking for a foothold, and give us a way back into the game. One is no square passes, with Joe having pinpointed that these are the passes from which we're most likely to concede. This becomes the soundtrack to our early training sessions. 'SQUARE BALL!' he'll boom in that Australian accent, if ever one of us slips up.

Most important to him is fluidity, and I have the confidence to cut inside knowing that someone will take my position so that we can create an overload. I start as a winger, but I float between the half-spaces and pockets as a number ten. From out wide, I can stretch the defensive line, which gives me so many options: I can take players on or combine with Viv, Danielle or Kim. The key is getting the pass away early before our opposition has had the chance to reorganise. We're confident on the ball.

In March, we reach the Continental Cup final, our run having taken me back to Sunderland for our quarter-final. My move from Sunderland to Arsenal was the first time I'd moved from one senior club to another and had never had to face so many old teammates before. We stayed at the Hilton next to the Stadium of Light, and my former teammates Steph Bannon and Gemma Wilson came to visit me at the hotel. That night, we had a great catch-up – the kind where the instant they walk in the room, you know nothing between you has changed – and we talked about the old times. It made for a strange experience, but I received a warm welcome from the players and fans I'd known since I was sixteen. 'You've grown up so much now!' they'd say. I appreciated the kindness of those who had known me from the start, particularly from the fans, who demonstrated the same respect to me as they had done when I'd worn a Sunderland shirt.

I scored our final goal in a 3–1 win, but didn't celebrate because I respected the club that had done so much for me.

'Of course you had to score against us,' said the Sunderland manager Melanie Reay, when I embraced her at the end of the game.

'I'm sorry,' I laughed.

When you play your old team, it's like some things are fated, meant to happen. I've always felt that way about players scoring against their former clubs.

On the bus down to High Wycombe's Adams Park for the final, we were shown good luck messages from Arsenal's male players. As holders of the league title, the FA Cup and the league cup, Manchester City were tipped to retain all three trophies that season – until we came along. Half an hour into the game, Dominique Janssen breaks down the wing and finds me in the area. Viv and I have switched positions, and I take up the space of a number nine to flick the ball into the space behind me, knowing that Viv is ghosting in. She brings the ball down and rolls it between goalkeeper Ellie Roebuck's legs. It's a typical Joe Montemurro goal. I leap into her arms and that breakthrough – Viv's first opportunity of the game – is enough to seal my first piece of silverware with Arsenal.

I feel an enormous relief and joy. I've done what I was brought into Arsenal to do. I'm beginning to show my worth, after all those injuries and the pain of moving from Sunderland. It feels like I've truly turned a corner.

At full time, Joe calls us into a huddle. 'Now you've proved to everyone, with hard work, where you're at,' he says, prodding the air with his finger to emphasise each word. 'This is the platform. Now we want more trophies. Enjoy it.' At that, we leap into the air, bouncing with our hands held high. Joe waits at the end of the podium for me, then slings his arm around my shoulder as I collect my medal. Player and manager are united as one.

I stare at a Beth Mead twice my size, stretching from floor to ceiling. I'm in the tunnel at Wembley for the May 2018 FA Cup final, about to play in front of the biggest crowd I've ever played in front of. And the tunnel has been wallpapered with . . . me, in my Arsenal kit, dribbling the ball.

Before kick-off, I had my picture taken with the mural, and my parents have this, along with other key moments from my career, printed onto canvases that they've hung on the wall outside my old bedroom in Hinderwell. I think I look slightly taken aback on that canvas, and who can blame me? Who expects to find themselves on a wall at Wembley? How could I ever have dreamed of that, as a kid?

Did I dream of FA Cup finals, in front of 45,423 people? Did I dream of this, against Chelsea, for my first game at Wembley? How could I have? At Sunderland, we'd never been expected to make an FA Cup final. The club had made just one since the competition's introduction in the 1970/71 season, and that had been the one I'd been to see at Derby in 2009.

I've never been the kind of player to struggle with match nerves, and my overriding feeling, as I stepped out at football's home, was that I was lucky. So, so lucky. I sometimes find it really hard to understand how people can get affected in big games to the point where they really struggle. Any final is a chance for me to just put my heart and soul into something that I really love.

However, the magnitude of this huge occasion hits me with my first real bit of skill. I take the ball down on my chest and flick it over the head of the Chelsea defender Hannah Blundell. I hear the crowd crackle with appreciation and admiration. It almost stops me in my tracks. At that point in my career, I'd only ever heard a couple of hundred people by the side of the pitch; 45,423 sound just a touch louder. It instantly calms me.

I wish the whole day had gone like that for me. Instead, it became an afternoon of thwarted potential. One glance at any Arsenal teamsheet from my time here will tell you how talented our squad is, but we don't always produce in big games. It has always been an issue for us, and it becomes even more frustrating because we know we're not a million miles away from the likes of Chelsea and City.

This FA Cup final is a prime example. Chelsea's Fran Kirby has the game of her life, and splits our defence with a cutting pass to Ramona Bachmann. When she zings her shot into the top corner, we lose rhythm, and it feels inevitable that Chelsea will score again. They do, twelve minutes later, when Bachmann bamboozles our defence with another jinking run. That second goal feels like a dagger to our hopes. It hits me deep in my heart. It's the point at which I know we have nothing to lose, and it lends a new urgency to everything I do. I beat Blundell out wide and pull the ball back for Viv to make it 2–1, but our belief is short-lived. Kirby restores Chelsea's two-goal cushion in three minutes.

As I watched Chelsea lift the FA Cup, I honed in on the hurt broiling inside me. I was adamant that I would win the FA Cup one day. It pains me that I'm still to do it.

Dad has always been my harshest critic. 'They were the better team,' he shrugged, as I met him in the family and friends' lounge after the game. 'You didn't turn up in certain areas. They got the better of you.' That made it easier to move on. Finer margins are always more painful, but my family are so happy to have watched me play at Wembley, and that helps. This was an amazing experience for them, and for me.

We made it our aim to win the league the following season. That's the standard every year at Arsenal, and the expectation was no different under Joe.

We lay down an early marker with a 5–0 demolition of Chelsea on their own turf. It's one of the most complete Arsenal performances I've ever been a part of. It's one of my favourite Arsenal games ever. Have we ever dominated a game like that since? It's usually cagey against Chelsea, but we feel instantly comfortable against them. I'm filled with joy just thinking about it, because everything went right. We win an early penalty when Adelina Engman brings down Emma Mitchell, and Kim Little scores easily. Then Viv takes the ball around Magdalena Eriksson for our second, and it feels like every move forward will end in a goal. We press well and simply flood forward. *Today is a good day,* I think. *Things will just go right.*

When Jordan scores straight from near the corner flag, looping the ball over Carly Telford, I feel it sums up our performance. When does something like that happen? All the luck was with us. One of my shots comes off Telford and spins right back to me, and I have lots of time to slide it across the box for Viv to tap in from a sliding Jess Carter.

When Jordan scores our fifth goal, fifteen minutes later, we both slide on our knees to meet each other in celebration. The rain is pounding us, but you would never know from our excitement and joy. I fall on top of Jordan, almost folding her in half as we roll in the mud.

Our command of Joe's possession-based style had created such an aura about us and everything we did felt fluid and fun. On the pitch, I never had to look at my teammates to know what they'd do or where they'd be. I felt like I could play with them with my eyes closed. That whole season felt like a dream.

We secured the title in the penultimate game of the season with a 4–0 win over Brighton at the Amex Stadium, during which I scored our third goal and one of my favourites from my career. I cut inside off the left wing and drive the ball from twenty-five yards. As it floats through the air, I know it's one of the cleanest shots I'll ever hit, and I know that it will send the net bulging. It needs to, because the tiny part of me that's second-guessing myself has seen Viv running into space ahead of me. She'll kill me if I miss now – but I was never going to. I see Viv applaud me, but her eyes give me a look that says, *you hit that one well, but don't try it again.*

I run all the way to the bench to celebrate with Jordan, who had played such a crucial role in our title win before her ACL injury cut her season short so cruelly. I felt her pain and I wanted to be there for her. More than anything, I wanted to show her that she mattered to this team.

Jordan had been a big part of why we'd felt so confident from the get-go, and why we instantly felt – and played like – champions. Our results in those first few months of the season included a 5–0 win over Liverpool and a 6–0 win over Reading. Another part of that was down to Viv's contribution. She scored a hat-trick in that win over Liverpool in the first game of the season and no one was surprised when she finished as the WSL's top scorer with twenty-two goals. We'd known how good she could be, and now she'd shown the rest of England.

On the bus back from Brighton, we sang karaoke. We managed to get very merry, even over a short journey.

We felt so light ahead of the final game of the season against Manchester City and were brimming with confidence after winning the title. I was ecstatic when we won 1–0 and we finally got to lift Arsenal's first league title since 2012 in front of our home fans. Again, I made time for Jordan, and went over and hugged her tightly. We'd won the title, but I could tell that she was still on such a low because she knew that she would be missing the 2019 World Cup.

I became one of the few players to have won both the WSL 1 and WSL 2, now known as the Championship. The overriding feeling, as I hoisted the trophy above my head, was that I was hungry for more.

9

Like Being in a Rocket

Arsenal training is laced with excitement.

'I've heard Phil is going to ring around today about the squad,' someone says.

I sit on the Wattbike, my legs bouncing with nerves even as they spin with the pedals. It's August 2018. Phil Neville has only been the England manager for a few months, having taken over in January. I don't know how much he knows about me, or about the women's game in general. I don't know if I'll even be on his radar.

My first senior call-up to England, in October 2015, had been forgettable.

I'd flown out to China for the CFA International Women's Football Tournament, a three-team friendly competition between China, England and Australia. I knew that I'd only been picked because the Continental Cup final, between Arsenal and Notts County, fell the same week as the second England match, meaning all the regular names were unavailable for selection. The England manager Mark Sampson had needed to call up other players. I was a last resort.

The whole time I was at Sunderland, I never seemed to genuinely force my way into his thinking, no matter how well I did. I never understood why he didn't seem to like me, especially by the time I'd made it to the WSL 1 and he didn't have the excuse of me playing in a lower league. In my eyes, I was the best-scoring number nine he could have had.

The hotel in Chongqing was horrendous. It stunk of smoke. The food was awful. I didn't feature in either game. The whole thing felt like a waste of time.

Three years on, my hopes of playing for England lay with Phil. I thought back to the week he joined; how all the girls had been bemused when someone called 'Fizzer' had followed us on Twitter.

'That's Phil Neville,' we'd say, swiping through each other's phones. There were rumours in the media that he was interested in the England job, but I didn't know anything until he was appointed as head coach on 23 January 2018. A media storm followed. Phil had to apologise for tweets he'd sent about women as far back as 2012, and the FA received heavy criticism for hiring someone who had never worked in the women's game and had very limited managerial experience. My outlook in life has always been to never judge anyone until I know them completely and I adopted the same approach with Phil. I wasn't naïve – I knew he hadn't been successful during his time as Assistant Manager at Valencia – but I didn't know him as an actual human being. I would judge him on my own terms.

My phone lights up. *Phil Neville*. My nerves dissipate. Phil wouldn't be ringing with bad news, would he? I feel a tug of excitement.

'Hi, Beth,' he says. His tone is soft and his voice gentle. He's easy to speak to. 'You're in my squad.' I feel a thrill course through me. 'It's going to be your first call-up in a long time,' he continues, 'and there might be some talk about it. I'm just making you aware, but you deserve to be in the squad.'

I feel a mix of emotions. I'm so excited about proving myself at the senior level, finally. I'd been desperate to make the jump for years, even if those camps at youth level had always caused me stress and anxiety. I'm comforted that Phil was thoughtful enough to give me some warning about what the press might write – that was good of him – but I feel nervous, too. This will be my first camp since China. I want to go and prove my worth as a footballer, but I don't want it to feel like last time.

I have to finish training before I can call Mum and Dad. I hear the delight in their voices. They're clearly proud and overwhelmed. 'It's been a few years since the last camp,' I tell them, 'so it feels like this is my fresh start with England.' Most of all, they're relieved for me. I've finally been picked.

For the first game, I come on as a sub against Wales in Southampton.

'Beth!' Phil calls to me from the bench. 'We need something different. Bring me the energy. Show me what you can do.'

There are 30,000 fans there, and it's one of the few times in my career when I've actually been nervous. I can't believe my England debut is actually happening. I've spent years watching other people take their chances, watching from the sidelines or at home, and now it's my turn. I can't explain how good that feels, even though the game ends 0–0. I'm so overwhelmed, and the enormity of winning my first cap doesn't hit me until later, when I'm back in the hotel room. My first senior cap means so much to me. This is the start of my England career; 2015 had felt like a pity selection because no one else was available. I've won this cap on merit.

Phil selects me again for the 2019 edition of the SheBelieves Cup, an invitational tournament taking place in the States in February and March. Arsenal's Continental Cup final against

Manchester City takes place at Bramall Lane the day before we're due to fly out, so we lumber around Heathrow Airport with tired, glazed eyes. But I'm excited to go out there. I know that Phil is using the trip to monitor us, that this will be my best chance to audition for a place at the World Cup that summer.

It is at the back of my mind throughout the first few months of 2019. When we play Everton in the league in April, I ride a badly timed tackle from Abbey-Leigh Stringer. As I go to ground, I panic that I've hurt myself. Pain thrums through my lower leg. Is my World Cup over? Daan fears the same for me, and remonstrates loudly with the referee for not protecting me better. I feel relieved when I finally get to my feet. I'll confess that there are moments in those months when I think, *do I go in for this tackle? Do I avoid this?*

It's a worry for all of us because of what happened to Jordan. She'd been in the form of her life when, in November, she ruptured her ACL in our 4–0 win over Everton. She described it as an out-of-body experience, and said it was like time stopped when she heard the tell-tale pop. She knew right away what she had done – and that she wouldn't be able to make the World Cup. That was devastating for her, and we tried to help her in those gym and rehab days when she was feeling low.

I come off the bench for our first match in the States against Brazil in Chester, Pennsylvania. The game is a cagey and physical one, and it's 1–1 when I come on, Ellen White having equalised after Andressa Alves da Silva put Brazil ahead after sixteen minutes through a penalty. The legendary Brazil player Marta was darting into the box when Lucy Bronze forced her off the ball, and the referee gives Brazil a penalty. *It's a soft one,* I think, shaking my head as Alves da Silva slots past Carly Telford.

I've been on the pitch nine minutes when Fran Kirby breaks into space centrally.

Play me out wide, I think. *Play me out wide now.* The full back I'm up against, Jucinara Thaís Soares Paz, is so high that she's left yards of space in behind her.

Fran threads the ball to me, and I know that anything I hit across goal, with the gap yawning open in front of me, could go in. I strike across the ball so it spins, as though I'm aiming for the back post. It lifts higher than I expect it to but whirls through the air and right over the goalkeeper, Aline Villares Reis, and settles in the top far corner of the goal.

In the coming days, this will be known as my 'crot' – a cross stroke shot – and all I can say about this one is that I promise it was a shot. In the moment, though, I don't think about giving it a nickname. I spread my feet apart and roar in the face of Ellen White, who is the first to come and celebrate with me. She cannot believe what she has just seen, and I'm not sure how many of the 5,954 fans in the Talen Energy Stadium, usually the home of the MLS side Philadelphia Union and which backs right onto the Delaware River, can process it, either. That most of them are American means that we don't get the celebration we'd have enjoyed if I'd just done that in front of the England fans, but it's a wonderful moment nonetheless, and Phil is over the moon for me. I know already that he wants the best for me, and after that goal I really feel as though he is proud of me.

Which is why I was so crushed when Phil announced the team to play the US in our next match. He pulled me aside before the meeting, and my shoulders sagged immediately because I knew what he was about to say.

I'd be on the bench. The fact that Phil took me to one side to tell me this showed how close I was to starting, which made the whole thing worse. I was annoyed. I didn't accept it right away. I didn't expect to start – this was, after all, one of my first camps with Phil – but I had wondered if I was close after my performance against Brazil. *What is a girl meant to do?* I thought angrily. I was hungry to play. *Let me go and prove myself.*

Phil was studying my body language. He smiled. I later learned this was the reaction he wanted from me. In the moment, I told him to shut up.

For the most part, I enjoyed working with Phil. We have a similar sense of humour and got along easily. I like his outgoing and bubbly nature. He also understands how footballers feel. 'I don't do long meetings,' he'd say, 'because I hated them as a player.' He backed us whenever we met with the FA to ask for more resources. 'This is what you guys deserve,' he'd say. 'You have the right to ask for this.'

I got the sense that he wanted me to progress and was eager to help. Phil said that I could be a matchwinner, but that I lacked confidence – that he got the sense that I always assumed that other players would be better than me. I agree that I was lacking faith in my own ability, and I did worry far too much about what everyone else was doing. But hearing it and believing it are two different things. I looked a lot to my teammates for reassurance and encouragement. I can give that to myself now.

'If you find that self-belief,' Phil kept saying to me, 'you could be a star.'

That first camp with him was a whirlwind because SheBelieves saw us travel to so many places. We toured the whole of Eastern America, flying from London to Philadelphia, Philadelphia to Nashville, Nashville to Tampa. It was like being in a rocket – up, up and off.

Phil had only worked in the men's game before he took over as our coach and he was still relatively new to coaching as well. He was obsessed with fitness testing and being the fittest team – something that had probably been ingrained into him from his days with Sir Alex Ferguson. We would do fitness tests every Wednesday. By far the worst was the MAS test: ten runs up and down the pitch as fast as you can. People would feel a lot lighter once those tests were finished.

Phil's worry was that I was too nice. He wanted me to be tougher, and his view was that I played best when I was angry and was fighting to prove a point. 'You need a bit of nastiness to cut it at the top level,' he said, and he wasn't sure if I had that in me yet. He believed that sometimes you had to suffer and struggle to develop that side of your game.

'I've seen you when you've been aggressive and confident,' he said. 'You need to get angry before playing every game. The Beth Mead that's angry is going to be a superstar. The Beth that's not angry is just going to be an average WSL player. What do I need to do to get that? Piss you off before a game?'

But at that time, I didn't know how to channel that emotion; I didn't know how to bring that to my game. Inevitably, that meant that Phil and I had a love–hate relationship. The easiest way to get an angry Beth Mead is to leave me out of the team.

'I'm not playing you today,' Phil would say. 'You need to be annoyed about it. I want to see a reaction.' It was his way of trying to trigger me.

I come on as a substitute for our 2–2 draw with the US and run my heart out against one of the most athletic teams in the women's game. The crowd of 22,125 is made up mostly of US fans and I relish being in the lion's den. Phil tells me afterwards that I deserve to start the last game, against Japan, and I reward his faith by scoring the final goal of our 3–0 win. Keira Walsh plays the ball out wide to me, and, as I run down the outside, I scan the box for someone to pick out. No one seems to open up.

Why not go for it yourself? I think, and I pull back my left foot. I catch the goalkeeper off guard. I'm thrilled to cap off my tournament that way.

What's going on? I think, as we go 3–0 up by half time. Japan have always been a good footballing side in the women's game. To be running the show against them feels like a significant step forward for us, and means that we win the SheBelieves Cup. We stay to watch the second game before taking to the stage to celebrate with the trophy. My rebooted England career has got off to a great start, as has Phil's.

10

The World Cup

I wrap my arms around myself as I shiver in my sleeping bag. In the dark, I can see the outline of Nikita Parris's face inches from mine. She butts my head whenever she moves in her sleep. Condensation drips down the inside of the tent. It's barely past midnight and we're already damp.

We're in the final weeks before flying out to France for the 2019 World Cup and Phil has invited the Royal Marines to St George's Park. As night falls and I brush the side of the tent every time I roll over, I'm half seething. *This is another one of Phil's bright ideas.* Nikita hadn't been much use when it came to erecting our tiny tent – I'd been camping as a kid, so it fell to me – but she had been good at chatting my ear off as I'd slashed open the food sachets and cooked them over the fire we'd built. The FA had taken our phones away from us for the weekend and we'd had no contact with the outside world. Many of us had been dreaming of making an escape under the cover of darkness to our rooms back at the hotel.

We'd be well able to, having spent the day learning survival skills, including carrying soldiers back to base on stretchers. I joke about our camping trip, but there was a point to it. As we sat around a main campfire with marshmallows and hot chocolate, the marines told us stories of the horrors they'd faced in their conflicts. They already knew many of us because some of them followed women's football. They were eager to share what they knew about handling pressure and being a leader.

The run-up to the World Cup is new territory for me. Our main media day falls in the same week as the marines' visit, and hundreds of journalists fill the Futsal hall at St George's Park. It's a speed-dating format, and we spend a few minutes with one group of journalists before the whistle blows and we move on to the next ones. They cluster around me, Dictaphones and cameras extended. 'What are your expectations?' they ask me. I don't know what to say. I've never been to a World Cup before.

The email to confirm my place on the plane to France had arrived in May. I'd felt desperately anxious beforehand, my stomach heaving. *At least I'm at home,* I told myself, bouncing my phone on my leg as I waited for the email. At least no one else will be looking. I can process it in whatever way I want to.

When the email finally lands in my inbox, my heart races. My eyes shoot about in search of the key word: congratulations.

In the days before we fly to France, Phil calls each of us into a room to present us with a gift and a letter. He hands out jewellery boxes. Inside is a silver necklace. The words 'France 19' glisten as I slide it out of the box. He often shows his emotional and sentimental side, and is open about how much the World Cup means to him.

When we touch down in France, young England fans greet us in Nice, waving flags as we arrive at our hotel. *Wow,* I think, *this is going to be bigger than I thought.* It's a moment we're pulled out of ourselves to be reminded that the world will be watching, including millions back home.

Toni Duggan, my competition on the left wing, is nursing an injury, meaning that I start the first game against Scotland in Nice. I walk out and am overcome with emotion. I battle to hold it in. As the national anthem plays, I can feel my eyes bubbling over. *Beth*, I tell myself, *you need to control this.* I deliberately look away from my parents for that reason. These are the moments you live for – all your emotions come out when they actually happen.

Those feelings evaporate as soon as the whistle goes. I'm in my safe space again, as engrossed as that kid running rings around the boys on the pitches at Hinderwell.

We go into the break leading 2–0, thanks to a penalty from Nikita Parris and goal from Ellen White. The heat is oppressive and I come into the dressing room at half-time feeling like I've just been cooked. Phil is about to begin his team talk. He opens his mouth before he pauses, staring at me with wide eyes.

'Jesus, Beth – your face,' he gasps. 'You're so red you look like you're going to explode. It's incredible.'

Thirty seconds into the second half, I think I've scored when Ellen White pulls the ball back to me. I hit it cleanly but, just as I bend my knees to leap into Ellen's arms in celebration, the flag flies up. Ellen was offside, something she still apologises to me for now. She told me later that Callum, her partner, turned around in the stands and apologised to my parents. If you read this, Ellen – it's fine. Stop worrying about it!

The 2–1 win over Scotland gets us up and running, and, on our final day in Nice, we walked down the promenade and a couple of us raced into the sea. Our security team on the shore were wincing and cringing as the waves lashed higher and higher. 'You'll be sucked out to sea,' they called, bringing the whole thing to an end.

I start our second game against Argentina and I'm pleased with my performance. My link-up play with Alex Greenwood wins us a penalty – I lay her off inside the box and she draws a foul from the defender – and, though Nikita Parris's shot is saved, it's really only the excellence of the Argentina goal-keeper Vanina Correa keeping us at bay. Nonetheless, we find a breakthrough on sixty-one minutes when Fran Kirby's sharp pass sends me scurrying down the left. I hit a low, first-time cross to Jodie Taylor, who finishes at the far post for her first England goal in fourteen months.

As we wheel away to celebrate, we spot Jordan in the media area, where she is working as a pundit for the BBC. I form a love heart with my hands and hold it up to her. I wish that she could be on the pitch with me – that I could be sharing this with one of my best friends.

In the days before our final group game, Phil took me aside.

'We're going to save you,' he said. 'You've done well in the games, but we've qualified.'

That's fair, I thought, and Phil kept his word, not using me against Japan.

But then I didn't play in our 'round of 16' game against Cameroon either. Toni Duggan took my place. At this point, I was filled with frustration. *What's going on?* I wondered. I hadn't had any communication from Phil. I was baffled and really annoyed.

I'm not somebody who is very good at being angry at people. When it comes to football, I think I'm like most players – I like clarity, reasons, details. Phil had given me none of those things. I didn't understand why I didn't feature in the very game I was meant to be resting myself for. I felt resentment towards Phil for not communicating with me properly. This trapped me in my head. *What have I done wrong? Have I upset him? Does he even like me?*

Phil knew that I was annoyed. But he's the kind of coach who smiles on his way past or cracks a joke to make you laugh. *Nah*, I thought, *I'm not having that*. I avoided him because I knew that is what he would try and do. Whenever I saw him in the hotel or at the training ground, I darted away and changed direction. *If he won't give me an explanation*, I thought, *I won't go looking for one*.

But I did. Ahead of our quarter-final against Norway in Le Havre, we stayed in Deauville, a seaside resort in the Normandy region about fifty minutes from the stadium. Once I found out I wouldn't be starting that game either, I padded to the white marbled lobby and found Phil and his assistant, Bev Priestman, in reception.

'I'm really confused as to why I'm not playing,' I began, my voice cracking. I was worked up because I've never been good at confrontation. Phil told me that he wanted more experience for those games, even if I was arguably playing better football. He was matter-of-fact, unemotional, and wanted me to respect his decision.

My view was that you always have your most in-form players on the pitch. That's what I'd do if I was a manager. But I wasn't. It was Phil's call, and I couldn't hold a grudge against him over any of that. The lack of communication before then, though, was difficult. I only got that meeting with him because I'd asked for it. Otherwise, I wouldn't have had any communication with him between the second group game and the quarter-final.

Looking back now, that's the biggest contrast between Phil and Sarina Wiegman. She keeps everyone in the loop at all times. She lets us know what's happening. Even those who don't play under her know their place and that sense of belonging is conveyed throughout. I struggled when I didn't start at the World Cup. I was lucky enough to be a starting player at the 2022 Euros, but even if I hadn't been, I think I would have felt a lot better off the pitch than under Phil because of the way Sarina handled that side of it.

On the day of the Norway match, we played games on the beach. We played Twister, falling over each other and landing in the sand, and with Nerf guns. I was the shooter and the girls had to catch my darts in their plastic cups. It felt like we played this game for hours, because we're so competitive. It helped to keep us relaxed, keep our nerves settled, because there was such a huge expectation on us. We wanted to win the World Cup, but, as players, we had never wanted to go out and say that publicly. We always felt that sounded arrogant and maybe people viewed us that way, but it was never us driving those kind of statements. We had to jump on board with that mentality because that's what we were doing.

We had three special guests before the quarter-final: David Beckham, his mum Sandra and his daughter Harper. It felt really surreal to know they were waiting on the floor below to meet us. Growing up, I had adored David Beckham. I loved who he was at Manchester United, and I loved what he helped make the number seven symbolise for me. I can't remember now if it was me or Ben with Manchester United curtains in our bedroom in Runswick, but whoever it was had showed commitment to the cause because they certainly didn't keep out much light.

We walked down the hotel stairs to a meeting room. Rachel Daly was the first to notice David coming down the corridor. She announced this to everyone, then turned bright red.

'Rach, man!' I moaned. 'You've just made it awkward for us all!'

Harper was quiet and didn't say much, but she is a huge football fan and you could tell she was enjoying the visit. She was holding hands with Georgia Stanway as we lined up to have our photograph taken with them.

'Please keep inspiring the nation,' David said. 'Look at girls like my daughter – you've done a good job so far.'

Then Ian Wright walked into the room. 'MRS. B!' he called, wrapping his arms around David's mum. 'What's the point in me being here?' he laughed, as he turned to face the rest of the squad. 'Nobody cares about me with David being here.'

I don't start against Norway in the quarter-finals, but I come on in the fifty-fourth minute, when we're already 2–0 up thanks to goals from Jill Scott and Ellen White. Lucy Bronze has spent the previous fifty-four minutes single-handedly skinning the Norway defence and my job is to come on and match the intensity that will see Phil dub Lucy 'the best player in the world, without a shadow of a doubt' at his post-match press conference. I've been on the pitch for just three minutes when I pull the ball back across the box for Lucy to rifle a shot home from outside the box. It flies into the roof of the net like a bullet and in response Lucy stands still, her arms wide as we race towards her, and soaks up our hugs and fist pumps. The images of David Beckham high-fiving Harper, and then high-fiving Sue Campbell, the FA's Director of Women's Football, in response to Lucy's goal end up going viral. They're among my strongest memories of the game, beaten only by the celebrations. We hold hands, run towards the fans and jump, screaming and shouting towards strangers. To reach a semi-final in such clinical fashion is unbelievable.

'Well done, Beth,' Phil said to me afterwards. 'You did well.'
'Great,' I replied. 'Thanks for bringing me on.'

Our win over Norway set a new peak TV viewing record for women's football in the UK: 7.6 million people watched us, and the semi-final was due to be shown in primetime slots on BBC One. Not that we knew that at the time. We were kept in such a tight bubble that we didn't know or see how big all this was.

Globally, though, the US commanded most of the spotlight. Searching for their fourth World Cup win, they were yet to slip up. They began their campaign with a 13–0 win over Thailand in which Alex Morgan scored five goals. Everyone was talking about lilac-haired Megan Rapinoe and, in her press conferences, the media clung to her every word as she advocated for LGBTQIA+ rights, criticised Donald Trump and vowed not to meet him at the White House if the US won the tournament. She also kept the team's fight for equal pay in the spotlight. The US were the best athletes in the competition, and remain one of the greatest teams of all time.

Despite that, we were as calm as we could be. We felt our squad was good enough to beat them. Yes, they'd won the World Cup three times, but they had to fall off their pedestal eventually. Why not with a little shove from us?

Little outside noise reached me until I met my family for coffee in Lyon in the days before the semi.

'We struggled so badly to get a hotel,' Mum said. 'The Americans have taken over.' I told her that I'd been out for coffee in Lyon and there were American fans everywhere I looked. I think that showed their confidence in their team. They thought they would get to the semi-final no matter who they played. They'd had their hotels and transport booked months in advance.

In the days before the semi-final, someone at the FA caught two US delegates pottering about our hotel while we were out training. We don't know whether they accessed any of the meeting rooms where the messages and information about our tactics would have been – one newspaper said that they were asked to leave when they were found in one of our private areas. The US manager Jill Ellis said in her press conference that they were just scouting out the hotel as a possible place to stay should they beat us and reach the final.

Phil downplayed it in his press conference. 'It'll have no bearing on the game,' he said. 'To be honest, I found it funny.'

If anything, it gives us a boost. The US must be rattled if they feel the need to send in a spy.

Then on the eve of the game, Phil spotted someone watching from the bushes on the hillside at our Terrain d'Honneur training base. The security staff went to meet the man, who turned out to be a local on a walk. This didn't affect the players, maybe because we're not totally sure of all the details.

I learned shortly afterwards that Phil was going to start me against the US. My first thought was that I didn't understand him as a coach. I was overjoyed, obviously, but I'd been on the bench for the previous three games. Why bring me back for this one – one of the biggest games in the history of England's women's team?

I was aware of the enormity of the occasion as I readied myself in the dressing room beforehand. I visualised the game in my head, running through key pieces of analysis and passing sequences. It calmed me, even as we heard the noise of the crowd pulsing through the tunnel walls.

As we lined up, our faces were impassive, stern. The US team were the opposite: they shouted words of encouragement to each other, clapped their hands, stamped their feet. I was struck by the contrast between us.

We begin sloppily, and I'm given an early sense of what will come when the ball flies down my side and Kelley O'Hara and I chase each other so ferociously that I'm out of breath. *Wow,* I think, *we're in for a game today.*

While we struggle to keep the ball, the US easily turn it over to search for Alex Morgan and Christen Press in the box. It only takes ten minutes for O'Hara to find Press at the back post. Halting her run behind Lucy Bronze, she rifles a header into the top corner. My stomach lurches with deflation because it was such an avoidable, preventable goal, even against the US.

I know, though, that it's very, very rare for a team to dominate a game for the full ninety minutes. That promise of a route back in for us gives me hope, and I receive the ball out wide and shift it on to my left foot. I can see Ellen poised in the box and I drop a bouncing cross towards her. She hits it first time and I cannot describe the ecstasy that floods my body as the ball hits the back of the net. Ellen runs towards me and I seize her as we scream at each other.

I feel like we're gaining a foothold in the game when the US work their way down the right and Lindsey Horan directs a cross deep into the box. Alex Morgan times her run well against Demi Stokes, leaping to nod home for 2–1. The deflation hits me instantly. It's like a sucker punch. It feels like reaching the top of one mountain only to see the summit of an even bigger one stretching high into the sky.

The US manage the game very well. They fall over at the smallest tackles. They take the ball into the corner to run down the clock. They launch the ball into the distance. I groan with frustration. The game is on their terms and they're in control. I come off after fifty-eight minutes, irritated that I haven't been able to break them down.

Ten minutes later, I'm filled with elation. Jill Scott has flicked the ball to Ellen and she has hared through the US backline to equalise. I leap off my seat. The rest of the bench follows me as I soar through the air, dancing and screaming with them until it feels as though my lungs are about to give out. Then we pause. There will be a VAR check.

The wait feels like it lasts an hour. The longer it goes on, the more I feel like it will bring bad news. I'm right – Ellen was offside.

I hear euphoria exploding from the US bench to my right. I sink. I feel as though I'm falling. Falling and falling, right back down into the pit of my stomach where my heart now lies.

Maybe the injustice spurs us on; we stream forward with new desperation. Demi Stokes shifts the ball across to Ellen and I leap out of my seat, shouting. I'm sure Ellen will finish this. Then Becky Sauerbrunn trips her up, catching Ellen's trailing leg. She only receives a yellow card, which frustrates me. It seemed to me that she must have known what she was doing.

Penalty. A lifeline. I throw my head back, screaming into the sky.

My stomach clenches with nerves as I watch Steph plant the ball on the spot and step back. When the whistle blows, I don't dare breathe. I clench my fingers around my seat in anticipation.

But Steph mis-hits it. The ball crawls slowly towards the bottom corner and Alyssa Naeher drops down easily to smother it.

My heart plunges. Immediately, my thoughts turn to Steph. I know that she will blame herself. That's the type of person she is. She will blame herself for shouldering all of our dreams and dropping them with that one unlucky stroke of the ball. It's the last thing I want for her given all that is going on in

My biker gang days. Teaching my brother Ben how to ride a bike with Dad.

Backstage at the Whitby Pavilion, getting ready for my dance recital. The peak of my ballet career (second from left).

Riding a horse at Haggerston Castle, one of the Haven sites we'd visit when I was a kid.

Right: My ballet teacher called me a 'well-poised little dancer' in my pre-primary assessment but I wasn't patient enough for dancing.

Celebrating my eighth birthday in Grange-over-Sands, Cumbria, with a Manchester United cake. Who's going to tell young Beth that one day she'll score at Old Trafford?

Ben and me in Ibiza, in our typical night-time outfits: matching England football kits.

Another trophy to add to my early haul from Cali Boys.

Above and below left: With my teammates at California Girls.

Meeting England's Sue Smith, future Sky Sports pundit, at a Middlesbrough Centre of Excellence's presentation night.

With the under 10s team at Middlesbrough Centre of Excellence. Our team photo to start the season.

An early school photo from Caedmon.

Left: A family holiday to Turkey with Mum, Dad and Ben, at about ten years old.

Above: Graduating from Teesside University, aged twenty-one, in 2016. The university now offers a scholarship in my name to support female footballers juggling a degree and training.

Left: The legend herself, Jessie Mead.

Winning the PFA Women's Young Player of the Year award in 2016.

Playing for Sunderland against Doncaster Rovers Belles in September 2016, aged twenty-one.

First day at Arsenal. I hate these pictures because you can see how nervous I am about leaving home.

'Mine! Mine! Mine!' With Joe Montemurro at Arsenal.

Facing my old club: playing for Arsenal against Sunderland in 2017.

Celebrating Arsenal's first league title for seven years with Danielle Carter, Jordan Nobbs and Leah Williamson.

My senior England debut: battling against Wales in a 0–0 draw, April 2018.

In tears after our 2–1 defeat by the US at the 2019 World Cup. One of my lowest moments in football.

Coming off in our third-place play-off against Sweden. The beginning of the end of the Phil Neville era.

Celebrating with the fans after demolishing Norway 3–0 at the 2019 World Cup.

Two of my favourite pictures from my football career: celebrating with the fans during our 3–2 win over Chelsea at the Emirates, September 2021.

Enjoying training at London Colney, winding up either one of the girls, the staff or Jonas. He was amused regardless.

My poker face. Rueing a missed chance versus Chelsea, April 2022.

Walking with Mum and my dog, Rona Mead, on Hampstead Heath, overlooking the London skyline.

My parents' favourite child, and me. Mum made the cushion in the background of Rona in her Arsenal kit.

Talking tactics with Sarina Wiegman and Ellen White after our Euros opener against Austria at Old Trafford. It's a true privilege playing under a coach like Sarina.

Fulfilling a lifelong dream: scoring the winning goal at Old Trafford …

… and celebrating accordingly. England v Austria, Euro 2022.

The ecstasy of putting us 1–0 up in a Euros semi-final. England v Sweden, Euro 2022.

The hen party. Celebrating reaching a Euros final with Rachel Daly.

What a photo! The biggest crowd I've ever played for.

Leaving the pitch with a dead leg during the Euros final. I'd given all I had.

Climbing over the barrier into the stand at Wembley to share my joy with Ben.

Lift off! Winning the Euros was the best feeling of my whole football career.

The concluding night of Rachel Daly's concert tour, Trafalgar Square.

When you run out of trophies! Celebrating post-final with Ben and Dad.

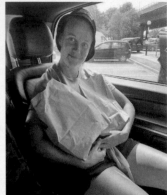

Above: The tried-and-tested hangover cure. A pitstop outside McDonald's, after Trafalgar Square.

Jordan, Steph and Jen. These girls always have my back.

Date night with Viv on our pre-Euros holiday in Ibiza.

Enjoying a training session with Viv at London Colney.

her personal life. The previous September – just ten months earlier – her husband, the former Liverpool and Bradford City defender Stephen Darby, had announced his retirement from football at the age of twenty-nine after being diagnosed with motor neurone disease. I can't imagine what it was like to receive and deal with that news, let alone to still be able to captain England.

Every day in training, we had practised penalties. The ones who scored the most or felt comfortable would be added to the list of takers for games. The ones who were successful would be placed higher, but we've always said that if someone is confident and wants to take one, then they should. Steph and I took loads and neither of us ever missed. You'd back Steph.

In that moment I make a promise to myself, as I'm sure most of the girls do, to rally around and be there for her.

We win as a team and we lose as a team. We conceded those goals. Whatever happens, her penalty was just one part of the equation. I hope she understands that. You just can't replicate the pressure of a World Cup semi-final. No training game or practice drill can ever come close. Those stakes – taking the penalty that would have drawn us level – are unimaginable. You can't blame her for anything, and we don't.

The US demonstrate their experience after that, with the same time-wasting they'd peppered the first half with. It feels as though they're in control. It feels like they win every foul, halting our momentum and slowing the game down to take all the danger out of our play. We become angrier, impatient, and Millie Bright picks up a second yellow because she's so desperate to win the ball back. That's when it begins to sink in that we might not be going through.

When the final whistle goes, I watch as our girls fall to the ground. The US celebrate in their typical, over the top way, but I hardly register those images. I sit alone on the bench before sloping onto the pitch to be with the rest of the girls. It's a moment of heartbreak so intense and searing that it is difficult to describe.

At some point, the US players come over to offer their commiserations. In my head, their words are white noise. I don't want them there, even if speaking with us is the respectful and sporting thing to do. It's how the game should be done, but I just want to be alone. *Go and enjoy your celebrations*, I think.

I'm barely conscious of picking myself off the pitch and shuffling to the changing room. It feels as though everything is happening around me, that someone else is moving me through the corridors and rooms of the Parc Olympique Lyonnais. I'm too lost in the turmoil inside my head.

An eerie silence hung over the changing room. No one made conversation. What could we say? We sat in our places staring at the floor, consumed by the what-ifs and if-onlys of our inner worlds. Some scrolled through their phones, thumbs swiping mindlessly as they searched for any kind of distraction. The room was claustrophobic with different emotions. I could guess the unspoken thoughts cycling through my teammates' minds because I was having some of them, too. What if this is my last tournament? What if I don't play well next season and am never picked again? What if something goes wrong for me in a few months' time and England want nothing to do with me? Heaviest of all is the sense that we've failed again, but we have to pick ourselves up because we have to play the third-place play-off in four days' time. I go through the motions of going to the shower, taking my shinpads off, packing my bag, but it's as though I'm not even there.

A World Cup final has been all we have dreamed of for years. We have been away from our families for eight weeks.

To fall short because of two headers that we could have easily avoided, and which would then have enabled us to equalise or even win the game, is frustrating. My thoughts were scattered. I blamed myself, replaying everything, but it was hard to wrap my head around the game when I was so full of sadness. The thing we wanted most in the world had been taken away from us and there was nothing we could do about it.

The silence continued on the bus home. Some of us blocked out the world with earphones. Music played quietly from a speaker and somehow even that seemed pathetic. Scrolling through social media was probably inadvisable, but it's what most of us were doing. It's where we saw what Alex Morgan did after she scored her winning goal. With her pinky outstretched, she put her fingers to her mouth and mimed sipping tea.

The celebration became famous around the world, endlessly debated and scrutinised. Was Morgan disrespectful? Would we even be asking that question if she were a man? The images of her with her head tipped back, as though swallowing the last dregs, is instantly turned into GIFs and printed on tote bags and T-shirts. In England, it's debated on ITV's *Loose Women* ('Were USA smug winners?'), on ESPN ('Was Alex Morgan and the USWNT too arrogant in their celebrations vs. England?') and forms the basis of a quiz question on Channel 4's *Big Fat Quiz of the Year*.

'Wah, wah, wah,' US winger Megan Rapinoe said of Morgan's critics. 'We're at the World Cup. What do you want us to do? This is the biggest stage, the biggest moment. I don't think anyone truly believes that we disrespect the game or disrespect our opponents.'

Morgan denied that it even has anything to do with England. She said she was copying one of her favourite actors, Sophie Turner from *Game of Thrones*, by referencing her catchphrase:

'That's the tea.' Sophie Turner made a video in reply, saying that she is honoured that Morgan thought of her in her moment of celebration.

I don't buy her explanation. I mean, why else would you want to do a tea celebration against England? She didn't do that celebration at any other time or in any other games. I feel like Alex thought about it all afterwards, calculated a story and then used that explanation as her get-out card. If you've just scored in a semi-final and want to do a tribute to England, that's up to you, but on that bus home, I found it a little bit annoying. I don't think there's any need for it, but we were all too heart-broken to really care about what Alex Morgan had done. All of our hard work had come down to nothing. We were far more heavy-hearted about that than we ever could be about Alex.

When I woke up the next day, the numbness hit me all over again. We only had one day to shake off our disappointment before we were due to move across to Nice for the third-place play-off.

Phil was hurting, too. He scheduled a meeting that day. None of us knew what to expect. A debrief? An analysis session? We were too numb to speculate.

What we got was the angriest version of Phil we'd ever seen. It seemed he had got wound up by a comment someone made. I'm not sure where it stemmed from but he'd allowed whatever had been said, whatever had happened, to get into his head. It was a very uncomfortable meeting. But OK, we thought – whatever. Let's move on.

The third-place play-off was a disaster. Against Sweden, we go 2–0 down in twenty-two minutes. Fran Kirby pulls things back to 2–1, but VAR disallows Ellen White's equal-iser – something that sums up the afternoon. Watching Sweden get their medals was a shit moment, but I stayed and watched. Why? To feel how much it hurts. So that I will remember this feeling – remember how badly I never want to feel it again.

Phil was criticised after the game for comments he made to the BBC in his pitchside post-match interview. 'Well done to Sweden but it's a nonsense game,' he said. 'We're probably showing in those first twenty minutes the disappointment we felt from the US game. We came here to win, not finish fourth.' He came under fire from former England players Siobhan Chamberlain and Lianne Sanderson, who were part of the 2015 team that won bronze at the World Cup in Canada. They felt that Phil had disrespected their achievement.

We'd never felt, as players, that it had been a 'nonsense game'. We had wanted to win. I hadn't been in that 2015 team; I didn't have a bronze medal. Many of my teammates didn't.

What Phil had meant was that there was only one game we'd wanted to play in, and that was the final. We'd wanted to be the best team in the world, and it was very hard for us to see past that. I doubt he's the only manager to feel that way. And maybe Phil's attitude towards that game rubbed off on some of the girls. Either way, as a team we felt flat before the game. The whole reason for being in a third-place play-off is because you didn't reach the final.

The game just had a different feel to all the others we'd played during the tournament. We were still hurting. We had nothing left to give. We'd spent so much of ourselves on the semi-final that it was hard, when football had made us feel as low as it was possible to feel, to lift ourselves for one more match.

Over the next few England camps, it felt like we were flatlining. It felt like we didn't really have an identity or way of playing. It felt like we were just putting things together as we went along.

These were the post-tournament blues, and they seized us for months. To come in touching distance of a World Cup final was one of the greatest highs of any of our careers. But, just ninety minutes later, we'd plummeted to rock bottom. It's the strangest thing to process, to understand that years and years of work and longing and dreaming can come crashing down in less than two hours. We felt like we'd failed. You start to question why you do it, because of how bad you feel. It's like we're stuck in the semi-final, living it over and over and over again.

It was a while before we were able to shake ourselves out of this mindset. Of our ten games after the World Cup semi-final, we won just three. We lost six times.

In March 2020, following our third-place finish at the 2020 SheBelieves Cup, one paper reported that Phil was preparing to leave. I wonder now if he had started to check out because he'd started to look at moving on. In camps, he started to let things happen that he wouldn't ordinarily have stood for. The way we as players held ourselves and treated each other in training made for an unpleasant environment. We were bitchy to each other on the pitch. We said things that we probably didn't mean. None of it was about pushing ourselves, or getting the best out of each other. It was all just malicious.

Phil never really addressed this or stopped it from happening. It just kept going and going until it began to affect some of us.

In one of the October camps, Lucy Bronze shouted something to me about what I was doing on the pitch. It was a harmless enough comment, and, on any other day, I wouldn't have cared, but I'd gone into that camp having learnt that the cancer diagnosis for Granddad Alan was now particularly bleak. He'd had leukaemia for several years, and his body was beginning to fail him.

I was sad and emotional, and Lucy's comment got to me. I'd told Phil about Granddad, not because I needed protecting but because he needed to be aware. He was there for me, and his support was great, but maybe he should have told the team so that people knew that I was vulnerable. It was another sign that the environment in camp just wasn't what it should have been.

I took a call from Mum on Monday. 'Granddad Alan has taken a turn,' she said. 'He's in bed, but fine mentally.'

Three nights later, Mum called to tell me she would stay in the spare room at Granddad Alan and Ninny's house. She told me that nurses were visiting, but that they were just looking after him, that he wasn't poorly enough to go into hospital.

I was woken at 6.30 the next morning by the vibration of my phone. It was Mum.

'Don't worry,' she said, her voice calm, soothing. 'Granddad's passed away. He fell asleep and just hasn't woken up again. It was peaceful.'

I messaged Phil and he replied right away, telling me that the FA have arranged a car for me to go home that day. I had spoken to Granddad on the phone earlier that week, and, as I packed my case, I thought over my favourite memories of him. I'd been obsessed with *Buffy the Vampire Slayer* and he'd nicknamed me Buffy as a kid. He used to sing to me: 'Buffy! Buffy! Buffy!'

Steph Houghton was up early that morning, too, and she sat out in the corridor as I cried on her shoulder. I didn't make it home before the undertakers came.

Phil arranged a squad meeting to clear the air over bad feelings, but I'm not sure if it was successful. The younger players were quiet. It's hard to speak up in front of people when you've only been part of the group a few months. Even though you want to be strong enough to say something, getting the words out can be quite hard. I wondered how they felt about the meeting, because from my perspective, it seemed that the more experienced players were the only ones speaking up.

Izzy Christiansen and I made the point that we wouldn't work well together with the way we were speaking to each other. Lucy Bronze responded that she had often worked with players who told her things that weren't easy to hear, but it always came from a place of them wanting her to improve and be better and served to get the best out of her. We all had differing opinions – neither Izzy's or Lucy's approaches would work for everyone – but it felt like we missed a chance to take a step forward because too many players just talked at each other. It felt like Phil was listening without giving enough direction. Then our next game, against Germany, which was scheduled for 27 October, was cancelled due to a Covid outbreak.

In January 2021, Phil confirmed that he was stepping down as our head coach. I can't remember the moment he told us. It might even have come from Sue Campbell, who often took the lead on big announcements. But we accepted it.

He could see how down we were – everyone could. We knew it was time for change and that we needed a fresh start with someone new.

The pandemic meant that even after Phil left, our England schedule was dominated by in-house games and behind-closed-doors friendlies. We hated them. We felt flat, disinterested. Few of us were enjoying our England journeys at this point.

Looking back, much of that time is a blur, including the World Cup. I can remember the stadiums, hotels, moments in the games. But other parts are just blanks. I've forgotten what training felt like, forgotten half the places we visited and what some of them looked like. So many moments passed me by. I never want to feel this way again at a major tournament. I didn't know then, but my next one would be unforgettable.

II

Sidelined

UEFA uses the World Cup as the qualifying tournament for the Summer Olympic Games. This year, the four home nations had agreed beforehand that England, higher than Scotland, Wales and Northern Ireland in the world rankings, would compete for the qualification place. When the US beat France 2–1 in the quarter-finals, and we knocked out Norway to reach the semi-finals, those results put England – and, by extension, Team GB – among the top three European teams at the World Cup. So it was job done. We were going to Tokyo.

The initial plan is for Phil Neville to manage the team, backed by his existing England coaching staff. That doesn't mean his existing England players will just walk into the team; my Scottish Arsenal teammate Kim Little is one of the most decorated and talented footballers in the game, and her compatriot Caroline Weir, from Manchester City, is in with a shout, too. At Wales, there's the gifted Jess Fishlock and Sophie Ingle, who runs the midfield at Chelsea. The World Cup consumes our thoughts, but we also all know that the selection pool is overflowing. Phil can only take eighteen players and four alternatives.

Women's football has been part of the Olympic Games since 1996, but this will be only the second time that Team GB has sent a women's football team to the Olympics. London 2012 was the first, when they fielded one to fill the hosts' automatic qualifying place. There was no British composite team at Rio in 2016 because the Football Association of Wales, the Irish Football Association and the Scottish Football Association were all opposed to the idea. In their minds, London 2012 had been a one-off. England's third-placed finish at the 2015 World Cup meant that Team GB could have competed in Rio if the governing bodies had wanted them to, but there are many intense feelings among the home nations and a lot of politics. FIFA declared that they all had to be in agreement about sending a Team GB squad.

Even though they're on board with sending a squad to Tokyo, the Scottish FA have announced that they will not actively support or promote the side. FA Wales have also said that they won't align themselves politically with the team. What will happen for the 2024 Olympics in Paris or the 2028 Games in California? The 2020 Olympics could easily be my only chance to be an Olympian.

I hate to use a cliché, but maybe you now appreciate why the Olympics really did feel like a once-in-a-lifetime opportunity. Phil always insisted that a Team GB side would play a huge role in growing the game, and we know where he's coming from – London 2012 helped to make a household name of Steph Houghton, who scored in each of Team GB's three group stage games. That last goal came against Brazil at Wembley in front of more than seventy thousand people. Watching her celebrate to those crowds felt amazing and those are my strongest memories from that Olympics. I couldn't believe that women's football was being projected to such a big audience. I'd met Steph at various functions over the years – despite her having left Sunderland several years before I joined – and it felt surreal to watch her become an Olympian. From that moment, I wanted to be one, too.

The England team were in the US for the 2020 SheBelieves Cup when Covid began to shut down the world. I was at home in England, completing my rehab for a knee injury, but I spoke to the girls regularly. Toni Duggan was playing in Spain back then, and their league had shut down. There was an outbreak in New York, close to where the England squad had been training. The situation was beginning to get serious, but none of us could have foreseen how all our lives would change over the next two years.

Over the next few days, the WSL was suspended and, along with the rest of the world, we were plunged into a time of uncertainty. Life quickly felt like one long Zoom call with Arsenal's general managers, who knew about as much as we did about whether the league would resume. The training ground closed and I had to have rehab at home, joining a Zoom call with the Arsenal physio every day. In the end, the WSL was cancelled and Chelsea won the title on a points per game basis. As a team, we were deflated. We knew we could have won if the league had carried on. In the time play was suspended, my knee injury healed completely, and the Olympics were postponed until the summer of 2021. It meant that I hadn't missed anything, but it's a lot of change to cope with at once.

In August that year, the Mead family welcomed a new member to its ranks. We had debated getting another dog since losing Jess, and we finally did when one of Mum's friends began breeding working cocker Spaniels. We had always wanted a little brown one and, when Mum got the first pick of the litter, she fell in love with one in particular. We named the puppy Rona, after the pandemic, and, to begin with, she was no bigger than my forearm. She is a typical spaniel: chilled in the house but wild outside. When I was allowed to visit family in Whitby, I fell in love with her immediately. She is the most loving, loyal dog you will ever meet. She loves jumping on the couch and settling down to snuggle and sleep alongside us. We don't even mind her habit of barking at the broom whenever Dad is sweeping the kitchen.

It was unclear when life would return to normal again, but, over the next year, something did become certain: Phil would no longer manage Team GB. His contract with England and the FA was set to expire in July 2021, almost a whole year before the rescheduled European Championships and when he stepped down for definite in January 2021 to go to Inter Miami, the FA began looking for an interim head coach who could lead the Lionesses – and Team GB.

The FA unveiled Hege Riise as the interim England head coach in January 2021, along with the former Canadian international Rhian Wilkinson as her assistant. From her CV, you can see easily why the FA hired Hege. She helped the United States reach the World Cup final in 2011 as assistant coach, then won Olympic gold with them the year after. In her native Norway, she'd turned LSK Kvinner, a women's football club from Lillestrøm playing in the top division, into a real force, winning six consecutive league titles since she began managing in 2017.

She also has 188 international caps, an Olympic gold medal, a World Cup winners' medal, a golden ball from a European Championship and a World Cup. It's an impressive haul from a golden period in the 1990s when Norway were big hitters on the international stage. Now, she'd come to England.

I didn't know a whole lot about Hege as a coach or a person when she was announced and I didn't have any preconceived ideas. I approached her arrival with the mindset I give to all managers – that it's a fresh start.

That mindset didn't last very long because I didn't make the list for Hege's first England squad. I learnt this via an email, which told me to be on standby but gave no real explanation of where I'd gone wrong or how I could get back in. I didn't respond kindly to that.

I was in St Albans with my mum when, two days into the camp, my phone rang. Hege. I ignored her.

'She's ringing you,' Mum said.

'I know,' I replied. 'I'm eating.' I speared a forkful of steak and chips. 'I'm actually going to finish my food, and then I'll ring her back.'

I can now admit that it was far from the right attitude – it was petulant, childish, overdramatic – but I was hurting and proud. I felt hard done by, and I'd never experienced being dropped from a squad without explanation. We all know that sort of thing is natural as an athlete, but it doesn't mean that you always handle those situations in the right way.

There was a spell of silence before the phone vibrated a second time. Hege was trying me again. This time, I picked up.

'Can you jump in a car ASAP?' Hege asked. Fran Kirby and Millie Bright had dropped out of the camp through injury, and Hege said there was an opening for Manchester United's Millie Turner and me. 'This is your time,' she continued, 'to prove to me why you deserve to be here.'

'It's not as if I've been sat waiting and ready for this call,' I retorted. I was way over-the-top. 'I need to pack. I need to get there.'

Grudgingly, I agreed to head across to St George's Park, and I drove there that night in my England kit. That first rejection had hurt me. *Ha!* I thought. *So, you want me now?*

Because someone's injured? Wrongly, that's where my head was at, even though it's routine for players to drop out because of injury and others to fill in.

By the time I arrived at the camp, I'd let go of those feelings. *I know how to handle this,* I thought. All I need to do is be myself and show them what I'm capable of.

In training games, Hege played me out of position, at left back. When she rejigged the formations and players switched positions, I stayed languishing in defence, with no idea of how to break back into her thinking. Hege was generally very quiet, and I didn't receive much feedback or any information on what I needed to do. In that training game, I was facing Rachel Daly and my plan was to do all the things that I hate when I'm playing against full backs. But each and every attacking drill, I played left back, with Millie Turner at centre half to my right. I'd never played that position in my life, and now I was doing it at an England camp which was essentially an audition for the Olympics.

Deep down, I was struggling. I felt like I wasn't supposed to be there. I felt that Hege's management team didn't really want me there. I tried to mask my emotions for the good of the team, but I went back to my room each night feeling extremely low. That's where I would let out the feelings I'd been hiding all day: anger, confusion, sadness. I felt I was never given a chance, and that they never wanted to give me one.

The game rolled around and England were predictably brutal against a Northern Ireland team made up of mostly part-time players: we were 3–0 up inside half an hour, Ellen White had scored a hat-trick by the forty-ninth minute and we went on to win the game 6–0. But with thirty minutes left, I was one of only two outfield players to be told they wouldn't be playing. Millie Turner was the other.

Pitch-side, I ran and ran, with so much emotion and anger that I find out later from the stats team that I completed more high-speed runs than anyone actually on the pitch. That says a lot about how cut-up I was inside during all this. I had no idea what I'd done wrong or what I needed to do to be better. This was new territory for me – and it all felt so far beyond my control. I didn't raise it with Hege because I didn't want to come across as abrupt and question what she was doing at my first camp. That would just make everything worse.

The heaviness lingered in me as I went back to Arsenal. The experience with England had affected me deeply, and it showed in my football over the next few months. I felt stale. The things I'd done naturally weren't happening. Although I was playing consistently and my stats were still favourable, I knew within myself that I could do more.

In March Hege was confirmed as the Team GB head coach, and in my mind, despite everything that happened at that England camp, I was still in contention for the Olympics. Chloe Kelly had just had a terrific season at Manchester City as a right winger but she suffered an ACL injury just as the season ended, ruling her out of an Olympics she deserved to be at. I was heartbroken for her. As a player, I always want to *deserve* to be in a squad; if Chloe had gone at my expense, I'd have had no qualms about that. As it was, her injury reduced the number of out-and-out right wingers playing regularly in that position. I felt I had a good chance of being selected for the team.

The day after my birthday, I took a call from Jordan Nobbs. She told me that Hege had just been on the phone. My stomach dropped and I was seized with nerves.

'I'm- I'm not going to the Olympics,' Jordan sighed. I could sense the emotion in her voice. 'And I'm not even a reserve.'

I was flooded with sadness for her. Jordan was in the best form of her career when she ruptured her ACL in the run-up to the 2019 World Cup and missed out on that experience. I can't imagine how hard that would have been for her, especially when her involvement in the 2015 World Cup had been limited because of a hamstring injury. She'd struggled mentally in that tournament and was so frustrated by the way her body kept letting her down. To lose out on another major tournament felt deeply unfair.

My thoughts then sprang to my own chances. The realisation hit me that if Hege called me today, it wouldn't be with good news.

I was restless and twitchy all day, rippling with adrenaline. My phone felt heavy in my pocket and I alternated between checking it every twenty seconds and just wanting to throw it away. My heart was hammering as the evening crept around.

And then it happened. My phone glowed and I snatched it up. The name on the screen sent my head spinning. Instantly, I knew. My stomach plunged. I felt as if I was falling. I felt like that for a long time.

'Just to let you know,' Hege said, as my vision blurred and my heart stammered and stuttered in my chest, 'that you're not going to the Olympics. Let my assistant know if you want to have a one-to-one conversation about why you're not going.'

I sloped from the end of my bed and landed on the floor. I stared into space, numb. I didn't care about anything else going on in the world except the emptiness inside me. Daan came into the room and saw what had happened – she knew the moment the call came from Hege. Silently, she hugged me. It was the lowest I've ever felt in football. I have never known a blow as big as this in my career. As day turned to night, it felt like the dark outside came in to fill my head.

The squad was announced publicly the next day. Team GB posted a futuristic video on Twitter, with a footballer drawn in neon lights backed by electronic music. Hege named five players from London 2012. My Arsenal teammates Kim Little and Leah Williamson made the cut, and Lotte Wubben-Moy was a reserve. Three of Chelsea's Champions League final squad were in there, too, and ten players from Manchester City.

My mind turned to the one-on-one meeting I'd arranged with Hege for the following day. Beforehand, I spoke to Daan and asked her to sit in on the conversation. I knew I would be angry and emotional, and maybe wouldn't listen properly and would misconstrue Hege's words. I needed her to provide a second set of ears.

I opened my laptop and notebook and joined the call with Hege and Rhian. I could see Hege poring through her own notebook for answers, before raising her head and fixing me with her gaze.

'You're not going because your player report card isn't good enough,' she said finally.

'What's a player report card?' I asked. I'd never heard of that in all of my time at England. If the report card was going off stats, I still had good ones as a winger. In the WSL rankings from that season, I was in the top five when it came to assists; I was joint-second for through balls, third for fouls drawn, fifth for crosses, fifth for passes into the penalty area, sixth for crosses into the penalty area, eighth for key passes, eighth for carries into the penalty area and ninth for carries into the final third.

'The second component is that you're too aggressive,' Hege added.

Mentally, I reeled back. I wondered if the hurt showed on my face. *Too aggressive?* The words struck me like a slap. It was really difficult to hear. Nearly every coach I've ever had has told me that I play my best football when I'm aggressive – I've controlled it, obviously, but I've always played on the front foot with fire in my belly. As Phil Neville used to joke: 'I need to find a way to make Beth angry.' That was what he wanted from me – a reaction. It's so fundamental to my game and who I am as a player that I couldn't register Hege talking like this.

Hege brought up the red card I'd received against Manchester United that March. I was joint-top of the WSL red card charts, but only because seven of us all had one each. Mine was two yellows, eleven minutes apart, both for challenges at the wrong time because I was so competitive. The first one was for a challenge on Lauren James: I'd had my hand on her back and gone to shepherd her away from the ball. It probably wasn't even a yellow, but sometimes it appears that players get protection on the pitch and you often hear rumours that managers discuss this with referees. I've never been privy to any discussions but I shouldn't have got a yellow for that challenge and whenever that happens it makes you wonder if the player was being protected. The second yellow was for a tackle from behind on Lucy Staniforth when I was trying to recover the ball – a mistake I'd like to think I've learned from now.

I have nothing to lose right now, I thought. *I'm not a reserve. I'm not travelling. I'm going to get to the bottom of this.*

'Please tell me about the player report card,' I said.

Hege spluttered her words. Her reasons were hazy, devoid of specifics. Then I asked her about the aggressiveness and the red card.

I prefer managers to turn around and say that they don't like me as a football player or human being instead of giving me what I think are bullshit excuses. I thought Hege's reasons were a big cop-out.

If I didn't fit the bill and I just wasn't part of her plan – and that's the top and bottom of things with some managers – she should have just said that. Tell me *how* I'm not good enough. Tell me that I don't fit the style of play. Tell me what I need to get better at. Make it plain and simple. If I was ever a manager, I wouldn't bullshit my players. I'm sure she wouldn't have wanted that as a player. I struggle with that. Sometimes, just being straight is the best way forward. I don't think that the excuses she gave to me fall in line with me as a player.

I've always insisted that you have to earn your right to be somewhere. I was brought up to never expect anything to be handed to me. I never expected to be in the squad, never assumed I'd make it; what I did expect was better reasoning and better communication from Hege.

Daan was watching me from the couch as I signed off from the call. 'I don't even know what to say to you,' she said. 'What I know about you as a footballer and see day in, day out – she has contradicted this completely and said the total opposite.'

Parents can always be a little bit biased, but my dad knows his football. He knows his stats and he knows my game inside out. I spoke to him and he couldn't fathom Hege's reasons. I called some of the other rejected players and we wondered why we didn't even make the reserves list. Maybe they thought we would kick up a stink if we were reserves. I'll never know, but that Zoom call was the last conversation I had with Hege – and also the only real conversation I ever had with her.

Around this time, Phil gave me a call. When he left for Inter Miami, he had told me that I was 'on the line', one of a handful of players whose position in the Olympic squad could go either way.

I don't know if this conversation will help me or not, I thought, as I saw the call come in, because he was no longer the GB manager. It doesn't matter if he'd have taken me. It doesn't mean anything to me now.

'You've got two choices now,' he said. 'You can just become an average player in the WSL. Or, if you use this to become fitter and more ruthless, you could become the best player in Europe. But it's on you. Stop making excuses. Are you going to be the Beth Mead who stays in her comfort zone and just plays OK? You can be up there with the best but you don't have that self-belief yet. Don't just accept being OK.'

During this time, I vented to Jordan. We were in the same situation and we read each other's feelings instantly and understood each other's pain, coming up with a plan to keep ourselves occupied. It wasn't easy because we were into the second year of the pandemic and couldn't leave the country, but we were resolved to step out of the women's football bubble for a little while.

Part of that involved going to matches at the men's Euros. We got tickets for the final at Wembley between England and Italy and sat in the friends and family stand along with Bethany England and the former Lionesses Casey Stoney, Rachel Brown-Finnis and Kelly Smith. They told me to try and find my enjoyment in playing again.

'Sometimes, a comeback can be even sweeter,' said Kelly.

I didn't register that comment right away. I was so switched off from women's football that it didn't even click that our Euros final would be held at this stadium in a year's time. Moreover, I didn't even know if I'd be in the England team twelve months from now. How could I even think about playing at Wembley when I'd been omitted from our most recent major tournament? I'm always willing to work hard, but I know now that that doesn't guarantee me anything. I had worked hard throughout last season, and something still didn't click.

The men's Euros played a huge role in helping me heal from the disappointment and fall back in love with football. It was an incredible summer, and I made a vlog of our celebrations during the semi-final. We went hard in the stadium, joining in with all the songs and leaping for joy. The atmosphere was unlike anything I'd experienced before. We'd wanted this kind of success for England a long time.

It took me about a month to even start to process everything. I was in a dark frame of mind and I felt incredibly lonely. I was sullen, angry and brooding. I didn't feel like myself. I've always been good at putting things into perspective and I'm a positive thinker, so I couldn't work out why I'd taken this so harshly. I loved all the girls in that squad, but because of how I'd left things with Hege, I didn't want her to do well. Going to an Olympics was a big dream for me. This could have been my only chance. I felt like it was taken away from me, so why should the one person I really didn't like at that time get anything from it? Why should they feel good?

Those were hard thoughts to deal with because I'm not that type of person. Every time they won, I felt blasé and indifferent.

With the time difference in Japan, the games were shown early over here. I'd generally catch the first half and then come back from training to see the full-time score.

Great Britain 2–0 Chile

Japan 0–1 Great Britain

Canada 1–1 Great Britain

Each time, I just didn't care. They were knocked out by Australia in the quarter-final, losing 4–3 in added time; they were coming away with nothing after all. My attitude made me hate myself even more. I almost lost myself in this period, my outlook was so dark and changed.

All my anger, though, was just hiding the fact that I desperately wanted to be there.

I headed back to Arsenal having got most of my anger off my chest and determined to knuckle down in pre-season. I decided I wouldn't make any big statements in the press or put myself out there; I'd just do what I needed to do and the new England manager could form her own opinions. My depressed, helpless anger had subsided into a determination to prove everybody wrong.

My Arsenal teammate, Lia Wälti, was one of the first to notice how I was moving a little differently. 'I couldn't understand why you couldn't kick into another gear last season,' she said. 'I felt like that once and it's what happens when you're so inside your own head. If you're in your head, anything physically that you try to do won't come off.'

It helped that we had a new head coach at Arsenal, too. We'd felt good with Joe, but I think he was unhappy off the pitch and was struggling during his final season, the 2020/21 campaign. He wasn't the same Joe: he was on edge and didn't seem present all the time. When he told us he was moving on because it was best for him and his family, we had the ultimate respect for him. He was eager to wish us all the best and remind us how much he had enjoyed his time with us, but we were gutted. Some players might welcome the fresh start, but I was crushed because I liked Joe's style and he liked me. Would the next manager feel the same about me?

My only regret from my time with Joe – and I'm sure lots of the other girls feel the same – is that we would psych ourselves out when we played the top teams. In Joe's second season – the one postponed due to Covid – we lost to Chelsea in the Continental Cup final and twice to them in the league. The year after, we lost 2–1 at home to Manchester

City and 2–0 away at Chelsea in the space of three days. Clearly, we weren't in the place we thought we were if we couldn't beat those teams. Despite what the scores suggest, I never felt as though we were a million miles away; more that little moments let us down. If anything, that made the gap feel worse.

We looked back over those games for hours. We dug into the analysis and pored over the goals. We knew we would create chances as a team to go forward, but we really needed to hone in on being a good defensive team that's hard to break down. We have the ability as a team to be the best in this league, and we play great football, but it's about whether we do it consistently against every team. That's the main thing for us to work on.

Our Swedish coach Jonas Eidevall arrived in June from FC Rosengård, who have been something of a talent factory in the women's game over the last few years. Jonas won three league titles there and they'd always been involved in the Champions League, while producing and developing very skilled young players. He thinks deeply about football and wants us to play a high-tempo possession game, moving like a well-oiled machine.

Jonas will admit that he's an intense man who wears his heart on his sleeve. He lives and breathes every beat and kick of the game as vividly as if he's on the pitch himself. I like that – why not celebrate the good moments? – and it became clear to me very early on that he was a family man with good morals. Despite his passion for the game, he made it clear to us that there is life beyond football and that he cares about us as people. You don't always find that combination, but he reiterated throughout the season the importance of family. I felt a comfort and trust with him from minute one, and we were on a similar wavelength from the get-go.

I got my first real introduction to his way of thinking early on, in one of our attacking drills. I was running at the full back and picked a safe, backwards pass. His whistle screeched and he stopped the drill right away.

'Beth!' he cried. 'What are you doing?'

'Keeping possession?'

'You are in a one v one situation. You're one of the best people when you're running at defenders at speed. Do not turn back again. You have my full backing to make mistakes, but if you don't get at players when you have a chance, I'll be really disappointed.'

It might have been a small thing from him, but it was a massive boost for me to know that he believed in me like that. Those first few sessions were intense – he was on it, angry, and I found it a lot to take at first – but he gave me so much confidence.

'You're good at driving at players,' he said. 'Do it more.' I stopped worrying about people being angry that I'd lost the ball because I got used to hearing Jonas clapping over my shoulder, urging me to try again. 'Defenders always switch off once they've tackled you,' he added, 'so tackle them back. Win balls high up the pitch.'

It was nice to be finding my confidence again. Without even realising it, I was rediscovering my joy in football. I started to feel lighter, like I was growing up as a person – and there was another big reason why.

That summer, I received some news that changed everything.

12

Mum

Cancer. It's a horrible word. Awful and utterly terrifying to hear. Even worse if you're the one who has to say it.

Cancer is a terrible, terrible disease. It's brutal, uncertain and indiscriminate. You never, ever want to hear about it in relation to someone you love.

And that's what happened to my family in August 2021.

Instinctively, I want to shield and protect my mum. That's one of the reasons this chapter is such a difficult one to write, because I know that sharing this with the world will impact her life and open her up to the public in a way she won't be used to. People will want to ask her questions, and, though they mean well, having her body and illness discussed in any kind of detail is a tough burden to place on her. I've given so much thought to this, but I cannot tell my story, with all the highs and the glories of 2022, without also including my mum's illness. It backdropped every moment where, on the pitch, my wildest dreams came true. And I kept it hidden from the general public, who had no idea of the darkness and the terror waging on in my personal life.

In the wake of my Olympic disappointment, Mum came to stay with me in London during pre-season to keep an eye on me. She was worried about how I was doing, given how hard

I'd taken all that had happened with England and Team GB. What's more, she wanted to get fit and we'd planned to do that together. I had made a fitness plan and circuits for her, and each day I talked her through sessions on my exercise bike.

Anyone familiar with cancer will know that the disease initially manifests itself in different ways, some of which seem harmless. Living in such close quarters, we found ourselves joking about her body. We laughed that they were signs of her getting old. Neither of us could imagine that her body was betraying her in a more menacing way – that these things would later turn out to be symptoms.

As the season drew closer, I waved her goodbye and she went home to Whitby. I trained, went out with teammates and lived my life, completely unaware of what was unfolding back home: 230 miles away, my mum was meeting doctors, undergoing tests, going to appointments and scans. During what must have been the most frightening time of her life, she strove to protect my brother and me from all of it. We had no idea.

I was in the bath when I found out. My phone rang with a FaceTime call. As her face flickered into focus on the screen, I could tell immediately that there was something wrong.

Her voice quaked.

Then came that horrible, horrible word. Mum had only found out herself that day, and now she had to break the news to me.

We all know that cancer exists, but how often do we think of it, day to day? We live most of our lives barely worrying about it beyond hoping that it will never impact us – until it does.

Only months earlier, my Arsenal teammate, Jen Beattie, had returned to football after being diagnosed with breast cancer. I remember the day she told us of her cancer. We cried with her as she explained what her treatment would involve. Carrying that burden, and having to tell that news to a group of people . . . I don't know how she found the strength. Just a few days after her diagnosis in October 2020, she scored during our 5–0 win over Brighton and we all huddled together in celebration. She was upset, and so were we, but it was a moment of strength, too, in which we could remind her just how happy we were for her to be on the pitch with us. During the warm-up for our game against Manchester City in December 2020, we'd worn shirts with her name on the back so that she knew we were behind her.

Now cancer had come for someone else I cared about. To someone I loved. To my own blood. To my mum.

I felt dazed, winded. I put the phone down reeling with shock, unable to register everything Mum had just said to me. My tears mingled with the bathwater until I couldn't tell which was which.

I couldn't process what had happened, nor that I'd been so unaware of it. I felt guilty that I'd not been around for her to lean on and for not knowing that something was amiss. I stared at her face on the call and thought, you're Mum – you're just exactly the same. But whatever was going on inside wasn't good. I knew I had to go home and be with her.

I called Jonas, my voice croaking.

'Beth, get yourself home,' he said instantly. 'There's far more to life than football.'

I drove the four hours home without stopping. My close friends from Arsenal who would become the people I'd rely on most – Jordan Nobbs, Steph Catley and Jen Beattie – spoke to me on the hands-free.

'I'm heading home now,' I said to Jordan. I was numb, but each time I went to say the words, I welled with emotion. Getting them out was horrible. It exhausted me. Each one was like a weight I had to haul from deep inside my chest. Each one broke my heart.

'I won't be in tomorrow, but I don't want everyone asking where I am. Tell me if this is too much for you to do, but if you could make people aware . . .'

It was a difficult thing to ask of Jordan. She knows my family well and this was huge news for her to take. However, I had wholehearted trust in her to handle this. She promised that she would stand in front of the squad and tell them what had happened – that I'd gone home because I'd learned that my mum had cancer. As soon as any player is missing, the questions start. Everyone is desperate to know where they are and what they're doing. I couldn't handle those kinds of questions.

Jordan's assurances slowed my racing, panicked mind a little, but I still felt trapped in a haze. So much was clouded in uncertainty. This felt like a step into an unknown that I could never, ever have been ready for.

'I'm so happy you're here,' Mum said, enveloping me in a hug as I stepped into the kitchen. 'We'll process this the best we can and then you'll go back tomorrow night.'

My mum had already shown incredible strength in hiding her illness from my brother and me, and she was just as brave and pragmatic when I arrived home. 'Nothing's changed,' she whispered, as we sat on the couch together. 'Your season is starting. You need to show them what you're about. I'm ready to kick cancer's arse, so you need to kick arse on the football pitch. Make me proud.'

'I want to stay home,' I told her.

'You're not staying here, moping around,' she said. She was so positive about the plan in place for her. She made a Sunday dinner, my favourite meal.

It was so difficult to drive away. I didn't want to leave her, but I took comfort in the conversations from the night before. 'If you need anything, you come home,' Mum said, 'but go and give me a reason to smile.'

In an instant, I flushed the GB disappointment from my mind. *You're being silly*, I scolded myself. *Put things into perspective, Beth. You might not have a mum soon. Her life could now be cut short. Stop overthinking everything. Stop being so angry.*

At that moment, I resolved to make my mum proud. I knew that I wanted to make new memories with her. After all she had sacrificed for me over the years, she deserved that; I should be focusing on giving back to her, instead of being an angry 26-year-old who was just being childish.

Mum ushered me back to London. On my first day back at the training ground, Jonas put his arms around me. 'We're here for you,' he said. 'You don't need to do anything on your own. If you need to talk, if you need a cuddle, if you need a moan – you let us know. If you need a break, you take one. You do what you need to do.'

His outlook touched on something we tell ourselves all the time but, in reality, struggle to practise because we're always so wrapped up in the present.

With huge relief, I realised that I was never going to be punished for going home. I already felt like our family was being punished, so I didn't need more suffering heaped on top of that because people in football were penalising me. My teammates understood that I would have to vanish at certain points if my mum needed me – that I might come back and play a game after missing a couple of training sessions – and their respect for that saved me from going too far into my own head. *Do they hate me because they've trained all week and I'm still starting?* I could easily have spent days lost in that rabbit hole in a less supportive squad. That resentment wouldn't have been what I'd deserved, but that issue never came up because of the safe space Arsenal had created for me. Because of that, I've always trusted Jonas.

Relaying all of this to Mum helped her, too. Her biggest worry for me during that time was that I was being looked after. I had a second family away from home and was surrounded by good people who were equally as ready to keep me occupied on the days when I needed a distraction as they were to catch me in my down moments. I was never on my own.

Knowing that was of so much comfort to Mum, and it helps me to know that she has Rona, who quickly became one of the best things that's ever happened to our family. Rona is amazing for Mum and helps to keep her strong. She is like a free therapy dog.

I was still a little bit stubborn when it came to opening up to others, and I was adamant that I wanted to manage everything in my own personal, quiet way. I didn't want to discuss things in detail with the Arsenal psychologist or a therapist. What was the point in sitting down and talking about how unfair life was? I didn't want to unpick all of that and delve so deeply into it. Psychologically, I felt that my friends and my family were the people I needed, not somebody who has a degree in how to bring things out of me. My football, at least, was going to plan, so why would I fix something that wasn't broken? It was what I felt was best for me at the time.

The psychologists kept watching me, nonetheless, and always knew what was happening. During training drills, they'd wait at the side of the pitch and I found myself dashing over at points to clear my head for a couple of minutes. Early on, I found that my emotions were always heightened. I'd lash corners into the box as viciously as I could, blasting balls into empty nets just to vent some anger. I must have spent hours slapping and punching the boxing bags, converting all of my emotions inside into something physical, feeling all the sadness and frustration drain out of me with each movement.

I was once so angry that I booted a ball into the distance and hit our goalkeeping coach. I'd known Leanne Hall for years and raced over to apologise.

'It's OK,' she said, calmly but with obvious meaning. 'Go get the ball, take a minute and reset yourself.'

Losing small-sided games in training would fill me with a kind of fury and I'd collect myself for a few minutes. I'd snap and throw my arms about if I lost the ball. I had to get better at reacting, instead of wasting time internally blasting myself for a mistake when I could be using those same moments to put it right. That was more advice from Leanne. I learned dozens of little coping mechanisms, like literally pulling my socks up if one fell lower than the other. That was a way of pausing everything and grounding myself. Actions like that bought me little pockets of time to find and reorientate myself; to feel human again when it felt like the world was crumbling inside me.

During this time, Jonas taught me a saying: lightning strikes faster than thunder. You can stand there waiting for the thunderclap and all of its noise and bluster but – flash – the lightning just hits. I was thunder, moaning and crashing about the training pitches, instead of being the lightning that strikes right away. Immediately, that resonated with me. It stopped me from overthinking. Every second is a new one. It changed not only how I moved on the field, but my thoughts on everything else going on at this time.

The most positive influence of all was Mum. Not once did I speak to her and find her fazed. She held the fortress up for me, my dad and Ben, even though she was the one going through it all. There were so many unknowns ahead, but Mum deflected them by encouraging us to take each day as it was. 'One day at a time,' she'd coach us, and that was all we could do. 'One day at a time.'

We followed her lead, and her outlook helped me approach football with a new urgency. In a half-hearted way, we always tell ourselves that we should seize and appreciate every moment, that we never know when life will end. We treat those words like clichés, and sometimes we just let them bounce off us without taking them in. But Mum's illness was the biggest wake-up call ever. You genuinely never know what day will be your last. In seeing how fragile life truly was, I found a new motivation to enjoy every aspect of life, and live every moment. In football, I found a genuine joy and real happiness. I've been so happy, despite everything.

I wish I'd had that perspective much earlier – not at twenty-six or twenty-seven. I'd just walked blindly through so much of life and so much of football without really feeling and relishing every moment. At the 2019 World Cup, I'd been so wrapped up in my inner world that I'd let so many things – the crowds, the places we went, the things we saw – pass me by. I didn't take enough in.

It's a huge regret. I really wish it didn't take something so drastic to happen for me to appreciate life. My message to you is to love life before something bad happens. Life is hard, but it's worth living. There are so many moments to enjoy. Life is full of ups and downs, but it makes me feel alive still because of those moments.

We opened the 2021–22 WSL season against the reigning champions Chelsea at the Emirates. In recent seasons, we'd been close to Chelsea's level but we kept falling short and we hadn't comfortably beaten them since that 5–0 victory under Joe. We were energised, determined to make up for lost time. It felt like we had a point to prove. What better way to start the league than to be three points ahead of Chelsea already? This game could set the tone for the season.

It was only the second WSL game to be shown on Sky. Falling just as Mum was beginning her chemotherapy, it would be one of the first times she hadn't been able to watch me in a big game in person. The games bring her so much joy – not just the matches, but everything around them. Since I was six years old, I've been her sole reason for being involved in football. For a while, her Facebook profile picture was a photo of her and Phil Neville taken after a game. She enjoyed showing that off to her friends, winding everyone up by telling them that David Beckham was there but had just been cropped out. When she came to England games, she always joked with me beforehand: 'Let Phil know I'm here!'

I wanted to make Mum happy and give my family memories that would last for ever.

That was the new incentive for me that season. I had been told been that I wasn't going to the Olympics because I was too aggressive, but I knew, as did various coaches throughout my career, that a balanced aggression often fuelled my best performances. I was angry at my mum's situation, and angry for her, but I was ready to channel that into my football instead of my emotions. Big signings had come in at Arsenal, including Tobin Heath, the two-time World Cup winner, and Nikita Parris, once the WSL's all-time leading goalscorer. Without realising, they unleashed a new competitiveness in me. I wanted to be impossible to ignore, because, clearly, that hadn't been the case for Hege. My opponents wouldn't have a moment to breathe, I decided.

I found the first half a little cagey, but we went 1–0 up inside a quarter of an hour. Katie McCabe finds Viv down the left wing and she weaves a dangerous, purposeful run into the heart of Chelsea's defence. She times herself perfectly, pushing from her left foot to her right and tucking it between Jess Carter's legs into the bottom corner. Then, with a minute to go before half time, Chelsea's Melanie Leupolz picks out Erin Cuthbert, who has drifted in having just taken a corner, to slot past our goalkeeper Manuela Zinsberger.

You have games and halves as a footballer where everything goes right. We can all name five to ten iconic individual performances that we'll never forget, where players seem to fly through on a different pane to everyone else. Everything comes together and they deliver the most complete performance possible. That's how the second half felt for me – like a dream.

When Viv plays a teasing ball between the Chelsea centre halves Millie Bright and Magdalena Eriksson, I know even before I meet the ball that I'll get away from them both. My first touch takes me wide and I can hear the fans quieten because they think I've missed my chance. But I know I haven't. I just feel good. I strike the ball and the roar of the crowd blasts through me. I ride on the elation.

Only twelve minutes later, I can feel the buzz growing around us. I try to stay onside as I know that Mana 'Buchi' Iwabuchi will find me. She spins the ball on a plate for me and, as the Chelsea goalkeeper Ann-Katrin Berger runs off her line, I think: I need to get there first, either for her to take me out for a penalty or to get around her. I take the perfect touch to drag it past her leg, then chop back to cut out Erin Cuthbert. An open goal gapes before me and I slot home easily.

I throw my hands in the air and let the girls run toward me. What is going on right now?

Chelsea bring on Fran Kirby and Sam Kerr. But we are in this space that footballers enter sometimes where they just refuse to lose. Even when Pernille Harder scores for 3–2, I never doubt us. We are never going to let those points go. And we don't, 3–2 is the final score.

After the game, the Chelsea goalkeeper Berger came up to me and said: 'I didn't know you had a left foot like that.'

It was the WSL's first introduction to Jonas and viewers couldn't take their eyes off him. He'd dressed as though he was going for a run, in a white Adidas T-shirt and black shorts, and by the end, he probably felt as though he had. He hurtled up and down the touchline, rippling with adrenaline. After Viv's goal, he raced off, bouncing from foot to foot, fizzing with joy. I'm not sure a WSL manager had ever offered the fans such an animated display. Maybe that's why the images of him dropping to his knees and roaring in relief at full time went viral. The whole internet was talking about them. I ran to him and he scooped me into a hug, lifting me off the floor.

That was the first time we'd seen that side to him, and it spiralled into a thread that ended up running throughout the season. When Chelsea won the title in May, some of their players copied that last pose and posted the pictures on Instagram. I get that they were taking the mick out of him a little bit, but we'd just won a big game against Chelsea. It was huge. Why wouldn't he celebrate? Yes, people can be overdramatic, but if that is their way of letting out their emotions, so what? Fair play to them. Why not celebrate the good moments? It's very English of us not to – we're more inclined to dwell on the negatives for a long time than allow ourselves to revel in anything we've achieved. And those highs don't last for ever. The previous month had taught me that.

I've played so many games in my career that have blurred the moment they finished, and soon dropped out of memory. That's what happens when you drift through life, barely drinking in the moments you take for granted. Not this time. I can remember every beat of that first game of the season. The roar of the crowd will stay with me for ever. After all I had been through, it was wonderfully affirming: this is what I'm good at.

I came back from my post-match interviews to find my teammates waving their phones in my face.

'Beth! There's this amazing picture of you online. You have to see it.'

I thought they were joking because I often hate the way I look in football pictures. I doubt I'm alone in that – you never know what kind of face you're pulling. But I loved this one right away.

Rachel O'Sullivan, a photographer from the women's football content platform GirlsontheBall, had caught my celebration for my first goal. Arms outstretched, I'm wheeling towards a block of Arsenal fans, who glow and jump in the background in a flurry of cheering arms and gleeful smiles. Taken from behind, you can make out my name and number beneath my swinging ponytail. The Chelsea goalkeeper Ann-Katrin Berger is blurred out of focus in the foreground, watching the ball roll to a stop.

I love that picture so much because it's celebrating to a packed-out crowd. To me, those are the most iconic pictures in football because you see so many different celebrations: a young kid, a grown man, a woman, grandparents. In women's football, we don't celebrate that much directly to the fans, but on this occasion you get to see both sides of my goal. You see how they felt in that moment as well as how I felt. It's one of my favourite photographs from my football career.

That photo has a twin, from right back in my days at Sunderland. It's the same celebration, shot from a similar angle, but back then no one is there apart from my family. I'm always taken by the contrast between them: running to four members of my family versus a crowd at the Emirates, sharing a similar moment with people I've never even met. It shows how far I've come, and how far women's football has travelled in just a few years.

It also disguises the turmoil going on in my life at that point.

At Arsenal, everything felt fresh. In that first month, we were unstoppable. Nothing was going to tear us down.

I won Player of the Month for September and Jonas won Manager of the Month. At the photoshoot, the photographer asked us to look at each other. I didn't want to because Jonas always stares at you so intensely. *He won't be taking his eyes off me*, I think. In the end I couldn't stop laughing, and probably ruined the picture ten times.

In previous dips in form, I'd felt trapped in my own head and clouded by my thoughts. I'd envisage doing something on the pitch but my legs and arm wouldn't follow. This season, I just felt lighter. Being tackled made me feel alive. In the past, I'd lumbered myself with so much pressure. A goal or an assist was the difference between a successful day or an unsuccessful one. Now, those parameters had changed. In light of everything, just playing football was a successful day.

There were times when I found it harder to process things. I think that was the case when coming back after Christmas. Over the winter break, I visited Mum, and it was a tough wake-up call. While in London, I'd seen her on FaceTime for just an hour a day. I didn't see how many tablets she was taking, or how tired she could get, or all the things Dad and Ben would have to do for her. I didn't see how frail she was.

That realisation hit me harder than I expected – how could I have prepared for that? – and the reality of her illness sat heavily on my shoulders.

I knew that Mum would be going through tough times and lonely moments. But seeing it brought that fact home. I tried to cling to the knowledge that I was still able to play football and do something that I loved, and I continually used that as my reset point. Life can suck and it throws things in your way, but it isn't there to be easy. I was making Mum proud by doing what I love, so I had nothing to complain about. Someone always has something else going on – you're never the only one suffering.

I did countless interviews and met scores of fans who'd ask me: 'What's the secret right now? What are you having for breakfast?' The irony was that nobody knew that I was actually going through the hardest time of my life.

And I don't know what the secret was – maybe just really appreciating life and letting go a bit more easily. I don't hold on to anger, grudges and pain now; I don't let it swirl inside of me. I will analyse myself, but the angry Beth who screamed and shouted over not going to the Olympics is a different Beth to the one who just wanted to prove the doubters wrong, be herself and find her love for the game again. I don't waste time being angry at things beyond my control: my anger is purposeful now, directed at the things I'm able to change and spurring me on further.

I'm more empathetic, too. I'm far less quick to judge – I'm living proof that you never know what's happening on the other side of the highlights reels and goal compilations. Life is there to learn from, and this year has taught me more about myself than any other. It truly made me grow up. There's no perfect formula for that, but we all reach a point where we feel comfortable in our skin and understand ourselves and how much we're able to cope with. I found myself thinking a lot of one of my favourite scenes from *The Lion King*, the moment when Rafiki whacks Simba on the head with a staff. 'It's in the past,' he says. 'The past can hurt, but the way I see it, you can either run from it or learn from it.' I love that film – maybe I've always been a Lioness.

Football has always been a safe space for me, right from the beginning. As my mum deals with her illness, it's my safe haven where I forget about everything. I don't think about anything else in the world. Nothing worries me. Nothing touches me. Nothing hurts me. I still feel like a six-year-old in a 27-year-old's body. I love what I do. Every aspect of it, and all the emotions it brings. Sometimes, that's all the therapy you need.

13

The Sarina Wiegman Effect

The fans sway and leap around me in a wave of orange. I'm in the Netherlands fan parade in Utrecht before the opening game of Euro 2017, being swept from the fan park to Stadion Galgenwaard. The energy is incredible; numberless rows of fans dance below the stage to a song called 'Links Rechts' by a Dutch party act called Snollebollekes. Over the next few years, it will become their anthem, like their version of 'Sweet Caroline', soundtracking parades over bridges and through cities before so many big matches.

'Naar links!' boom the speakers, and we sidestep to the left until the next line prompts us to dance to the right. When the thumping drums kick in, we all bounce on the beat, waving our arms and spinning in circles.

I'm here with Leah Williamson to support my Arsenal teammates: first the Dutch ones, who open their tournament against Norway, and then the British ones playing in England v Scotland in three days' time. The Dutch have thrown themselves behind the Euros and a ball hasn't even been kicked yet. The fans are very, very crazy, and, at the 2019 World Cup two years later, the authorities will close a road in one of the host cities, Le Havre, so that more than ten thousand Dutch fans can march behind a bright orange double-decker bus. A DJ on the top deck pumps out their favourite football songs as fans, in high spirits wearing orange wigs, high-five the policemen watching them from either side of the road. The fans trail the bus and stretch back like a tail far into the distance.

This is the Sarina Wiegman effect. Over the next few weeks in the Netherlands, I'll watch her team, the Oranje Leeuwinnen, or 'Orange Lionesses', win the European Championship on home soil. The tournament helps turn some of their best players, including Viv, Daan and Lieke Martens, into huge stars in their home country. Martens is crowned the UEFA Player of the Year, the Best FIFA Women's Player and wins Player of the Tournament. They're an utterly phenomenal team, conceding three times and scoring fourteen, and they beat England 3–0 in the semi-final. And their nation falls in love with them, those passionate fans bringing real energy to the matches. Sarina is the mastermind behind it all.

I meet her for the first time ahead of the World Cup semi-finals two years later. By this point, I'm dating Daan. The Netherlands are playing Sweden and, in our down time, I go to the hotel to wish Daan luck. I see Sarina across the lobby. As I'm speaking to Daan, Sarina makes a point of coming over to shake my hand.

I almost feel a touch intimidated, even though she's the smallest woman in the world, and she congratulates me on how well England are doing. She had already achieved so much and she'd got everything right throughout that Euros campaign. I have so much respect for her, even as the Netherlands lose 2–0 in the World Cup final to the US.

The following summer, I find out from Viv and Daan that Sarina has told her squad that she will be leaving after the 2020 Tokyo Olympics.

'But she never said where she's going,' Viv says.

Immediately, my ears prick up. I had *loved* what she'd done with that Netherlands team. No, they weren't the best team in the world at that point, but she'd made them who they were. She didn't need all the absolute best players; she just needed a team of women who were willing to fight and care for each other, and she created that culture, bringing people together to appreciate the collective. That's a very special skill to have. Until she left, I don't think the Dutch players realised how much she'd got right. Maybe the Dutch team isn't as tight as it was when she was there.

I would love play for her, I think, hoping, with Hege only ever hired on an interim basis, that Sarina might be on her way to us.

The FA announce Sarina as the new England head coach in August 2020 – thirteen months before she is due to take over in September of the following year. She wants to take the Netherlands to the Olympics first, we're told, for one more shot at a trophy with her home nation, but the four-year contract between her and England has been agreed. We learn of all this in a meeting with Baroness Sue Campbell, who plays us a video message in which Sarina is wearing an England kit. Until she joins up with us, her full focus will be on the Netherlands – but I'm full of excitement. All she'd done for those Netherlands teams was exactly what we needed for an English team.

The Olympics is a mixed one for the Netherlands. They top their group and Viv, with ten goals in four games, finishes as the top scorer, but they lose on penalties against the US in the quarter-finals. Canada takes gold, Sweden silver and the US bronze.

I don't see Sarina again until her first England camp. I've been focused on Arsenal, and I'm on my way to the Hilton

Hotel, adjacent to Southampton's Ageas Bowl, when I take a call from our photographer.

'How far away are you?' he asks. They want to film each player arriving. 'Sarina is waiting in reception.'

I gulp. *This is the moment*, I think, as I pull up outside. I want to salvage my England career after the disappointment of the summer, and the thought of doing it with a coach I admire and respect as much as Sarina inspires me. But it also means I'll be even more crushed if it all goes south.

'You're doing really well,' says Sarina, shaking my hand. We sit down together and one of the first things she says is that I deserve to be in this camp. Hearing that is something of a balm given how the camp under Hege went. I am still nervous because I know from the Dutch girls at Arsenal that Sarina is direct and to-the-point, but I like this about her. She outlines what I can improve on, the things I can turn into 'super strengths'. I don't want to divulge all the details of that conversation because I don't want the whole world knowing our winning formula, but it's instantly clear to me that she will make me a better player. I leave buoyed and filled with hope.

We learn later that Sarina had already let the FA know what she was about. In her first few days as England manager, she went on a guided tour of St George's Park and they showed her everything: all fourteen outdoor pitches, the full-size indoor 3G pitch, the Sir Bobby Charlton pitch – which replicates the Wembley surface – all the sports science areas and the 228-room hotel on the campus.

'And this is the men's pitch,' said the tour guide, gesturing to turf behind him.

'It doesn't say "men's pitch",' Sarina said. She's right – almost all the pitches at St George's Park are named after England legends, including David Beckham and Kelly Smith. There's a beat of silence. 'Is this the best pitch?'

'Yes.'

'Then we should be training on here,' concluded Sarina. 'The men train on it, so why shouldn't we?'

An FA staff member told us that story. You won't be surprised to read that, yes, Sarina got us the main pitch instead of one of the dozens around it. They had no right to refuse her. Later, when we're readying for the Euros at the same time as the men were playing in the Nations League, we are given priority. The men don't care. It's just about respect.

Sarina played during a very different era. She juggled her playing career in the Netherlands with a job as a PE teacher, and returned to her home country after a spell playing in the US to find that women's football wasn't as advanced as she'd hoped. As an England squad and manager, we can fight for the right things in part because we're all on the same wavelength. We've had lots of meetings where she's asked us what we need, expect and want. She was eager to understand the whole picture of the last ten years and that's where players like the recently retired Ellen White and Jill Scott, who made her senior England debut in 2006, and Lucy Bronze, who had played in four major tournaments even before the most recent Euros, were so insightful. How had the game changed for them? What was it like for players like me and those a few years younger? We have a leadership group of players who filter our concerns through to Sarina.

'I've disagreed with coaches before,' Sarina said. 'I lost my captaincy for it at one point.' Immediately we knew that she was someone who understood our challenges and pressures. Phil got us, too, given his background as a player, but, as a woman, Sarina just gets us that little bit more and understands many of the situations and feelings we're dealing with.

In my first one-to-one meeting with Sarina, I told her about Mum. 'If I react angrily to something or storm off, I apologise,' I said, 'but this is just where my head is right now.'

Emotions were already heightened at this camp. Rachel Daly had lost her dad, Martin, earlier that month.

Sarina told me that she had a family member suffering from cancer. We had a mutual understanding from day one.

'Are you happy for other people to know?' Sarina asked. She wanted to protect me from having to give the uncomfortable news to different staff members and players over and over again. I told her that I was happy for others to know, and she took that burden from me. 'If Beth wants to talk to you about it, that's her choice,' she said to the doctors, physios and performance analysts, 'but I want to make you aware.'

Later, I talked directly about Mum to Sarina's assistant, Arjan Veurink. Arjan had worked with Sarina since 2017, before which they'd actually been rivals – he was the head coach of FC Twente when Sarina managed ADO Den Haag, and their two teams were battling for all the major trophies each season in the Dutch leagues. He was superb at briefing us on the opposition, but he was also deeply empathetic and I felt comfortable talking to him about Mum. He was there for me and understood how what was happening at home could affect me. Arriving into camp, the first thing Sarina asked me was how my mum was doing. The staff hugged me. It felt like a safe space, and I didn't feel judged when I got upset.

Over the first week in Sarina's England camp, I came to relish her brand of honesty. She's as direct and forthright as they come.

In an early drill, I shied away from a one-on-one, turning back to plump for an easier option.

'Why didn't you get at her?' Sarina probed.

I realised I didn't have an answer for her. 'I was trying to keep the ball,' I offered. 'I was trying to play it safe.'

'Why?' She gave me the same speech as Jonas had weeks earlier. 'You have my backing to make mistakes in that area because that's the whole point of your position. I want you to get at people. You'll never have a 100 per cent success rate – but now you know what I want from you.'

With Sarina I'm free to improvise, and, when I do, she encourages me to be even more inventive. We wouldn't be playing for England if we weren't good players, and Sarina reminds us how we're capable of thinking for ourselves on the pitch and should express ourselves more.

'No one's going to tell you off for making mistakes,' she says. 'They're going to happen.' It sounds like such a minor thing, but we put so much pressure on ourselves as players that we often forget this. At the end of every speech and team talk, she always closes with the words: 'Go and enjoy yourself. Go and enjoy football.' For Sarina, a happy footballer is a good footballer.

In another drill, focused on crosses and timing, Sarina wanted me to go at the defender and cross first time. Instead, I chopped back, then crossed. We scored.

'I was going to call you up on that, for cutting inside,' Sarina said. 'But it turned out perfect. What am I supposed to say now?'

We opened our 2023 World Cup qualifying campaign with an 8–0 win over North Macedonia and followed it up three days later with a 10–0 win away at Luxembourg.

For many years, there had always been a few grey areas when it came to our playing style with England. We'd been good enough to get through tournaments, but we'd never had a plan B or C. Sometimes it felt as though we concentrated too much on the opposition, instead of honing in on us as a team. Sarina covers every eventuality. Even when the style feels unnatural, she's able to adapt it to our skills as players. It's crystal clear now, and it suits us as a team. We're quick-thinking and can adapt quickly. Yes, people expect us to score a lot of goals against these lower-ranked teams, but it can be harder than you think because they pack eleven players behind the ball. We play good football and find solutions; in the past, we wouldn't have done that. People would have overdone and overthought things, or would have tried to do things on their own. Now, we play for every single one of us. It's so simple, but managers can complicate things. I'm not ashamed to admit that with other coaches, their meetings have gone on for so long that some of us have switched off.

All of that said, I was not a happy footballer when Sarina benched me for our next game at Wembley against Northern Ireland.

'I just want a little bit more from you,' she said.

I was filled with that classic Beth Mead anger that so many of my previous managers had liked. *I'm giving you my all*, I thought. *I'm doing well for my club – can't you give me a break?* I thought I'd earned the right to be starting in that team.

But it was just the right thing to say to me. I come off the bench in the sixty-fourth minute determined to prove a point.

It's been a cagey game, and we've peppered the goal but haven't been able to break Northern Ireland down. When the ball drops to me inside the box having pinballed around the area, I lean backwards and with my first touch, curl the ball into the far corner. I scream. All the feelings pour out of me in that moment. As the girls jump on me, I can hear their joy. Finally, someone had scored. I look over my shoulder to see Sarina raising me a thumbs-up. *This woman knows what she's doing,* I think afterwards. *You have to trust her. She has it together, and she'll get us together.*

I feel so, so happy, like everything I touch will go right. Things feel so easy, so instinctive, when Lauren Hemp's cross finds me on the edge of the area and I easily volley in my second. When Bethany England's shot ricochets straight to my feet and I apply the finish, I'm ecstatic. Sarina got what she wanted. Maybe that was the plan all along: for me to score a hat-trick in fourteen minutes. Added to a goal from my fellow substitute Bethany England, we win 4–0.

By the time I finished the post-match interviews, the Wembley pitch was empty apart from the media team and me. I rolled the match ball between my hands and gazed around at the rows of deserted seats. I took in the stillness, before flicking the ball into the air and juggling it with my feet. I felt like a little kid again, drinking in Wembley. I was on such a high that there could still be 90,000 people screaming at me.

Over the next few months, Sarina created one of my favourite environments. We're grown adults, and, outside of camps, we went about our day-to-day lives without a second thought. Sarina knew that and we quickly earned her trust, and, in turn, she gave us the boundaries to freely express ourselves as people and show who we are. That made us feel so much lighter. As a player, you didn't feel like you were in a military camp or on a time limit. There was no micromanaging, ordering us to be in bed at a certain time. We already knew the right things to do.

'I'm waiting for there to be an issue,' she became fond of saying. 'At some point, something always happens. I'm still waiting.'

Sarina won every single one of her first six games in charge. The aggregate score was 53–0.

During the February and March international break, the FA hosted the first edition of the Arnold Clark Cup, an invitational tournament to sit alongside competitions like America's SheBelieves Cup and the Algarve Cup. Over six days, we played Olympic champions Canada, rising force Spain – home to the Ballon d'Or winner Alexia Putellas – and eight-time European champions Germany. The tour provided Sarina's first big test as England manager.

During our stay at the Rockliffe Hotel in Darlington, Sarina invited some special guests to come and speak to us. Professor Jean Williams, an expert on the history of women's sport, visited along with a handful of former footballers: Kerry Davis, one of the first women of mixed heritage to play for England; Carol Thomas, the first woman to win fifty England caps and England's top scorer until Kelly Smith, and then Ellen White, broke her record; plus three women who played at an unofficial World Cup in Mexico in 1971, Leah Caleb, Christine Lockwood and Gill Sayle.

In 2018, Jean had worked across the women's and men's departments at the FA with Phil Neville and Gareth Southgate respectively. Jean delivered elite performance psychology sessions, where key trigger words – think 'resilience' and 'courage' – were laced through a presentation on the history of women's football. Kay Cossington, the FA's head of women's technical, arranged a meeting between Jean, Sarina and Arjan and they all just got each other, right away. There was no question that Sarina would bring the players to meet us. That is typical of Sarina's approach – the behaviour, habits and mindset all come first. They're more important than the aim. Get those right and winning will follow. On top of this, Sarina wanted us to feel the power of what these players had to say. She wanted these players to put football and life in perspective, and for us to recognise how we must keep pushing the game onwards; for us to look to something bigger, and think about our impact on the women's game.

At the Rockliffe Hotel, Jean and the players relayed their stories.

From 1969 to 1993, the Women's Football Association governed the game in England. The FA didn't take over until 1993. The WFA was riddled with in-fighting, particularly over whether players would be allowed to compete internationally in overseas tournaments. One committee member, Harry Batt, was adamant that they would, and took a team to an unofficial European Championship in Italy in 1969. When those players returned, they were warned that if they went on another trip with Batt, they would never be picked for any future England team.

Then Harry took a team of players to an unofficial World Cup in Italy in 1970, and another team to a World Cup in Mexico in 1971. Eventually, he was banned. So were some of the women who travelled with him. Leah, Christine and Gill were only teenagers when they received their bans. Some of their older teammates got longer bans and were frozen out by the players who went on to form the first official England team. Some gave up football completely.

It was tough to hear of another ban, around fifty years after the FA infamously banned women's football for being 'unsuitable for females'. We all knew that story, but some of us had never heard of these players or what they went through. Lucy Bronze was one of the few who had. Many of us felt angry on the players' behalf – not only for what they endured for wanting to play internationally, but at how they were unable to tell their stories for so long. This was the reaction Sarina wanted us to have. Gill's daughter is in her late thirties but didn't know about her mum's involvement in the Mexico World Cup until 2018. That's how shameful and upsetting the ban was for Gill.

It was a big moment of realisation for me. I knew women footballers had never had it easy – just look at everything I'd endured with Sunderland – but the stories never stop being shocking. It reminds us of the legacy we have to continue, of why these women are so invested in seeing us do well.

Jean has written a book on this, and she handed out copies to each of us. We asked the players to sign them and they joined us for dinner afterwards so that we could hear their memories of playing for England.

'Don't wait fifty years to tell your story,' Jean said to us. 'The time to do it is now.'

Sarina bought a trophy for the winners of all the training matches and squad competitions we had while away on camp: everything from 5-a-side to darts, table tennis and snooker. We called it the Carol Thomas trophy.

The quizzes were particularly competitive. Arjan was the quizmaster. We sat in designated teams and our captains had to wear an armband. There was a karaoke round, and to finish Sarina had to perform to the group. She told us how she missed her family – she has two teenage daughters – on camps, which was why she was so keen for us to become a family away from family. It's not easy to balance that with being such an authority figure, but she managed to retain an aura. I lost count of the number of times we walked into meetings to find her stern-faced and tight-lipped.

'We're in trouble,' the players would think, glancing at each other in a panic.

Then Sarina would smile, laugh and get on with the meeting, and we'd all be left on our toes. She was similarly blunt with

Arjan. He would suggest something on the pitch, only for Sarina to respond 'Erm – no', and vice versa. They took it easily because they knew exactly where they stood with each other, and they weren't afraid for us to see that. Things like those quizzes gave us a sense of regular life even while we were in camp. Sarina and Arjan seemed to know when we needed a pick-me-up or a moment away from football.

While good, Arjan's quizzes had nothing on Wendy Taylor's, our former media manager. Her quizzes were exceptional. She set up a big screen in the ballroom and had someone filming her as she walked down through St George's Park, like we were watching an *X Factor* judge make their way to us from backstage. With Millie Bright and Rachel Daly flanking her as her bouncers, Wendy made her entrance in a full gold outfit. Then she'd run around the room high-fiving people, like she was Paddy McGuinness or Keith Lemon.

'I've got a few messages for you,' Wendy would say. She used to work at Newcastle, and invariably a video would pop up on the screen of Georginio Wijnaldum or Rafa Benítez. 'Hi, Lionesses. This is Rafa Benítez, and I've got a question for you. In what country did . . .' She set a high bar.

Our next stop for the Arnold Clark Cup was one of my old haunts, Middlesbrough's Riverside Stadium, for our opening match against Canada. We were rushing through drills at Middlesbrough's training facility when I heard a voice boom across the fields.

'Oi! Beth!'

It was Lee Cattermole, who had remembered me from my time at Sunderland and was now working at the Middlesbrough Academy.

'You've not changed, have you?' he shouted.

'Neither have you, by the sounds of you!'

'Look at you now, pottering around on our main pitch like you own the gaff,' he said, gesturing behind me and laughing. We'd been given the show pitch and they'd been placed on one of the side pitches. 'We normally train here and you've taken it straight off us. Look at us training at the side of you.'

He had kind words for me about my football career and it was nice to reconnect, however briefly, before we began the tournament with a 1–1 draw with Canada. I start the following game, against Spain at Carrow Road, and I come up against Barcelona's Alexia Putellas. I slide for a ball and she all too easily flicks it away from me, while I end up sprawled at her feet. She casts her eyes over me and I feel minuscule in that moment. I'd slipped, missed the ball, was on the floor and the first woman to win the UEFA Women's Player of the Year, the Ballon d'Or Féminin and the Best FIFA Women's Player in the same year is peering over me. It didn't stop us from swapping shirts after the game, though, and we got on when I saw her around St George's Park, where the Spain team was training.

Added to our 0–0 draw against Spain was our 3–1 win over Germany in the final game, which meant we won the tournament. Millie Bright's two goals across those games made her the tournament's joint-top scorer, tied with Putellas. They were jointly presented with the trophy, which Alexia promptly gave to Millie.

'*Of course* she gives it to me,' Millie said. 'I'm sure she's got better ones at home, but I'll take what I can get.'

'Any chance of you strikers turning up?' we all joked.

Now, Euro 2022 was looming. Sarina had already seen the impact that winning a home Euros can have. She knew how important it is. In 2017 the media reported that eight out of ten people in the Netherlands watched their country's 4–2 victory in the final against Denmark.

'When you go out for a warm-up,' Sarina said, 'and you see people in the stands, I want you to wave at them and clap for them.'

We were a little uneasy when she first suggested this. We'd always appreciated fans in the women's game – we were known for staying behind after games for autographs and photos with supporters – but wasn't this a little . . . big time?

'No!' Sarina said. 'You're just showing appreciation for them as much as they're showing appreciation for you. Appreciate the fans first, then focus on your warm-up. After the game, you go around the pitch and you appreciate every single one of them.' I can now see why the Netherlands fans flooded the streets for her.

It was a different perspective on how we interacted with the fans. We had been very English about it, worrying about looking like divas. The pandemic, and the difficulties of playing games in empty stadiums, had made us realise how important crowds were, but Sarina's words – to appreciate people and appreciate moments – resonated with me because of my new resolution in light of everything going on with my mum. It was like she was seeing life through my eyes. She reiterated the standards I was living by. It was another thing that drew us closer.

The league, meanwhile, was nearing its conclusion, and on the final day, the title was to be decided. Chelsea were a point ahead of us and had Manchester United at home; we were away to West Ham and needed to better Chelsea's result. After losing to us on the opening day, Chelsea won eighteen of the next twenty-one games. Since drawing 0–0 with us in February, they won their next nine league games. We'd been ahead in the league until March. Since returning from the winter break, we'd dropped too many points against our fellow top five teams, only managing draws against the two Manchester clubs. But the thing that really punctured our hopes was a 2–0 defeat by bottom side Birmingham in January.

We were too naïve that month. We lost four players to the Asian Cup – Australia's Caitlin Foord, Steph Catley and Lydia Williams, and Japan's Mana Iwabuchi – and Jonas was very critical in the press of the decision to restart the WSL while such a big international tournament was taking place. We weren't playing the kind of football we were at the start of the season, and I was enduring my own down moment, struggling to process my mum's illness. We were still in the running, but we went into the final day knowing things were out of our control.

Both games kick off at the same time. The Arsenal fans have come out in force and our families are in the stands. We are comfortable and are playing our style of football, so, although our match is goalless at half-time, we're not fazed.

We'd decided beforehand that we didn't want to know the score, but, walking back to the tunnel after half-time, we hear the crowd cheer. The PA system has just announced that United are leading 2–1 against Chelsea. It's a new flicker of hope. United are no bad team.

The adrenaline increases. I roar with hope when Viv plays a delicious through-ball to substitute Stina Blackstenius, who sets herself well to slot home into the bottom corner after being on the field for just a minute. Then Catley caps off a brave solo run with a fierce strike from inside the area, putting us 2–0 up with twenty-four minutes to go.

The whistle goes and we know instantly that we haven't won the league. The crowd are too quiet. Our instincts are right – Chelsea have come from behind to win 4–2.

I'm fine, I thought, as we huddled as a team. We said all the usual things: that we'd accepted beforehand that we weren't going to win the league, that we'd still had a good season, that we could be proud of everything we'd achieved. I clapped the fans.

I only began to cry when I got to my parents. Mum reached out her arms and I fell into her, weeping on her shoulder. I felt like I'd let her down. Winning the title would have been such an amazing feeling to give to her, and I couldn't do that. I'd wanted to win the league with her and for her. She'd asked me to make her proud, to make her happy and give her a distraction. To fall short by a point was devastating. I'd put my heart and soul into this season, had given as much as I could.

I always say that the true emotions come out when you see those you care about. In that moment I allowed myself to accept that I truly was gutted. Which games had hurt us? I played back key moments, key matches, over and over again in my head. How could my best still not be enough?

It meant that the Euros were my last hope of silverware that season. As the tournament drew closer, I thought back to that parade in Utrecht. I'd seen a home Euros from the fans' side, I'd been there as a supporter. But what about as a player? Would I get to see that view? Would Leah? How weird would that be? Could we win this Euros together, four years after we'd watched those Netherlands players do it?

14

Golden Ticket

It's always been a phone call. Or an email. That's how we're used to learning if we're in the England squad. That's how we like it: at home, where we can easily find some quiet if it's bad news. Not like this. Not in person, at St George's Park, in a one-to-one with Sarina.

'You'll get a text when I want to see you,' she says, before leaving us to suffer for the day.

Have I got a message yet? Have I got a message yet? We obsessively check our phones.

We scatter ourselves in our rooms, trying to spot patterns that aren't even there – is it defenders first? When are the midfielders up? I haven't got a call yet – does that mean the squad is full?

Chloe Kelly tells me she's been sat on the toilet for most of the day. I sit with Jill Scott and both of us are jittery with nerves, barely able to stand the tension.

'Jill,' I tell her. 'You've been in this position ten times over. You'll be fine.'

Literally ten times over, I think. This will be major tournament number ten for Jill, should she make the cut. She made her tournament debut at the 2007 World Cup in Japan, aged twenty. Fifteen years on, the possibility of a home Euros – she

172

played in the last Women's Euros hosted on English soil, in 2009 – means as much to her as the first. The uncertainty isn't any easier to bear.

'Shhh,' she replies. 'You've had a great season. What are you bothered for?'

The day continues like this, with players trying – and failing – to reassure each other as much as themselves. I never expect to go to anything, especially after the Olympics. Everyone earns the right to be where they are so have I done enough?

Only one of us is not nervous – Lucy Bronze.

'Obviously you're not worried!' we jokingly snap at her.

I'm jealous of the first girls to be called. *At least they'll know,* I think, and won't have to endure this suspense for much longer. We find out later that the early meetings are with the ones who haven't made it, and they pack their bags and leave immediately. It's that cut-throat.

My message arrives at 4.13pm. It's from Arjan. 'Hi, Beth. Can you come to the drum now please?' I don't even reply. Immediately, my heart speeds up.

I'm shaking as I head up the spiral staircase to the drum, a dimly lit lounge above the reception of St George's Park. It's been set up as our games room for the past few months, and the jungle theme – there are fake palm trees and artificial grass – feels incongruous with the churning in my stomach. Sarina peers at me from a chair a few feet away, inviting me to join her. Her face is impassive as I sit across from her.

'So,' she says. 'Are you nervous?'

'Nervous?' I splutter, in disbelief. 'Beyond nervous. That's an understatement.'

'Why?' she says. 'You've had a great season.'

'Well . . .' I pick at a loose thread on my tracksuit. 'This time last year, I was told I wasn't going to a major tournament

– the Olympics. I never expect to go to anything now. Until you tell me, and I hear it coming out of your mouth, I don't believe I'm going to this tournament.'

'Oh, right,' she says. She sits in silence for a while. I scrutinise her face. I've always felt Sarina would make a great poker player. My insides twist.

I dare to look up. Her face breaks into a smile.

'Congratulations,' she beams. 'You're going to the Euros.'

It feels like the final whistle of the biggest final I've ever played. Inside, I collapse with relief as Sarina hands me a golden envelope. I turn it over to read the inscription on the front: 'Congratulations!' it says. 'You're going to the Euros.' I slide my finger beneath the seal. Out falls a sticker. Sarina leads me to a nearby table, where the FA have made a replica of the Panini Euros sticker album.

'Stick yourself in the book,' Sarina smiles.

I dash back to my room and call my parents right away. They cry as soon as I tell them the words, and I cry, too. It's a huge relief after such a tough year, and I'm so grateful that I'm not calling them with more bad news. I can feel the weight lifting off my parents' shoulders as I tell them – that's how much this means to all of us. I don't think Sarina realised right away just how nerve-wracking the day had been for her players. That was the way she'd always done things – including with the Dutch team – but it was a draining, testing day. Mentally taxing, too.

Later that night, Sarina leads us back up the spiral staircase and shows us a video that the FA has prepared ahead of the public squad announcement. The opening shot is of a music box in a little girl's bedroom, with a figure of a footballer turning where the ballerina would usually be. There are Lionesses posters on her wall and she pastes Mary Earps into her sticker album. Then her bedroom walls fall away, and she's racing from her local park to Wembley. Throughout, players appear on stickers, swapped and traded by Ian Wright and David Beckham. 'This is our family,' says the narrator, 'and family comes first – through thick and thin, rise and fall.'

Sarina says little after that. She doesn't need to. After all, perhaps we've been guilty of saying too much in the past, in camp and to the public. We already know how desperately each of us wants to win. That's what we're here for. Nothing less. We can feel that urgency, that need, rippling through the room. Why do we need to voice it?

'Let's just have the best summer,' concludes Sarina. 'Let's enjoy this. Let's take it all in.'

In the coming days, Sarina also sets the place on fire. Sort of. She and her staff project a campfire onto one of the big screens, turn down the lights and serve us hot chocolates while we sit on comfy beanbags.

'Go and find out a little bit more about each other,' Sarina says.

We all surprise each other with how open we are. It's a great sign of trust when you're willing to share personal things with people you might not have spent a great deal of time with. It sounds contrived, but the conversations feel natural.

I, for example, had argued with Lucy Bronze in the past. She'd once called me out for a loose pass in a game, and I'd felt hurt.

'I expect more from you because you're a such a good player,' she tells me by the flickering virtual fire. It's not an easy conversation, but it pulls us closer. It's one of the steps Sarina takes to make us comfortable in being more honest with each other. In some squads, it can feel like certain players have authority over the others, but that's not the case now with the Lionesses. We all want the best for each other.

There's also been a huge development in my personal life – Viv and I have started dating.

I'd broken up with Daan in October. When I'm with someone, I like to think I'll be with them for the rest of my life. If not, what are you both doing it for? I'd never experienced genuine heartbreak before and I didn't know what my future would look like. I thought I was never going to find that kind of love again, that I'd never find someone who meant as much to me as Daan did.

I channelled that pain into football, which was by then carrying so many of my emotions and fears. All of my hurt over the Olympics, all of my pain at Mum's illness and now the upset from my break-up, were being pumped and pumped into my season. In April, I became the WSL's all-time assist leader. I made the shortlist for the FA WSL Player of the Season, the PFA WSL Fans' Player of the Year, and I won the Arsenal Player of the Season Award and the Arsenal Women Supporters Club Player of the Season Award. All I'd been through had shown me that life was too short. This was just me making the most of it.

Viv and I had known each other for five years; but we hadn't really *known* each other, we realise now. Although we'd always played well together, we had both been wrapped up in our own relationships and probably hadn't given each other the time we should have. I'd always thought that Viv was my total opposite. She would sometimes sit with Steph and me on the bus and complain that we were being too loud, leaving us to go to the front with a book or her university work for her Master's in Business, Marketing and Sponsorship. She tells me now that she loves that side to me, but only wants it at certain times. She has conceded, though, that when we're at home together I'm more relaxed than she would have expected. Viv is naturally introverted and inward-looking, whereas I've normally gravitated to people who are as outgoing as me.

Those of you who have watched her on TV will know what I'm driving at. In interviews, she looks very stern, and can come across as aloof sometimes because she's so humble. She rarely celebrates her goals, preferring instead to respect the opposition when they've just conceded. When it comes to Viv, we tend to view any tiny show of emotion as a celebration.

I remember taking a photo after one game with a fan who was terrified to approach Viv.

'Could you . . . um . . . just ask Viv to . . . er . . . come . . .' they stammered to me.

'Why don't you ask her yourself?' I smiled.

'Well . . . she's just a bit scary, isn't she?'

She really isn't. Beyond that veneer, which people mistakenly interpret as bravado, she's a soft human being – even softer than I am – who feels the pressure that comes with achieving all she has. She's truly a once-in-a-generation talent. By the time she was twenty-two, she had become the Dutch national team's all-time leading goalscorer of either gender. She holds the record for most goals scored in an Olympic tournament (ten) and is the WSL's all-time leading goalscorer. Her most memorable performance came against Bristol City in our 11–1 win in December 2019, a match that now has its own Wikipedia page. Viv got six goals and four assists in that game. I just sat there applauding everything she did. 'Let's clap that cross. Let's clap that finish.'

She scored her 100th Arsenal goal in just 110 games. I put the ball on a plate for her, and I said as much in the changing rooms at Slavia Praha, where we took photos of us making the number 100 with our fingers. It was low-key for the enormity of Viv's achievement, but that's just the way she likes things. 'You didn't hit the first defender for once,' was Viv's way of thanking me.

Maybe that's why people assume that Viv wears the trousers in our relationship, but it's absolutely the other way around. 'It's definitely 70:30 to Beth,' Viv tells people.

But even I didn't know about that side to her until recently. Viv has never been a social butterfly – unlike Jen, Jordan, Steph and me, who live in each other's pockets – but she suddenly began making more time to socialise with us. Many of her closest teammates had left. She was softer, more approachable, had more time for people. She wanted to be a part of things. As her teammates, we started to see a new Viv.

It was comforting to see her around, joining us for coffee and days out. It felt like she cared more. She always did, but we never felt as though we'd seen that.

'So, this is you,' we'd say. She is laser-focused when it comes to football and has high expectations of all of us, and maybe we were guilty of reducing her to just how she behaved in training. She's a strong character who is direct in team meetings and isn't scared to stand up to managers and speak her mind. Spending time with me was starting to bring her out of her shell outside of football.

'Have you been here?' I'd say to her, showing her pictures of restaurants and London landmarks.

'No.'

'Right – we're going.'

Over the winter break, I had reached out to Viv to make sure she was OK. She had just broken up with her partner. Having just been through that, I wanted to be there for her and keep an eye on her. I let her know that I was there for whatever she needed. If you'd have told us then that we'd get together in the next year, we'd have laughed – but we continued to grow closer. I enjoyed the new, more sociable Viv. It was as if I was seeing her for the first time. Our time together felt deeper, more meaningful, than everything we'd shared in all the years before. We bounced off each other effortlessly and connected on a new level.

In the spring, we had our first kiss. I was dropping Viv back at her house and turned off the engine to say goodbye. As she unbuckled her seatbelt, she turned to me and it happened. It wasn't planned, and I was more than a little nervous. We were both still trying to process the fact that we felt that way about each other, considering how long we'd been teammates. But it felt right.

We both laughed, then Viv got out of the car and went home. It was the classic movie cliché.

While I was away for the Arnold Clark Cup, Viv and I kept calling each other. That had never happened before, but I wanted to know how she was, what she was doing. Most of all, I missed her. That's when it clicked. Maybe this was more than just being there for each other, I thought. Something was happening here. There were deeper feelings involved. She made me happy – and I really, really cared about her.

Towards the end of the camp, Sarina handed out the schedule for the next few months. There it was, right at the bottom: England v the Netherlands, Friday 24 June, Elland Road. *Of course*, I thought, stunned by the irony. In four years with Daan, I'd never once played the Netherlands. To get them when I was feeling all kinds of things about Viv felt ridiculous. What a fantastic time to be alive.

On 24 March, I made the decision to tell Mum about Viv. She had come down to London to come out for dinner with Viv and me. As far as Mum knew, Viv and I were just team mates, but I needed to tell her how I was really feeling.

Mum, Rona and I went for a walk through Longacres Park in St Albans. By the entrance, there's a bench Mum and I call the 'talking bench'. It's where we always sit when we want to open up about what's been going on in our lives.

'It's early days, Mum,' I said, 'but I've really been getting on with Viv. "Getting on with Viv" in a way that feels like we're more than friends.'

That was the first time I'd told Mum about someone so early on in a relationship. I texted Viv to let her know.

Well, I can't run away now, she replied.

Viv met Mum and me that night at Prime Steak and Grill, one of my favourite restaurants in St Albans. I wanted to go all out and got ready to order three courses. Mum and Viv were more restrained and shared a starter. Their calamari had just arrived when all the lights went out – there had been a power cut. The staff brought out candles and Mum and Viv chatted away while we waited for our main courses to arrive. They never came. We sat there for three hours, which made them regret sharing. But they chatted easily and have the same sense of humour. Mum loved Viv right away.

The Netherlands match was our final one on home soil before the Euros. A fan captured a video of Viv and I walking into the tunnel with our arms around each other, way before the public could possibly have known about our feelings. I like that clip because it shows how happy we were to see each other. Even though we'd only been apart for two weeks, it had felt like for ever. Our feelings had grown so big. Did she feel the same after we beat them 5–1, with me scoring two of the goals? You'll have to ask her.

England then gave us the weekend off, and Viv, staying in Manchester with her Dutch teammates, had the afternoon free. I met her at the Marriott Hotel and we walked along the Bridgewater Canal together, enjoying each other's company.

We walked between overhanging trees, past the canal boats taking tourists on river cruises, to a sun-dappled spot set back from the towpath. The Horsebox used to be a literal horsebox;

now it's a café, and we ordered coffees as we watched the boats a while. Neither of us could stop smiling at the other. *This feels like the right time*, I thought, *and the right place*.

I knew what was coming even before Viv said it.

'I love you,' Viv said simply. It's the first time either of us had said the words.

'I love you,' I replied, without a pause.

We smiled at each other – wide, toothy grins. We sat for a few moments, laughing.

'Viv . . .' I began.

'I know,' she said.

'I refuse to ask you to be my girlfriend,' I replied. 'You're going to have to ask me.'

'Maybe not,' she said. That dryness is classic Viv. 'You just put two past us.'

Even though I was the outgoing one, Viv had taken the lead for much of our initial relationship. She'd instigated that first kiss. She'd been the first to say 'I love you'. We joke now that I had to make her feel wanted in some way. That's why I'm the one to ask.

'Of course I'll be your girlfriend,' she grinned.

We'd already seemed to know what was going to happen. Maybe that's why we were so smiley, so giddy. I always call Viv a 'big awkward tattie' – an awkward potato – because I'm always so happy to see her and she's shy until she's warmed up. 'Beth, I'll still be like that in six years' time,' she says. I've never been great with romantic moments either, but we never have to say too much to each other.

Since then, it's just been easy. When you've had your heart broken, you think you're never going to find that happiness again. But it's a different kind of happiness, and a different kind of love with somebody else.

A lot of women's football fans were very invested in my relationship with Daan, as we were open about being together. Despite that, we never officially announced our break-up. Why would we? It was personal and we needed to get through it in the best way we could, but it meant that there was lots of speculation for a long time about what had happened between us – and lots of rumours about my dating life.

It amuses me sometimes to see who fans put me with. Someone thought that I was going out with Amelia Dimoldenberg, best known for interviewing footballers as the host of the web series Chicken Shop Date. Amelia is one of the presenters for Lionesses Live, the England Women magazine show that runs on the FA's YouTube channel, and she mentioned this to me.

'Have you seen the fanfiction?' she asked. 'There are TikToks about me and you. I'm here for it.'

It's not uncommon for players in women's football to date their teammates, but in every dressing room I've been in, those involved have been very good at keeping things professional. It's like any other workplace. Yes, you have disagreements, but you've got to be disciplined and leave those at home. Pick them up again, if you need to, away from the team. No one wants people to feel awkward or weird around them or their partner.

That said, I've noticed I tend to get particularly emotional and angry, in a game, with the person I'm with. I've always said you take things out on the person you care about most. Luckily for Viv, that's her.

15

Panini Stickers

A few weeks before I leave for the Euros, Mum buys me a present. She is staying with me while I finish the season with Arsenal. As I leave training for the day, she takes me to WH Smith, where she sneaks off between the aisles and I lose her for a few minutes.

'I've found some,' she says, when we get home. She dips her hand into her carrier bag and pulls out the Women's Euros Panini sticker book. She fans five packets across the table, like a poker player showing their hand. Wordlessly, I smile. I don't need to say anything because we're both casting our minds back to the same thing – to those days when the elves would leave Match Attax on my bed at home. Now we're looking for a sticker of me.

It's a mind-boggling moment. Panini had made a sticker album for the 2019 World Cup but I hadn't been in it because they go to print weeks before the squads are actually announced. I think back to that young girl in Hinderwell, and the hours she spent slipping cards of her favourite Premier League players into her collector's album. I think of the kids today who will now be pressing me into their own sticker books. It feels very special.

The break following the Netherlands match is our final chance to spend time with our family and friends before our Euros journey begins in earnest. Mum and Dad have rented an apartment in Wakefield and they hop across to Leeds to visit me for lunch, and we have dinner out before I spend the night with them. The next day, I drive down to London to get ready to fly to Switzerland for our final pre-Euros friendly. We win that 4–0, with goals from Alessia Russo, Georgia Stanway, Bethany England and Jill Scott. Those are our first nights away from home. We know that we won't be in our own beds again until we're knocked out – or come home as champions.

After touching down in England, we went to our base for the next few weeks. The Lensbury Hotel is a 102-year-old resort with twenty-five acres of gardens and grounds, situated on the banks of the River Thames. It's an imposing building, the reception area hidden behind white columns that meet a high pointed arch. It has history, too, and we're not the first professional sportspeople to train there. In the 1970s, Steffi Graf would go to the Lensbury before Wimbledon. Phil Tufnell, Mark Ramprakash and Andrew Strauss are among those to have played in cricket matches there.

'Resort' really is the right word. The FA wanted us to spend the next few weeks in a bubble, closed off from distractions and criticism, but they made sure that we never felt trapped because there was so much for us to do. The Lensbury grounds roll down into Teddington Lock, where there were kayaks and boats for us to ride. When the weather was at its hottest, I jumped in with Rachel Daly, Millie Bright and Ellen White, and we had fun splashing each other. By the pond, the FA built the set for Lionesses Live, the daily magazine show that ran on YouTube during the tournament, adding a wooden stage and sofas next to the bridge. We had breakfast most mornings on the terrace. The environment they created felt like a holiday camp but also quickly became a place to call home.

Nike helped to design the relaxation room, and there was a table tennis table, a pool table, a dartboard, basketball hoop and beanbags. Everyone's favourite activity was volleyball, and so many of us joined in – including our doctors, physios and media team – that the ball never hit the ground unless someone really messed up. We felt light and full of joy.

We checked in to our rooms on the first night to find envelopes on our bed. At the FA's request, our family and friends had written us letters. Mum even wrote one from my 'proud sister' Rona and drew around her paw. Family friend Lorraine mentioned the fountain at Beacon Farm. 'The magic water needs to come into action now,' she wrote.

That was the point at which a lot of us got emotional; the people who cared so much, who have been there for much of our journeys, have sent us something so special. Over the next few weeks, our families got to know each other, too. They met up for meals beforehand, with Sarina's family attending also. They bonded as much as us players.

I thought back to the FaceTime call I'd had with my parents a short while before, when they'd been in the middle of decorating the house with England flags. Dad was literally up the stepladder when I rang.

'This is a bit over the top,' I said.

'My daughter's playing in the Euros!' Mum responded. 'I'll do what I want!'

Take all of this in, Beth, I told myself, turning the letters over in my fingers. *Take in every single thing.* I thought I'd done so at the World Cup – I really thought I'd drunk it in. But I hadn't. This time, I was determined to enjoy the full experience.

Nike had also left some trainers for us, and, that night, we went to Nike Town, the flagship store on Oxford Street. The store was closed completely for us and decorated for the

Euros. There were huge banners showing the girls in action –
Georgia posed under one that says 'shine like Stanway' – and
Lionesses scarves, including one with Lucy's face on and the
words: 'Bronze by name, Bronze by nature'.

The top floor was turned into a changing room and this
was how we learned our shirt numbers, seeing them hanging
above messages from fans all over the country. On each floor,
there were activities for us. We customised our own shirts and
I added a decal of three Lionesses to mine. On another, there
was a jewellery-making workshop, and we crafted colourful
phone charms and bracelets. We were asked to choose a word
or a name that gives us strength. I never actually finished
mine because I was too impatient. I gave up on threading the
string through the beads. We made collages of each other, too;
Georgia made one of Leah Williamson and glued a crown on
her head, adding the caption: 'A life of firsts'.

A drummer played us out, and we saw the shoppers on
Oxford Street craning their necks, wondering what was going
on. I don't think they were totally sure who we were. It would
be interesting to see if that's still the case now, or if they realised
when Nike projected images of us across English landmarks,
including Tower Bridge and Battersea Power Station.

Our first game was against Austria and, two days before,
we flew to Manchester, staying in a Hilton Hotel in the city
centre. On the drive to the stadium the night before, Lucy
told us to look out of the window.

There were moving screens with Lionesses graphics. We
caught ourselves on billboards. Hotel Football had a banner
of some of us pasted across its front. That was when it hit me
– the Euros were about to begin. *This could be huge.*

I took a moment to look around the stadium, and remembered how I'd been a handful of times to watch United with my

dad. I'd forgotten how steep some of the stands are. I thought back to my own visits, and how the players had looked like dots as I'd watched them from above. It felt bizarre that, the next day, people would be watching me.

Ella Toone, a Manchester United fan and now player, kept bending over and stroking the grass. She interrupted my train of thought.

'Carpet, this,' she cooed. 'Absolute carpet.'

I never struggle to sleep before a game, but that night I was gripped with nerves that had been building for most of the afternoon. We would open the tournament in Group A. I thought of all that would hold for us, and the games coming up against Austria, Norway and Northern Ireland. *We've been preparing for months*, I thought, as the realisation hit that the work we'd put in had to come to something the following day. All eyes would be on us, and the magnitude of the match and the expected crowd – we were told to expect close to 70,000 – made me extra desperate for us to start with a bang. I slept fitfully before eventually dropping off properly.

The coach journey to Old Trafford was quieter than usual. There was a nervy edge to the atmosphere. Our UEFA bus didn't have tinted windows and we could see the fans waving at us from the road below. We waved back, but even the busy streets gave us no inkling of what awaited at Old Trafford.

The tunnel was soundproof, deceptively quiet. As we walked out for the warm-up, the roar of the fans rolled towards me in waves. I thought of Mum, because I knew how much it would mean to her to see me achieve my dream of playing at Old Trafford. I looked for her in the stands, a ritual that always settles me. When it came to singing the national anthem, I was overcome with emotion. Leah Williamson told me after the game that she didn't want to look up because her mum, Amanda, was crying and that would have set her off. I did the same. I focused instead on the energy that rippled towards me from the crowd.

The game begins. Sarina had told us to make runs in behind to stretch the Austrians. Our opposition set up well and the opening moments are cagey, as the first games of tournaments often are, until Fran picks me out perfectly with a ball over the top. It comes at me with such power that all I can do is take it on my chest. In the next second, my mind flashes with thoughts. Am I onside? I have just one more touch before someone is up my arse. I see the Austria goalkeeper, my Arsenal teammate Manuela Zinsberger, closing in on me and I know that one of her strengths is stopping low shots. I go for a lob. I wince internally as I watch the ball soar above her. Is it too high? Then I see it drop, and it seems to do so agonisingly slowly. From my vantage point inside the 18-yard box, I will the ball to edge over the line.

The roar of the crowd tells me it has.

The ecstasy is indescribable. In my mind's eye, I see Mum soaring to her feet, waving her flag. I feel Ellen White and Lauren Hemp rushing towards me, then, as my teammates retreat, I put my thumbs and forefingers together to form a love heart. I hope that Mum sees it.

My goal, on sixteen minutes, gives us a moment to pause and catch a breath, to rein in the adrenaline of playing at Old Trafford in the opening game of a home Euros. The ground roars when the attendance of 68,871 is announced – then a record crowd for a match at a Women's Euros – and I feel them with us constantly. When I walk near the corner flags, I'm greeted with a flurry of boos from the Austrian fans. The England supporters respond, overriding them with chants of 'MEADO! MEADO!'

We know that we can be more ruthless and this is a source of regret for us, but we largely reduce Austria to half chances and come away with a 1–0 win. On the coach back to the

Lensbury, many of us beat ourselves up. We hadn't shown the world everything we could do. It's Lucy Bronze who put everything in perspective for us, reminding us that the most important thing was that we won and we could now relax into the tournament.

I thought of Viv. That we were playing in different groups made being at a tournament together easier – and I took Viv's shirt from the Elland Road match with me. I wore it while I watched Viv play against Sweden in her opening group game, and she did the same when she watched me play for England. Although we both love playing for our country, you also feel strongly for your other half. If we were to be knocked out, the Netherlands are who I'd support. That's not because I don't care about England, but because you support the one you love.

Not that it's always easy. I'd sit bolt upright in bed, wincing every time Sweden mounted any kind of attack. I'm a terrible supporter and was on edge the whole time.

'Viv!' I shouted, covering my eyes. I winced, paced about the room, looked anywhere but at the screen. Each close call or missed shot sent a jolt of terror across my abdomen. I just wanted the best for her. When the Netherlands finished second in their group, Viv and I knew that we would not play each other unless we both made the final or the semis. We vowed not to worry about it unless it happened.

My sticker collection was coming along well, and two others joined me on my quest to collect all 366 – Rachel Daly and Millie Bright. Over the course of the tournament, we spent hours in each other's rooms, sprawled across the floor and the beds and rooting through piles of stickers. I was ahead of them given my early start, so I had the biggest swap pile and spent those early days throwing my duplicates across the bed towards them.

'I need number sixty-seven,' Rach would call.

'Yep,' I'd say. 'Got that one over here!'

By the end of the tournament, Rach and Millie's books were close to full. Lauren Hemp joined us, but my collection was the biggest. As I write this, I need just two more stickers to fill the book.

Collecting stickers wasn't the only way we prepared for our game against Norway which would take place in five days' time – imagine if it was. We knew that this would be our hardest group game. Much had been made of the return of Ada Hegerberg to the Norwegian national team, just in time for the Euros. Ada was the first-ever winner of the Women's Ballon d'Or and the all-time highest goalscorer in the Women's Champions League, but she stopped playing for Norway in 2017. It was her way of telling the Norwegian Football Federation that she was unhappy with how they were treating women's football. She refused to be called up for the 2019 World Cup, which was a huge story but would have been even bigger had it happened in the men's game. Imagine one of the world's best players refusing to play in a World Cup because they don't feel they're being treated equally and with dignity.

When Ada told the world, in March 2021, that she was ready to return to international football after meetings with the NFF, it was a huge moment. In many people's eyes, this turned Norway into serious contenders. Add in Chelsea's Guro Reiten and Barcelona's Caroline Graham Hansen and their attacking threat only increased. All of us knew the magnitude of the game we were about to play. 'This is going to be *the* game, girls,' we said to each other. 'We need to be on this.'

We felt ready. In the days before, I felt at peace. We stayed in the Malmaison, a boutique hotel along the Brighton seafront. We breakfasted on terraces overlooking the marina, so close to the boats that it felt like we could reach out and touch their sails. As I walked along the promenade one evening, a handful of locals and tourists waved at us. 'Hi, girls – good luck!' they called. It gave me a sense of what was brewing in the outside world, but things felt calm. My teammates felt the same. There was no sign of what would happen in the next twenty-four hours, the dizzying high that would see us produce one of the finest and most one-sided performances in football history.

We have no inkling of what is to come even as the game kicks off. As the whistle blows, the few nerves I have leave me. For the first five minutes, the ball seems to bob in the air above us. Then, I feel a shift. I can almost hear it, the smooth click as we glide into top gear. We seem to know, amongst ourselves, exactly what we have to do. I feel filled with a kind of super strength, a weightlessness, free from doubt.

The game is not even fifteen in when Ellen White wins a penalty against Maria Thorisdóttir. Latching on to Fran Kirby's through ball, she begins to spin away from Thorisdóttir, whose left arm seizes Ellen by the shoulder and waist to send her to the floor.

We know before the referee blows that it will be a penalty, and we know that Georgia Stanway will take it. We protect her in the build-up as the Norway players protest, but I have total faith that she will score. She always leathers her foot through her penalties in training. It's no surprise to me when she does the same here, putting us ahead after twelve minutes (1–0).

Norway's forwards and defence are split, distant from each other. It is exactly how Sarina predicted – this will work perfectly for us to overrun them in midfield and cause overloads in the wide areas. Lucy and I will be able to go two v one against Julie Blakstad. We've worked on our partnership to the point that our connection feels telepathic. I understand what Lucy is going to do before she does. I can read her body language, know where she will run, what pass she wants to play.

Sarina had also warned us that Ingrid Engen would pop out of midfield to act as an extra defensive player. What it means is that, when we win the ball high up the pitch against her, Norway won't have any answers.

Lucy releases me into space on the wing and I can tell by Blakstad's body language that she doesn't know whether to press Lucy or follow me. That moment's hesitation is enough for me. I'm away. Blakstad scrambles to make up lost ground, but she's on the back foot. I know she is panicking and that all she can do is block any shot I have, so I chop the ball back, opening up space for myself. I'm ready to shoot until I see Lauren Hemp standing on her own inside the six-yard box. I know she's onside, and I flick the ball across to her to tap home (2–0).

Behind me, the flag flies up. Lauren halts her celebration, but I know that we will be fine. Lauren is twitchy as she waits for confirmation from VAR, but explodes with joy when the goal is given. I know that she needs it because her first tournament has been overwhelming for her, particularly with all the expectation on her following a terrific personal season with Manchester City. I understand how she will be feeling, and what a catalyst this moment will be for her.

Thorisdóttir had already taken a few dodgy touches before I began to close her down on twenty-nine minutes. She has her back to me and mis-hits the ball as I close her down. She claws the ball away from me, but spills it right into Ellen's path. Ellen barges forward, leaving Thorisdóttir sprawled on the floor. I have no doubt that Ellen will score and finish. I'm the first there to celebrate with her (3–0). She plants her feet apart and roars into the crowd.

Then Ellen turns provider for me, hunting the Norway full back Maren Mjelde all the way into the 18-yard box. Ellen easily snatches the ball from her and ushers it in the direction of Lauren Hemp. As soon as I see Lauren take it on her left foot, I know she is readying herself to cross. I commit to my run and my heart leaps as I see the ball surge perfectly towards me to head it into the back of the net (4–0).

I race over to the girls, laughing unabashedly. 'I can't believe it's come off my head!' I shout. I never score headers. Maybe that goal should have told me what kind of game this was shaping up to be.

Ellen had spent most of the week laughing at me because I'd injured my wrist in training and had some strapping on my thumb. Every time I went anywhere near her, she'd give me the thumbs-up and roll her shoulders and wiggle her hips, moving from side to side. As soon as I score, she's straight over to me, with the express intention of winding me up. I throw my head back with laughter and copy her. By the end of the tournament, all the girls will be dancing like that with us.

It's not until I score my second that the enormity of what we're doing settles upon me. When Fran Kirby plays me into space on the right, a deserted 18-yard box opens up before me. As Blakstad tries to delay me, I think of the words of every single coach I've ever had. They echo through my mind, ringing through my head. *You're so good when you're running fast. You're so good when you're aggressive, when you get at people.*

The voices push through my head, pumping me with adrenaline. *Get at them*, I can hear them demanding. I move in time to their words. I have nothing to lose.

I drag the ball easily across Blakstad. Fran's run draws away Engen, who only realises how much danger Norway are in once I'm even closer to goal. Maren Mjelde is haring into the box, scrambling to make up the lost ground. I see a gap open up, and the goalkeeper Guro Pettersen steps to her right.

Gotcha. 5–0.

All of that happens in a couple of seconds, but my mind processes so much more in those moments than some people's will in minutes. I think of every single manager who's ever told me to terrorise a defender. I think of Fran's run. I keep up speed. I keep the ball at my feet. I trickle in and out of players. I know every inch of the space around me, almost as if I'm part of it. I know that Engen can't touch me without fouling me. I know that Thorisdóttir won't commit to me. I know that Mjelde is running to catch me. I know that she is too late.

I hear the excitement surging in the crowd as I get closer to goal. My mind whirs, yet I feel calm. I know when to pull the trigger. I know that this will be one of my favourite goals of the tournament.

How does it feel, to be in charge of a game like that? You feel bolder, braver, as though nothing can go wrong. You put balls through from angles you wouldn't ordinarily try and they float and glide perfectly into the best areas for someone to tap in. You can feel the confidence radiating through the team, as if you're floating on cloud nine while it's happening. Those days happen sometimes. When they do, you feel untouchable. Nothing can bring you down.

Most of us know what it's like to be on the other side of a performance like that – every bit as excruciating as you might imagine. The simplest things feel like a battle, like an exhausting uphill struggle. Your limbs feel heavier, disconnected from your mind and out of your control. Your mind then betrays you in its own way. Everything seems muddled, disjointed. You second-guess yourself. The decisions you've made thousands of times, that have come as naturally to you as breathing, seem to desert you. You're emotionally exhausted. What's the point in playing on when you've no way of getting back into the game?

When that realisation hits, you just wait for the game to end. You convey that with your eyes, with your body language. I can see it in Norway now.

Ridiculously, we have time for one more goal before the break when Fran curls the ball to the back post for Ellen to slide in (6–0). This is the point at which it all gets overwhelming, and Ellen, just as I did, breaks into incredulous laughter.

'What is happening right now?' she screams in my direction. How can we be 6–0 up after forty-one minutes? This was supposed to be our hardest game, yet everything we're trying is working. Every flick, every combination, every rotation. We're fast, ruthless, deadly. Not one of us could have dreamed of anything like this.

I want to keep going. I don't want the whistle to blow for half-time. I'll play all the way until the end. I could play like this for ever.

We enter the dressing room in a stunned haze. We look at each other, eyes wide and mouths agape, as if daring someone to point out that none of this is real. Stunned laughter bounces off the wall as we wait for the only person who will be able to make sense of this.

'Well,' Sarina begins. 'We didn't really expect that.' Her face splits into the widest smile and we laugh. This is the happiest half-time dressing room any of us have ever known.

'I didn't expect this team talk,' Sarina continues. 'But this is the level we've set. You've got to do that again in the second half.' We're all in agreement with her. I think that approach – to go out just as hard – demonstrates much more respect for Norway than just sitting back and chilling would.

Another goal – it still feels ludicrous to write, even now – arrives at sixty-six minutes, when Alessia 'Lessi' Russo rises in the box to knock in Lucy's delivery. We'd practised laying balls off for Lucy and me to hit first-time crosses dozens of times in the weeks leading up to this moment and Lessi had been one of the best at finding space between bodies and jumping above everyone. She makes this finish look easy (7–0).

Fifteen minutes later, I watch from the edge of the area as the ball ricochets off the goalkeeper Guro Petterson towards me. I know that Petterson was too committed to her save from Walsh to get up in time to deny me. I glance back over my shoulder to check the lineswoman and, when I realise I'm onside, lift the ball over a prostrate Petterson for my hat-trick (8–0). It's pure striker's instinct, a throwback to those number nine days. Only this time I'm playing at the Euros, and have just scored one of the easiest goals I will ever get.

I run towards Chloe Kelly in a haze. 'Does that mean I'll get an assist?' asks Keira Walsh, as we look around the stadium to see England flags flying and the first choruses of 'Three Lions' surging from one end of the ground to the other.

Scoring that many goals, in front of that many fans screaming my name, was the biggest rush of blood I'll ever get in my career. I saw other people finding so much joy in what I'd just done, and it overwhelmed me.

Our families were to the right of the tunnel. I spotted them in the warm-up, as I did at Old Trafford. Throughout the tournament, Mum did so much dancing, swaying and flag-waving before matches that Leah and Keira began to look for her, too, because 'she always makes us smile'. They fell about with laughter when they saw her doing exactly the same at the end of the match, to Status Quo's 'Rockin' All Over the World'. We danced along with Mum, who copied our moves from behind several rows of overjoyed family members. I still look at those videos most days.

Lucy came up to me. 'This is what I've always expected from you,' she said, stressing each word. I thought back to that conversation around Sarina's virtual campfire all those weeks earlier, when Lucy had said the same thing. And she was right.

Maybe you should be the next manager of England, I thought.

When the whistle blew at an incredible 8–0, I wanted to stay out on the pitch all night. Instead, I was taken aside for my television interview as Player of the Match. In the corner of my eye, I saw the girls dancing with the fans. I could hear 'Sweet Caroline' booming over the sound system, thrumming through me. *This interview is terrible timing,* I thought. We had so much to celebrate in the next few weeks that we asked for the playlist to be changed so that 'Sweet Caroline' came on later and whoever was being interviewed had the chance to join in.

I came back from my media duties to find the changing room transformed into a disco, the girls dancing and swaying around me. I checked the group chat and saw the videos from twenty minutes earlier, and all the celebrations I'd missed. Never in the past would we have celebrated a group game like this, but Sarina had us living for the moment and relishing the times when we really did well. We accomplished something huge that day, producing the biggest winning margin in Women's Euro history. We equalled the record, which some of my teammates had set with their 6–0 win over Scotland at Euro 2017, by half-time. I'm struggling to put into words now how incredible we felt.

Sarina danced with us. 'Enjoy this,' she told us, just as she did at St George's Park all those weeks ago. And I really did take it all in. Everything felt vivid and vibrant. 'These are the moments you live for as a footballer. You've just done something historic,' she said.

We really had. Norway are a good team, then ranked eleventh in the world. Not one of us could believe that we made them look bang average.

On the bus in the early hours, we sang all the way back to the Lensbury. I FaceTimed Viv before we set off, and was flooded with warmth as her face filled the screen.

'Any chance of you putting those kinds of balls in for me at Arsenal?' she said.

When I crashed into bed, I immediately fell into a deep sleep. There were some stiff limbs the next morning, as if the power of the day before had been drained from us, but we snapped back into work mode instantly ahead of the Northern Ireland game.

Three days later, we sensed something was amiss. At our hotel in the Ageas Bowl, the team doctor was flying from room to room, his expression forlorn. The girls knew, even without saying anything to each other, that something was wrong.

We walked uneasily into our meeting room to see Arjan stood alone at the front.

'Sarina has tested positive for Covid,' he said.

I winced. We had all been around Sarina at training. What if it had got anywhere else? *I really hope I'm not next,* I think. *I don't want to miss these games.*

'It doesn't change anything,' Arjan said. A calm quickly descended as he reminded us that we'd been here before. Sarina was absent from one of our preparation camps following the death of her sister. She had already talked us through our matchday training and tactics. Arjan pointed us towards the big screen where a video message of Sarina appeared – the final time we'd see her until she returned from her quarantine.

'I'm feeling fine,' she said. She was sitting up at her desk, her tactics books spread out before her. 'Don't worry about me. You know what you have to do, and hopefully I'll be ready for the next game.'

We knew that Northern Ireland would present a different test to Norway – they would come out to frustrate us and make life difficult for us with their low block. When teams have that many bodies behind the ball, they're hard to unpack and you have to look for new avenues and solutions.

Fran Kirby gets us on our way before the break with a well-placed finish from the edge of the area (1–0), and, four minutes later, I'm ready to join her on the scoresheet. Lauren Hemp crosses from the right and the Northern Ireland defender Julie Nelson heads the ball towards me on the edge of the area. I collect it right away. It's that classic striker's instinct, of seeing a cross come in and being poised to scoop up the knockdowns.

As a line of green shirts form a wall in front of me, I'm filled with a sense of déjà vu. How many times have the girls shot early, only for the ball to ricochet off a body and become trapped by the Northern Ireland defence? I won't make the same mistake. As I bring the ball down with my right foot, I cut in front of Rebecca McKenna. In my peripheral vision, I can see my old Sunderland teammate Rachel Furness lunging towards me, but, by then, I've already decided what I'm going to do. As I follow through with my left foot, my shot pings off Rachel's splayed foot and slides low into the bottom corner (2–0).

Still, we know at half-time that we haven't been ruthless enough. That's the message from Sarina, too, as the staff relay what she's told them on the phone call from the hotel room where she's watching the game. It's odd to feel so thwarted when we'd ridden through the Norway game so effortlessly.

We throw that frustration into coming out swinging, and it takes three minutes for Alessia Russo to extend our lead (3–0). Ella Toone cuts a short pass across to me and I hit a first-time cross onto Alessia's head. It doesn't matter that Alessia and Ella replaced Ellen and Georgia respectively at half-time; things still feel seamless, and Alessia certainly isn't phased.

Her second goal (4–0) is the kind of finish you'd expect from strikers who have been playing on the world stage for years. Here it is coming from Lessi in her first major tournament. She receives the ball on the edge of the area from Ella, spins out of the reach of Nelson and, with the goalkeeper Jacqueline Burns haring towards her, makes the finish look easy. But it's all about the composure in her first turn, the coolness and speed of thought to drag the ball past Nelson as she uses the pace of the pass to get herself out of danger.

I'm thrilled that Alessia has shown Europe that she has all the signs of a world-class forward. It's testament to the calm environment that Sarina has created. Even girls without any caps at all would have felt comfortable among us. We feel protected by each other, like we have each other's backs.

Our final goal is an accident, and I can say that because I'm involved in it. I move centrally and lift the ball over the defence to search for Chloe Kelly at the back post, but the substitute Kelsie Burrows clips it into the net when she attempts to usher the ball clear (5–0).

We did what Sarina asked us to do, keeping up our winning run and demolishing another opponent even though we'd already secured our place in the quarter-finals. In his post-match press conference, the Northern Ireland manager Kenny Shiels said that we could go on and win the tournament. 'I think most people feel that way,' he added.

We left the pitch thinking of the adventures to come. I finished the group stages with five goals, which meant I led the race for the Golden Boot. Behind me, with three goals each, were Germany's Alexandra Popp and our own Alessia Russo.

16

A New Level

The day after our win over Northern Ireland, the operations team call a meeting at 10.30pm.

'I think Adele's coming to perform,' Jill Scott says. She's wired with excitement. The meeting is by the pitches instead of in our usual meeting room. 'That's definitely it,' Jill adds. 'Adele's here. That's why we're outside. That's why it's so late.'

We meet by the pitches, where we're told one of our goal-keepers, Hannah Hampton, has tested positive for Covid. With thirteen days left, Sarina has made the decision to cut our time with our families. It's just too risky. We all nod in agreement.

'Girls,' Jill then says, 'I don't think Adele's coming.'

Our quarter-final against Spain took place five days after our win over Northern Ireland. We thought back to our 0–0 draw with them at the Arnold Clark Cup in February. What it taught us was that we had to learn to be comfortable out of possession. That's always been the way with Spanish teams and it's no different in the women's game. They are one of the best technical teams, and probably the best international team when it comes to keeping the ball. But if they're bobbing the ball on the side of the field or the middle of the park, they're not hurting us, and we needed to remember that. Losing our heads trying to win the ball back could be the thing to kill us.

We weren't naïve about that. Maybe some teams need to relinquish a little bit of their ego when they play Spain – accept that they will not dominate the ball – but we were already comfortable in our own strengths. We knew what we were good at.

But it makes for a difficult game, particularly for me. Lauren Hemp and I feel suffocated by the Spain full backs, Ona Batlle and Olga Carmona. As soon as the ball reaches me, one of them is on me. There's no time to move, no time to think, and I can feel my frustrations build. I know that there is an expectation on me to be able to pop up and do something in every game – to do something great, to create something from nothing.

I feel that pressure, that sense of claustrophobia, immediately leave the game when Lauren Hemp's ball from a free-kick wide left fizzes into the area and into Ellen White's vicinity. Maybe Ellen knows what's happened before I do as she does not celebrate – the flag goes up because Lucy Bronze was offside in the build-up. My stomach plunges and my nerves become taut again. I thought we had them.

For all their possession, Spain rarely cut through us. When they do, though, they show how deadly they can be. Athenea del Castillo collects the ball out wide and glides easily past Rachel Daly, spinning the ball across to Esther González. She sets herself and, with her second touch, finishes precisely from inside the area.

It's the first goal we've conceded all tournament. 0–1.

I know most fans are panicked at this point. A home Euros is a huge opportunity for the game. To go out at the quarter-finals would be our worst finish at the competition since Euro 2013, when England were eliminated at the group stages. This would be a huge backwards step after back-to-back semi-finals at the last two major tournaments. The backlash would be brutal.

But we don't think about this. Not for a second. Maybe we would have in the past, but at no point in that game do we feel defeated. Most teams that go 1–0 down to Spain begin to prepare for a mauling. *Here we go,* they think, and the whole world knows why. How many times have we seen teams chasing recently vanished shadows when they come up against Spain? Too many to count. But we're different. We trust in Sarina's plan implicitly. We know what she has up her sleeve. We know of her back-up plan.

Part of it involves swapping me out for Chloe Kelly, Ellen White for Alessia Russo and Fran Kirby for Ella Toone. *Aaargh,* part of me thinks, *I was just getting going.* But the game needs new energy.

Sarina had not banked, though, on the energy that I was about to bring to the bench. Here's something this game is about to teach her: that I am comfortably the worst spectator in the world. We speak to psychologists about the mental side of major tournaments and the moments when the pressure will be at its most intense – who we can talk to, how we might feel. We try to cover as much ground as we can, but there's only so much they can give us, so much they can prepare us for. You can't compare those practices to the real thing. The emotions and feelings that come with a game can never be replicated. There's no way of doing it, ever – not that I've found, anyway.

One bit of advice is to 'find a spot', to pick out anything, from a blade of grass to a floodlight, and concentrate on it so hard that you forget about all your surroundings. That, of course, isn't especially helpful in a Euros quarter-final. Instead, I call on the breathing techniques and exhale deeply.

I joke about this with Kate Hays, the FA's Head of Women's Performance Psychology, who's sitting a few seats across from me on the bench.

'You didn't prepare me for this!' I shout. I'm a nervous wreck. The helplessness is the thing I hate the most. In that moment, you can't physically do anything to help the team, even if doing so is the thing you want most in the world. All you can do is try to get information, give them energy. This is the moment when something else clicks for me – that the substitutes have a job that's even harder, in many ways, than starting. My respect for them, at how they deal with this every game, shoots through the roof. Jess Carter talks me through the game: 'Do you need anything? Do you need to me to help calm you down?' I can't speak highly enough of how easy she made it look. In contrast, Ellen, Rach and I were absolute messes.

I can sense the momentum shifting in our favour. Our substitutions have taken us to a new level. Spain's haven't. They are stalling. Even so, as full time drifts closer, I worry about going home. I can barely entertain the thought. I'm simply not ready for our Euros to be over.

There are six minutes to go when Keira Walsh knocks the ball short to Georgia Stanway. Then Stanway finds Lauren Hemp, who switches the ball onto her left foot and sends it arcing deep into the box. I see Alessia Russo rushing to meet it, sandwiched between three red shirts.

Lessi, I think. *Get up. Head it. Head it.* I'm willing her to jump the highest with every fibre of my being. But if willpower alone could suck the ball into the goal, we'd have equalised an hour ago.

Alessia does. She flicks the ball towards the back post. Ella Toone bolts to meet it. When I see Tooney running, it's like my body knows what is happening before my mind does. The net bulges, and, as Tooney slides to her knees, Ellen, Rach and I grab each other and scream (1–1). I have never sprinted down a flight of stairs so fast in my life. We stop on the touchline as the stadium erupts around us. We shout in Ella's direction: 'Tooney! Tooney!' I hope she can hear me from where I stand. I hope she can feel the energy I'm trying to send her way.

It's at this point that my nerves ramp up even further. As the whistle blows to signal extra time, I can't stand to sit on the bench anymore. I stand up, go to the nearest set of stairs and begin chatting to the fans.

'You all right, Beth?' one says.

'Nope,' I say, tight-lipped and strained. 'But whatever!'

I don't know if I'm helping them or making them worse. I think they're just as tense as me, even though the momentum is firmly with us by this point. When Keira Walsh comes off with a calf injury, I stand up and offer her my seat. 'You sit in it,' I tell her. 'I'm not using it anyway.' I'm too busy pacing up and down. She puts her leg on my chair as I make conversation with anyone who will listen, desperate for a distraction.

After Tooney's equaliser, Spain's substitute goalkeeper Misa Rodríguez is incensed. She kicks the cool box containing Spain's water bottles. It tips onto its side and the lid flops backwards as she gesticulates angrily at the officials.

Many of the Spanish players are angry that the referee has given Ella's goal. They think there was a foul in the build-up, that Lessi had manhandled Irene Paredes when rising to meet the ball. Our video team show us the replay. We know there is nothing wrong with the goal, that things will be fine. As Spain shout and march around, we don't need to say a thing. We let it happen. We know and trust in each other, in our processes. We know they're wasting their own time. They're getting themselves in a state – and for what?

Six minutes into extra time, I watch Stanway collect the ball in the centre, carry the ball forward unchallenged until a crack yawns open in the heart of the Spain defence. Then she strikes. She will never hit a cleaner shot in her life. The ball arcs into top corner and I've never felt such an energy and pride run through me (2–1). I scream, running towards the pitch. After all this game has put me through in the last hour – all the tension, fear and panic – I wouldn't change any of it. I feel on top of the world. It is some goal for our 100th under Sarina Wiegman – the most significant so far out of all of them.

I know Spain can get a goal from anywhere. It's a tense, long time watching the clock. The subs we've made keep us exactly where we need to be. That's a real luxury. Some squads just don't have that.

The final whistle brings with it the biggest sense of relief. To get through that game – one we knew from the outset would be among the hardest we'd face all tournament – showed the world that we were a special side. I was glad that the nation had seen just how much I believed in these players. There are few teams that would have been capable of demonstrating the grit we did. That's what happens when you're not ready to go home. You leave everything out there.

This is the proudest I've ever been of this team, I thought, as I ran to celebrate with them. No one could say we had it easy. The nation mirrored my elation and pride: the UEFA ticketing portal experienced a surge in traffic after the game for tickets for our semi-final at Bramall Lane.

After the game, Hempo and I were called away to give urine samples as part of UEFA's anti-doping procedures. Players can be tested at any time, without warning, and Lauren was so exhausted that her legs were cramping. She spent the first ten minutes lying on the floor while a doctor shook her legs, but we felt electric. Nothing could stop our joy. Not even the two Spanish players sitting in the room with us.

Two days later, we learned that we would play Sweden in the semi-final. The following day, Viv was out of the competition as the Netherlands lost 1–0 to France in added time. Although I was crushed, I was so proud of her. We spoke on the phone throughout the tournament and I knew that she had been struggling. On 12 July – the day after our 8–0 win over Norway – Viv had tested positive for Covid and withdrawn not only from the Netherlands' game against Portugal on 13 July but from their final group game against Switzerland on 17 July. She'd come back into the team to play France and played 120 minutes. I knew how badly Covid had ravaged her body and I worried whether she'd been looked after properly or if they were rushing to get her back to the game. I felt she should be proud of herself for what she'd been able to do in those circumstances.

What this meant was that Viv now became my number one supporter, a role that would see her wear my England shirt out in public and join my parents in the stands at Bramall Lane. We knew that Viv's outfit had the potential to provoke a reaction – good or bad – but I'd love for her to be there, and she was adamant that she would be. 'I'm coming to watch,' Viv insisted. 'I want to be there. I'm so proud.'

I was grateful for a game in Sheffield because it's easy for my family to get to. That was the first thing I thought about. The other thing I dwelled on, as I walked across the pitch the night before the game, was what happened to me the last time I came here, with Arsenal. We lost to Manchester City on penalties in the final of the Continental Cup in 2019, in that final game before I flew out to the US for the SheBelieves Cup. To stand there and watch someone else lift a trophy, when you've earned the right to be there, is crushing. The thought of feeling so low again, in that same spot, horrified me.

'Girls,' I said. 'I've lost here once before. I don't want to do it again. Let's make better memories.'

We knew what Sweden were good at and what they would want to do. They would want to move forward early and get the ball to forward Stina Blackstenius, who would run in behind.

We had a meeting before the game and the assistant who ran it asked us for pros and cons to each of the Swedish players that we usually play alongside in our clubs in the WSL. It felt weird, because you had to tell the people that will play against them in the league their weaknesses, but when you're playing with an England team, they're not your teammates. If you can give any of our players an edge against them, it's what you do.

But it's easier said than done to prevent things that you know are likely to happen.

We realise that in the first ten minutes. Sweden start brighter, with Mary Earps denying Sofia Jakobsson with an outstretched foot just moments after kick-off. We're angry with ourselves because we should have known better, and maybe that inspires what happens next.

I feel the click again – that shift in our collective consciousness. The inaudible tug as we slide into top gear. Lucy sends a first-time cross into the area and I have time and space to hook the ball towards me with my right foot. Four minutes into the game, I'd met Leah Williamson's ball from deep and beat the defender Hanna Glas in the air. Although my header went wide, it was an early indication that I could achieve joy against her. I sense her hesitancy again as I turn to stroke home (1–0). We're thirty-four minutes in. The goal doesn't fill me with ecstasy; it's more of a sense of coming home, of settling down. Of doing what we did against Norway, and against Northern Ireland – and many other teams.

It might sound silly, given Sweden were ranked second in the world at that time – six places above us in eighth – but I can tell that my goal has scrambled them. They're continually out of position. Their thoughts seem slower, muddied; we seem to move two or three beats ahead of them, almost like we know what will happen even before it does.

'Beth,' Lucy says to me, as we come off the pitch at half-time. 'There's so much space in the backline. No one's marking me. You have to find me.'

She reminds me of this eighteen minutes later, when my corner finds her unmarked inside the area and she leaps into the header that really sends Sweden crumbling (2–0). 'I told you so!' she screams, as I give chase to celebrate with her. The final is in our sights.

Over the next hour, we will see Sweden unravel before our eyes. Most footballers know the feeling of when your body seems to betray you, you are second to every ball and everything feels utterly mountainous, a thousand times harder than it ever has. All those instincts, those things that have always come as naturally to you as breathing, seem to desert you and it's disorientating, dizzying. I see it in their body language after Lucy's goal, in the way they stare helplessly after her as she dashes away. You can see it in their eyes. I know what they're thinking: *we're about to go home*. We've blown all the air out of them.

Sweden have nothing left to give, but we've got so much adrenaline pumping through us that it feels like we're literally flying.

All these months on, I'm still trying to process what happened next, even though I can remember every little moment. I can replay the memory in my mind, at full speed or in slow motion, poring over each frame. I'm not the only one who does so. In the days after the final, the BBC Sport Twitter clip of this moment will be viewed seventeen times a second.

I run across to the front post as Fran Kirby prepares to cross inside the area. I know I'm too close to goal for Fran to pull the ball to me, so what I need to do is take a player with me, and Magdalena Eriksson duly follows me, opening up a gap behind us for Alessia Russo.

I'm the closest England player to Lessi, just feet away. I'll always be grateful for my front-row seat. After her initial shot is saved by Hedvig Lindahl, Lessi drags the ball to the byline and, with her back to goal, flicks the ball between the legs of both Linda Sembrant and Lindahl (3–0).

I chase Lessi as soon as the ball crosses the line. All I can do is scream. 'You are not OK!' I roar at her. 'That is not OK! You've just retired a keeper!'

'I should have finished the first shot,' Lessi says after the game. 'Fran set it lovely for me.' How can she care? What she did instead was ridiculous, and possibly the finest piece of improvisation I've ever seen on a football pitch. Who nutmegs two players with a backheel to score in a Euros semi-final? When has that ever happened before?

From that moment on, we're comfortable, sashaying around the pitch with assurance as we drink in the fact that we've made it to a final. It can't get much better than this, I beam, as Fran lifts the ball over Lindahl from outside the area to notch the goal her performance deserves (4–0). It feels like I spend the whole game running after my cheering teammates, our arms outstretched like wings, as if we're birds floating on air. We're up in the clouds, and I feel like I'm gliding and freewheeling on the wind for the final fifteen minutes of the game. How can reaching a final be this comfortable?

I abandoned my television interview to join in with 'Sweet Caroline'. *If there's one thing we've learned from all this*, I think, *it's that we're no good at interviews when that song is on.* I dropped everything to join in with the fans: 'Sweet Caroline, BOM, BOM, BOM.' I punched the air in time to the beat. Every single person in the stadium knew this song, and I wished it would play for ever.

Rachel Daly found a cowboy hat from somewhere. Ella Toone found another ridiculous hat – a blue, yellow and red cap with a propeller on top. Jill Scott, at 5 feet 11 inches, was wearing a puffer jacket several sizes too small for her, the wrists up by her elbows. I was draped in scarves the fans have thrown down to us from the stands.

'Look at us,' Jill said. 'We've just reached a Euros final and we look like we're going to a hen do.'

We rolled about with laughter. We looked like we were there for a good time, because we were, and we made sure we relished the moment. We danced in the changing room for what felt like hours, a hen party that had just made football history.

The semi-final was special for another reason – it marked the first meeting between my parents and Viv's for fifteen years. Remember that game in Zwolle, when I made my England youth debut for the under 15s? Viv's mum Caroline and dad René had met my parents out there. It felt like things had come full circle. They chatted away happily, remembering those games from 2007 – Viv's parents still had them on video, and Viv told me just days ago that she actually vomited the night before her debut because she was so nervous. I waved at them from the pitch, the first time I saw Viv's parents not as their daughter's opponent, but as her girlfriend.

'They're dating now – is that OK?' René asked.

'If they're happy, I'm happy,' Mum replied.

'I trapped you before the Euros started,' Viv said to me on the phone that night. Before I make history, she means. Before everyone wants a piece of me. Before the match that will change my life for ever.

17

The Final

It's 2am by the time we return to the hotel. The staff have made us each a personalised KitKat where one stick carries our name and the other says: 'You're going to the final'. Seeing those words written down still doesn't help them sink in. More than anything, this just feels unfamiliar. Some of the team are still twitching with adrenaline and they'd play the final right now if they could. The rest of us are grateful for the recovery time. I'm somewhere in between.

We're all trying our best to process what we've just done, feeling our way into what it really means. It's difficult to get a handle on it because we've spent the past eight weeks ensconced in the bubble wrap of the Lensbury Hotel, with outside noise rarely penetrating. It's like being on an island. Genuinely, we don't have a clue what's unfolding across the country.

There are moments we see things in the press, but the magnitude of what's happening still hasn't completely hit us. The next day, Ellen and I appear on Lionesses Live. In Sheffield, the TV cameras had picked out Tess Dolan, an eight-year-old girl in full England kit shouting every word to 'Sweet Caroline' and punching the air on the beats. Instantly, I loved that video. The clip goes viral, and Tess herself quickly becomes iconic, appearing on all the breakfast TV and radio shows as a symbol of what this means to young girls. On Lionesses Live, we video-call her and give her a signed shirt. She can't believe it. You can see instantly in her body language and expression how much it means to her and she is overcome with emotion. I receive a couple of videos of fans in pubs chanting my name, but it feels too crazy, too surreal, to be true.

Over the next few days, the surprises keep coming. We receive a video message from Björn Ulvaeus – or, as most of the team refer to him when it arrives, 'that guy from ABBA'.

He smiles back at us in a Sweden shirt. 'I understand that you celebrated your well-earned victory the other day with ABBA music,' he says, 'and I have to say that that makes the defeat a little easier to bear.'

A handful of our younger players don't actually recognise the ABBA songs when we put them on in the changing room, even though they're a staple of our pre- and post-match playlists. 'Go away,' we tell them. 'You're too young.'

On the night of 27 July, we met in the games room as a team to watch the other semi-final between Germany and France. Germany's Alex Popp was the star of the show and delivered a commanding performance, first with a thumping volley and then with a header, thirteen minutes from time, to pull herself level with me in the Golden Boot race on six goals. France had equalised when Kadidiatou Diani's shot from outside the area bounced back off the post and smacked in off the Germany goalkeeper Merle Frohms, but this was Popp's night.

We were willing to take either team because to be the best, you've got to beat the best. But Germany's win set up, in my eyes, a final between the two teams who most deserved to be there.

In the next few days, Lucy and I found ourselves trying to make sense of a Dutch game that the staff had us playing before the final: Foxhunt. I googled it while writing this book and I still can't make much sense of it. It's a kind of scavenger hunt, I think, featuring staff members in costumes, quiz questions and team-building games. Lucy and I just overthought the whole thing and got very frustrated. We didn't do very well.

At the end, we had to write a postcard to our partner and slip it in the post box for the staff to hand out later. It was easy to write about Lucy, and I told her how much of a pleasure it was to play with her, and how she made me a better player and person.

Although you're world class, you try and make everyone else around you world class, too, I wrote. *Hopefully we'll have lots more memories to make in the next game.*

I was in my room when I received Lucy's message.

I always knew you had this in you – you just needed to find it yourself.

In the days before the final, each player presented a shirt to a staff member as a memento of the tournament. Jill Scott took charge.

'Do you want someone specific, or shall I choose?' she asked me.

'I'm happy with anyone.'

For the past six weeks, I'd had to put up with every single one of my teammates calling me a teacher's pet. I picked up some Dutch during my four years with Daan – enough to understand and speak a bit – and I speak it with Sarina from time to time. Jill, of course, thought it was hilarious to give me Sarina.

We sat through the presentations, and each player gave a short speech thanking the staff member before giving them the shirt.

'Everyone knows who my shirt is for,' I began. 'I'm the biggest arse licker in the team.'

Everyone hooted and howled with laughter. Sarina was confused. She didn't know what an arse licker was.

'Obviously you have Sarina!' someone shouted.

'I didn't pick her!' I replied, hopelessly. 'I was given her!'

'Thank you for *alles* throughout the tournament,' I said. *Alles* means 'everything' in Dutch. I sheepishly presented the shirt to Sarina.

'I don't get why everyone laughed,' Sarina said, leaving the stage.

'They joke about me being an arse licker because I speak some Dutch.'

'What's that?'

I blushed. 'Do you know what a teacher's pet is?'

'No.'

'Well . . . It's someone who really . . . like . . . they're up your arse, basically.'

Sarina gasped in mock horror.

'The girls wind me up for speaking Dutch to you,' I explained, as she passed me the shirt to sign. She was very touched by the gesture. She had never known a team do that for its staff before.

We knew the final was sold out. As players, we received tickets from the FA for each of the games. We got four free, and then we could buy extras: six for the groups, eight for the quarters and ten for the final. I prioritised my family and friends, then gave my last two tickets to Jen Beattie and Steph Catley. They're two of my closest people and were supporting me at many of the games. I didn't want to swap them out for someone who had just jumped on the bandwagon.

For a lot of us, it wasn't easy deciding who to pick. Many of the girls wanted more than their allocation allowed and, throughout the tournament, those of us with spares transferred them across to those who needed them. Players from the England men's team called us asking for tickets and we couldn't help them, so the FA stepped in to find them some. We'd never known such a demand for tickets. Neither had the rest of the country. There were stories in the press of touts selling tickets online for £500 and £1,000. With four days to go, 3,000 extra tickets were released and they sold out in no time. The papers and social media were full of fans desperate to find a way to go. On the day of the final itself, when they eventually arrived at Wembley, my guests' FA Friends and Family lanyards had a picture of me on one side, wearing my England kit. Dad keeps his at home, in a pile with all the cuttings from the tournament.

But it didn't feel like we were at the centre of the universe. Looking back now, we vastly underestimated how many eyes were on us. People would throw TV viewing figures at us – BBC One alone got a peak audience of 9.3 million for the semi-final against Sweden and 7.6 million for the quarter-final against Spain, to say nothing of the viewers tuning in online – but they barely registered. We left the Lensbury on 30 July and the staff congregated on the driveway, waving banners and flags as we smiled back from the coach.

The night before the final, we stayed at the Myddelton Lodge, the living accommodation for players and support staff at Tottenham Hotspur. Half sunk into the ground to blend in with the landscape, the lodge is situated in the Spurs training centre – we could see the pitches from our bedroom windows – and if we'd been staying a little longer, maybe we'd have been able to enjoy its cinema room and video games room. It's shut off from the world, all slatted walls and floor-to-ceiling windows, and given the staff are used to seeing footballers, our departure felt low-key. On the bus, I sat where I always do – directly in the middle on the back seat so that I can see all the way down the aisle. Millie Bright was to my left and Rachel Daly to my right.

We didn't even begin to realise the extent of the interest in us until the coach pulled out and we found a convoy of six police cars ready to escort us to Wembley. I'd only ever known us to have one before.

We were en route when I heard the chug of helicopter blades and looked up to find one circling overhead.

Millie Bright turned to me. 'Is that a media camera or a security helicopter?' she asked. 'Is it following us?'

Then we saw the footage on Sky. The helicopter *was* following us – it was videoing us, and we had the surreal experience of watching our coach journey from above on live television.

'What's going on?' we said to each other, shaking our heads in disbelief. This was big, we realised. How many footballers get tracked by helicopter?

I sat back down, stunned and a little light-headed. Then my phone vibrated with a FaceTime call from Steph Catley and I held it up to Ellen White.

'She knows I have a game,' I said, slightly unsettled. 'Why is she ringing me? It's not as if it's not a big one.'

I answered quickly and was met with another picture of our bus. Steph and Jen were driving past us, and I looked out of the window to see them waving wildly from the back of an Uber. *We can't escape the cameras!* I thought, laughing as they tootled past, and my nerves were immediately allayed. I was around my familiar people, and, with the team laughing along, it felt like free adrenaline coursing through my body. I knew even then, my body rollicking with laughter, that I'd never be able to replicate the feelings I experienced that day.

The bus took the final turn, Wembley Stadium rising before us, and my breath hitched in my throat. Thousands of fans lined the barriers on each side of the road. Some clambered onto skips for a better view, holding up signs and waving flags. Drums thrashed and air horns tooted. More waved from the stairs and balconies several storeys up. The volume shook the windows of the coach. From behind the tinted windows, we waved, bemused, stunned, looking for someone to explain what was happening. We'd clearly inspired more of a frenzy than we'd given ourselves credit for.

The noise was still ringing in my ears as I walked out for the warm-up. There was another riot of sound, but as the volume rose, I felt a calm descend. *This is a once in a lifetime opportunity, Beth,* I told myself, skipping between the cones. I had such a staunch belief in Sarina and my teammates that it was impossible to rattle me. The only shock came from the cameraman, tracking me for the close-ups. 'Good luck, Beth,' he rushed, and I did a double-take. I'd never heard a cameraman take sides before. We were all invested in this.

I thought that would be the only surprise of the day, until Rachel Daly shook me by the shoulders just as I was coming back into the dressing room.

'Beth! Beth!' she panted. 'Popp's not playing! You've probably got the Golden Boot!'

She was out due to an injury. We were oblivious to the pre-match coverage, but we suspected that this story would now be dominating it. I took a moment to get my head around the news. I'd caught the end of Popp's training session with Germany on the Wembley pitch yesterday, just as they were coming off for us to take our turn. Nothing was visibly wrong. I was so in my zone during the warm-up that I didn't hear the teams or subs being called.

Part of me was gutted. I wanted Popp to play. I wanted to play against – and beat – the best. She deserved that final after all she'd done in the tournament. Germany wouldn't be there without her, simple as that. But their best striker was no longer playing. That, of course, gave us a boost, and the energy in the dressing room took on a new edge. Sarina was quick to distribute plan B, to combat the new threat of Lea Schüller.

That was almost the extent of Sarina's team talk. We formed a half-moon around her and the room was silent apart from her words. You could feel a power rippling through the room, the kind of power that comes with being zoned into the same goal. We nodded at every word Sarina said. Sarina was as calm, as still, as a statue. She smiled easily.

She has never overloaded us tactically at the eleventh hour – all of that work is already done – instead choosing to fire us up, reiterating how intensely we need to throw ourselves in.

In the end, she plumped for twelve closing words, as crystal clear as she could ever say it: 'We don't need to win today, but we really, really want to.'

We all nodded. She was right. We didn't *have* to win – we'd already transformed the landscape of women's football in this country. That was one of our aims, right from the beginning, and everything would stay changed regardless of what happened in the final.

But we wanted to win more than anything in this world. We were a team of players who had come through more heartbreak than you can begin to imagine in these competitions. We'd never got ourselves into this position before, never been this lucky. My mind flashed briefly back to the hurt and disappointment of the 2019 World Cup. Defeat was a possibility, and my stomach lurched even considering it. *No*, I told myself. *I can't – won't – let that happen.*

We got to the tunnel in time to see the end of Becky Hill's opening ceremony performance. It was a good tonic; we talked among ourselves, trying to work out who was on stage with her, and we probably looked like the most relaxed finalists ever. Our opposition were stern-faced, staring stonily ahead, which amplified the contrast.

'Ready?' called a stadium manager, as Hill's stage was dismantled. '3, 2, 1 . . .'

Goosebumps raced up my arm. We walked out to the biggest Euros final crowd of all time. There were 87,192 people there. The previous record for a Women's Euro final was 41,301, set by Germany and Norway for the 2013 final in Sweden. The men's record was set in 1964 when 79,115 watched Spain and the Soviet Union play at the Bernabéu.

The noise exploded and I was flooded with pride and happiness. We sang the national anthem and it felt as though every person in the stadium was singing with us, drowning us out. Knowing that people would be watching from their televisions doing exactly the same, I can't describe the joy I was flooded with at that point. *Football,* I thought, *is honestly such a special sport.* This is my sport, and I love it, and it brings me so much happiness. What would I say to that wounded girl, on the defensive and licking her wounds after missing out on the Olympics? That one day she'll be pinching herself over how much she loves this sport – at Wembley, in a Euros final?

We were so focused that it was almost like time became distorted. Weeks later, an interviewer showed me a video recorded just as the national anthems ended. I'm running for the pre-match team photo and the cameraman is holding his equipment just inches from my face, so close that I could have reached out and touched the lens. I don't remember that at all. I didn't even see him. That's how absorbed I was in the game, in my inner world.

It's a backbreaking game, far more physical than I'd anticipated. From the beginning, you can feel the emotions and nerves bristling through the air. The tackles crunch and we take it in turns to look at the referee in dismay. There's so much going on, and everything feels heightened. I leave everything on the pitch.

Fran Kirby breaks down the left-hand side and Ellen White is darting to the back post. With every fibre of my being, I'm willing Ellen to head the ball back across goal towards me, but she takes it on her own. I sigh inwardly, all those usual in-game frustrations magnified to a new degree. I've had a great tournament, and all I want, all the time, is to receive the ball in that position.

In the second half, Lucy plays a ball down the line to me. It's a touch too heavy, but the game has gone a little bit flat. *I need to get to this ball,* I think. I'll either protect us from conceding or reignite the game.

I dart in wholeheartedly. So does Marina Hegering, Germany's left-sided centre half. Some part of her catches my leg and pain shoots up my left quadricep as my body seizes up. My leg throbs with pain and I can feel cramp juddering and quaking through me. I lie flat on my back on the pitch, wincing in pain as Lucy Bronze massages my calves and the physio elevates my other leg.

'We need to know now if you're staying on,' says the physio, linking arms with me as I hobble tentatively to the sidelines.

I want to stay on. Desperately. This has been my tournament. More than redemption, I've felt indestructible. Throughout my career, I've played on with dead legs, but this is a Euros final. These are the highest stakes − of any of these players' careers. I know what's right. I know that Chloe Kelly, my replacement, will be able to give more.

'Bring Chloe on,' I tell them. I've given all I can.

I'm hobbling behind the sidelines, back to the bench, when I see Keira Walsh lift the ball, from deep in our half, over the heads of just about everybody. Ella Toone closes in on the goal. Alongside the pitch, so do I.

'Come on!' I roar, as I watch Ella track the flight of the ball and cushion it down. With her second touch, from my view from the side, I'm waiting for the net to ripple, just to be sure it won't swerve past the post. My leg is seized with pain, but then I'm running, running, running. I watch the ball dip and settle in the bottom corner (1–0). And it feels like I could run for ever.

It's instant medicine, like I've been fitted with new batteries. 'Get in there, Tooney!' I bellow, thumping the air. Then my leg gives way. *I'd better stop doing that,* I think, lugging it behind me. But I feel fixed. I'm so high I could run the length of the pitch with her. The temptation to invade the pitch is overwhelming.

I still have most of the crowd to walk past as the players take the ball to the centre circle. 'Come on!' I scream, clapping furiously. 'Give us more energy! We need this!'

The quarter-final against Spain proved that I'm a terrible spectator. But this is another level. I'm strapped to the ice machine to aid my recovery, totally pinned in place, unable to release my nervous energy. It feels like a lifetime of waiting. We're trying not to look at the clock, but it feels impossible. Every time Germany win the ball and pile forward, I'm seized with panic and helplessness. 'Girls!' I scream. 'Get near them! Kick it away!'

I'm so vocal that Jess Carter moves next to me and puts her arm around me. 'What do you need, Beth?' she asks. 'Can I get you some water? How can I help you?'

'How are you doing this?' I reply incredulously, hiding behind my hands. 'Genuinely, how?'

Rachel Daly is in the row behind, leaning forward. 'Beth,' she whispers, nerves as taut as mine as Lina Magull hits the post for Germany. 'I can't cope.'

There are twelve minutes to go when Tabea Waßmuth carves open a crack of space to pick out Magull at the near post. With a single touch, she flicks the ball through the sharpest of angles to equalise, sprinting off to blow kisses to the German fans now waving flags behind the goal (1–1).

The bench heaves the heaviest collective sigh of our lives. The girls had defended with everything they had for the past six games and we'd all put our hearts on the line. It's crushing, and the less emotional part of my brain can see that Germany has the momentum. We just need to settle again, and I know we can because of what we'd done against Spain eleven days earlier. It's a strange feeling; I feel wretched but full of faith. If anyone is capable of pulling this back, it's these players. That's my chief thought, as the game stands at 1–1 at the end of normal time.

We'd worked with psychologists and our backroom staff around how we wanted to handle extra time. Sarina had made that a part of our tactical meetings, intertwining the two instead of just spitting big psychological words at us. They'd given us a presentation on this before the tournament and it featured a team whose huddle had been, to put it politely, messy – and they'd gone on to lose on penalties. Now, we knew exactly where we were going to stand in the huddle, who'd be fetching drinks and recovery gels. The sense of the familiar quiets us before Sarina begins speaking. She knows we have the ability to beat Germany and manages to calm us down and fire us up all at once. 'We've got the character,' she says. 'We've got the willingness.'

Her final words are reassuring. 'Do the best you can,' she says. 'That's all we can do.' And she's right. She didn't demand that we go out and win the game, and she didn't have to – we know we've got the quality to do that. But with the prize as huge as it is, the mental and physical tolls are unimaginable. Sarina is so good at relieving pressure and she's always the coolest, calmest presence. I don't know what's going on inside her head, but she always seems to regulate herself. In moments like this, she soothes us all.

Sometimes, a bench is the worst place in the world from which to watch the game. I'm on the front row, level with the pitch, when Lauren Hemp's corner arcs deep into the box and meets a pack of bodies. There are so many people there that none of us on the halfway line can see. We watch the ball pinball around the area, literally from the edge of our seats. Then we see the back of the net ripple and the fans fly in the air (2–1).

We don't find this out until later, but the ball had been spilled to Chloe Kelly. With a poke of her right boot, she had sent it scurrying into the bottom corner – and now she is running to meet us in her white sports bra, whirling her top in the air like a lasso. I hurdle the barrier, screaming at full volume with the rest of the substitutes. We all jump on her, in a memory I know will give me goosebumps as long as I can keep it alive. The fans roar behind us and the joy and excitement pumping through me in that moment is beyond anything else I've felt before in football. It's the best feeling this sport has ever given me.

Chloe, a lifelong QPR fan, had told her parents before the game that, if she scored, she'd recreate what happened the last time she went to Wembley, when Bobby Zamora scored in the last minute of the 2014 Championship play-off final against Derby County to send QPR back into the Premier League. Over the next few days, she'll earn more comparisons to Brandi Chastain, who became known around the world when, after scoring the deciding penalty for the US against China in the

1999 World Cup final, she peeled off her shirt and fell to her knees in her black sports bra.

We're not thinking, then, of all that will happen in the next few days – how the sports bra Chloe is wearing will sell out on the Nike website and Chloe will appear on magazine covers wearing it. The moment becomes about more than Chloe celebrating and ends up carrying so much meaning. It will become a slice of history, but the significance doesn't dawn on us at the time. We're too busy riding the world's biggest high.

We clutch each other tightly on the bench. We have shown so much spirit and character over the past six games that I know these girls have got this, and, for most of the next eleven minutes, we keep the ball by the corner flag. Chloe draws a cheap foul, and there's a moment where she cuts inside, only to U-turn and go back to the corner, the defenders unable to get the ball off her. Lauren takes her time lining the ball across the corner quadrant. Lucy milks a throw-in for another sixteen seconds. They protect each other, sending the ball careering off Germany's players for countless throw-ins.

We never spoke about that before the game – we'd never worked on that kind of game management – but our young players know exactly what to do. I fill with pride. My mind flashes back to the US doing that to us in the 2019 World Cup final when they were 2–1 up. Did we pick it up from them, subconsciously? Maybe, but we are showing Europe that we can do everything. We can play good football, we can come from behind, we've got team spirit, we've got grit and we can play the ball in the corner and annoy teams. We've experienced it all and shown it all – and that's impressive for a team whose manager has been in charge for less than a year.

To switch instantly from the glee of Chloe's goal to that degree of focus is no easy thing to do. Unless you've actually experienced a final, with the kind of pressure and expectation riding on us, I don't think you can fully understand and appreciate just how much discipline is required to manage those emotions. Sarina personifies this. If she's feeling any fear inside, she never betrays it.

'Wahey!' the crowd cheer as we win another throw-in. It's probably quite comical and enjoyable for them, but for me, the clock feels like it's taking ages to tick down. I'm counting in my head. Seven minutes . . . Six minutes . . .

In the final few seconds, I pin my eyes to the referee. As soon as the whistle goes to her lips, I'm up. I'm running to the huddle in the middle, my dead leg gone. I'm totally stunned, overcome with relief. We've worked so hard – we were away for eight weeks in a confined bubble, putting in hours that no one else sees. Demi Stokes has been away from her newborn baby and I know she is reflecting on that as the whistle goes. We've given so much, and people were just so desperate for England not to fail again. The relief is an indescribable feeling.

We've just won a gold medal in a major European tournament. I drink it in, knowing I will never, ever be able to recreate these feelings again.

During all the madness, while everyone was still celebrating, I was presented with the Golden Boot at the side of the pitch. There was a quick picture, then I was off again, still running, still singing, still floating with disbelief and desperate to join the party.

A man in a suit approached us.

'Girls! Girls! Guard of honour!'

I made to go towards the podium before he stopped me.

'No, no – you need to come with me,' he said.

'Why?'

'You've won Player of the Tournament. The guard of honour is for you.'

I probably looked unimpressed on the TV footage as the reality slowly dawned. That award hadn't even come into my equation – we'd just become European champions. That was all I'd cared about. For the past six games, my teammates were probably more excited for me to win the Golden Boot than I was, but I didn't care about those accolades when I had a gold medal around my neck that I'd earned with this team. I cared more about being a part of this group than any individual award. They're bonuses. The girls can say I've earned them, but they helped me. I'm just the one getting the plaudits. They're proud moments but I wouldn't have won them without the team behind me.

My teammates lined up on either side and I planned to run through as quickly as possible because I always find these things a little awkward. But looking back now, I don't even remember walking through. There was just so much noise.

I went to the walkway to meet Prince William. 'I'm so proud of you and what you've achieved,' he said. 'What a great tournament you've had.' He's been a huge supporter of the Lionesses over the years – at a charity game once, Jill Scott slipped and ended up wiping him out with a slide-tackle, and they've had a special bond ever since – and he came to St George's Park for our final camp before the Euros.

As we walked across the podium, barely hearing the clack of our studs on the walkway given the noise exploding around us, the FA chair Debbie Hewitt enveloped me in a hug. By how tightly she squeezed me, I could feel how proud she was. I'm always taken aback by Prince William in general, but, as he slipped the ribbon around my neck, the realisation of what we'd achieved began to sink in. I took a moment to spin the medal in my hand and gaze at the engraving. The trophy is rendered in miniature, as though we're each taking home our own slice of what we've achieved.

We've actually done this, I thought. *It's not silver. It's not no-medal-at-all. It's gold.* I let it go and it hung there, heavier than I imagined it would be but sparkling in the late July sun.

I recalled Prince William's words to us from his most recent visit, long before we set off on this adventure. 'We're already so proud of you as a team, but this summer is going to be incredible,' he'd said then. 'Make it well worth remembering.'

That we did, I thought, as I stood on the back line of the podium with Keira Walsh. We put our arms around each other and squeezed each other tightly. So, so tightly. Leah Williamson crouched, the trophy a foot off the floor, then swung it through the air and lifted it high above her head as fireworks shot into the air behind us. I was screaming at the top of my lungs. 'Get in!' I shouted. 'Thank you! That's for England.' *Mic drop, see you later,* I added mentally.

The next thing Leah did was call Jill and Ellen to the front. 'Come and hold it with me,' she said. 'You two have been here so long. This is your moment to enjoy as well.' That humility is typical of Leah, who's always been a leader; the only difference in this tournament is that she wore the armband. She was incredible considering the expectation on us, on her. No England captain has led a team to a win for fifty-six years.

I thought then of my family, and all of their pride and emotions after the work they'd put in for twenty years to get me to this point. We'd been told throughout the tournament not to find our families in the crowd after games because of UEFA protocols. There were guidelines in place around keeping our distance from anyone outside of the England bubble, including ball boys, members of the media and stewards. I doubt there would have been too many worries once the final had finished, but, in any case, we were European champions – of course we were going to celebrate with our families.

I picked my way through the metal barrier behind the hoardings. I was so happy and relieved. Then I saw Mum, and my tears started. She was crying too, as was Dad. In that moment, we didn't need to say anything to each other. We huddled and cuddled and cried and cried.

Jen had taken a photo of Mum and Dad holding hands right after the final whistle. She posted it to Instagram with the caption: 'Point of view: your daughter's just won the Euros, player of the match and top goalscorer.' My parents had pulled at Jen and Steph's heartstrings throughout the game because their love for me was so obvious and so deep. Jen says that my dad was pacing up and down even before kick-off, and my mum, usually sat dancing with a flag and joining in with the music, was far more agitated than normal. Our families felt every ball with us, as they have for so long.

I gave my trophies to Mum and Dad. I would never be where I am without them. It's the best memory I could give them.

I picked out Popp among the deflated German players and went over. We both had things in our past that have really hit us hard. Popp missed the 2017 Euros due to injury and didn't make her Euros debut until this tournament, at the age of thirty-one. I'd always respected her even though I didn't really know her.

As I approached her, I could see from the shape of her body that she was going to embrace me, and in that moment we conveyed our mutual respect without having to say anything. I'd also been at the end of the line when we'd given Germany their guard of honour, and Popp had broken out to shake my hand.

'I have so much respect for you and what you've done,' I said. 'I know you've had hard journeys in the past.'

'You've done so well and had a great tournament,' she replied.

In my opinion, she was Germany's standout player through-out the tournament and would make things happen for fun. And she probably wasn't even supposed to be Germany's star until Schüller got Covid and they needed to rejig their frontline.

I looked around me and drank in the snapshots of ecstasy. Lucy and Jill took a quiet moment together on the podium, to reflect on not only their win but the length of their journeys to get there. Rachel and Millie danced among the confetti.

Our party continued in the changing room. We put the trophy on ice in the beer cooler. Then we danced with it, moving through every old-school banger you can think of. Some of the team just sat in silence, trying to process what we'd just done, but most of us took selfies with the trophy for the next two hours. We were singing and dancing. We formed a circle around Sarina and sang to her as she danced with the trophy. I'm not sure if she knew the song – the England spin on Atomic Kitten's 'Whole Again', with 'Southgate' switched to 'Sarina' – but she grooved along anyway.

At some point, a member of the media team told us that Sarina was in the press conference. At once, we all turned to each other.

'Come on! Come on!'

Someone began singing, and the end result was Mary Earps dancing on a table in front of a room full of journalists. And why not? We'd just won the Euros. We could do what we wanted. Although I think Sarina was more worried about her goalkeeper falling off and injuring herself than anything else.

Sky stationed cameras outside the Lensbury, where we danced on the grass while swinging the trophy through the air. We'd made friends with the hotel staff over the past few weeks and they were waiting outside to clap us in. In a really short space of time, they'd transformed the breakfast room into a party just for us – there were red and white banners, an arch of red, white and silver balloons, a cake decorated with a St George's cross and lion teddies for table decorations.

Our friends and family were waiting to greet us. I hugged Viv, my parents, our friend Lorraine, Ben and his partner Olivia, her parents Mike and Karen, and my agent Mags. We spent the night dancing, laughing and making memories together in front of a live band. Rachel seized the karaoke microphone and belted out a rendition of 'River Deep, Mountain High'. She'd sung it so much that it'd become something of her signature song in the past couple of weeks. She sang it on the bus after our win over Norway, using my Player of the Match trophy as a microphone as we all waved our phone torches in the air. Now we were singing it as European champions. And this time Rach was moving across the dancefloor, to the appreciation of everyone else on there.

When the music went off, Sarina grabbed the karaoke microphone. 'No!' she shouted. 'Not yet! We want more!'

'That's enough. Come on, Sarina,' we all said, but she persisted for ages. She was in such a great place. We all were. We were dancing on each other's shoulders. At some point, we moved into a different room because they needed to prepare for breakfast. Jill Scott and Millie Bright didn't get any sleep because they were too busy rapping. There were no quiet moments to take in what we'd achieved. We partied from the moment we arrived at the Lensbury to when we crashed into bed. Our feet never touched the ground.

I really hoped all the other guests were English and partying along with us. If not, they probably hated us, and I want to use this opportunity to apologise. We're very sorry, although not too sorry, because we'd just won the European Championships.

I can't remember what time my night ended – 4am? 5am? Somewhere in that region. I dropped off to sleep right away.

18

A Big Mac, Fries and a Coke

I wake up two hours later with my medal still slung around my neck. My first thought is that I need to make sure I can stand up – it's been a heavy night. Some of the girls will still be drunk. I glance down to see the gold medal in my hand, but it's like I can hardly process it. It's not even close to sinking in.

There's a red line on my neck where the ribbon has cut into my skin during the night, and I'm not the only one who has this. The material is actually quite coarse and the edge of the ribbon is sharp and rigid. This issue quickly eclipses any hangovers and 'my neck is in bits' becomes the soundtrack to the morning. We're all pulling our shirts high across our necks, trying to turn sports tops into turtlenecks.

Being a European Champion is not as glamorous as it looks.

We don't look anything close to glamorous that morning, and certainly nowhere near as invincible as we'd felt hours earlier, dancing in the dressing room at Wembley. With bleary eyes and raging hangovers, the immediate priority is digging out bucket hats to hide our faces for the England Champions Party in Trafalgar Square at lunchtime. Here, Georgia Stanway delivers in a big way. A sunglasses brand had reached out to her before the tournament and kitted us out with a pair each, although most of us can't really carry them off because they're an . . . acquired taste. They're like ski goggles – huge hexagonal lenses with an orange-hued tint – but Georgia and Lucy insist and the rest of us follow their lead.

Somehow, Jill Scott and Lotte Wubben-Moy manage to heave themselves out of the hotel and down the road to a coffee shop.

'We got five metres and someone stopped us,' Jill tells us when they finally return, a considerable amount of time later. 'Someone stopped us everywhere we went. It took us for ever.'

I picture the scene. One step. A fan. Another step. Another fan. 'When we'd been before, we'd walk past people and they wouldn't say a word to us,' Jill continues, sipping on the disposable cup. 'I think we've underestimated what we've just done.'

We had to give back our famous England UEFA bus with all the Euros branding. The regular coach gave us a degree of anonymity – the last we'd have for a while – but as we pulled into the car park behind Trafalgar Square, people realised who was on board and we brought Central London to a standstill. No one moved. People lined the streets on both sides, stopping to point and take pictures. There were fans in the middle of the road, waving flags, cheering and singing songs. *The commuters must hate us*, I thought, as we caused total carnage. We told the driver to pip his horn so they would know just how much we appreciated them.

I can't explain the buzz of walking out to 7,000 people, all of them screaming. I mean, when did we ever think that would happen? We couldn't see where the sea of people ended: it swept up the stairs of the National Gallery in a frenzy of flags. But all I could see was my family in the front row, and my mum mouthing: 'Beth! Beth!'

'What?' I said, cringing slightly.

'My head's burning! Has anyone got a hat for me?'

In my moment of glory, I was glancing up and down the stage, trying to find a hat for someone who just should have thought ahead and brought some suncream.

'I'm really sorry,' I said to Ella Toone, pointing to my mum and then to Ella's head.

'No, no – give it to your mum!'

'How about coming more organised?' I jokingly seethed at Mum, as she gratefully seized Ella's bucket hat.

We were still laughing as Rachel Daly started singing 'River Deep, Mountain High' again. It was the norm for us to join in during those dozen renditions she gave us throughout the tournament – now, we were on a stage in front of 7,000 people for the Rachel Daly Show.

'It's like your own concert,' we told her. 'Look at all these people singing it with you.'

A few of us were handed microphones and asked to speak to England defender-turned-broadcaster Alex Scott. Lucy tried to coax Sarina into a dance. Jill Scott interviewed the trophy, which was now wearing a bucket hat ('How d'you feel? How's it going?') and Ella told the fans that scoring her goal was 'the best feeling in the world'. The crowd cheered everything we said. 'The shirt's staying on,' said Chloe, after jokingly starting to lift up her top. 'I haven't stopped dancing. My feet just keep going.'

'This is the missing ingredient England was looking for,' Leah said of Sarina. 'She's a special person. She puts us all first as human beings and allows us to be who we are. You've seen us enjoy this tournament for what it's been and finally win.'

No one told me I was supposed to speak, so when Alex called me over and pulled me to the front, I was shaking, either from beer sweats or because there were so many people in the crowd. I'd lost my voice and I got a little choked up on stage.

'So many special journeys you got left out,' said Alex. 'You came back, and you've shown the world what you're capable of.'

'Sometimes, football sucks,' I replied. 'But I worked hard, and I feel so lucky to be part of this team and be a part of this group. I'm just so happy to be here. I'm so happy.'

The flags flew as the trophy came on stage, and the biggest roar of the day was reserved for Leah lifting it high one more time as fireworks flashed behind us and jets of confetti shot from cannons either side of the stage, settling around our shoulders like snowflakes.

'I don't actually know what we've just done,' Leah told the crowd. 'What have we done, girls?'

We'd definitely underestimated the scale of our achievement and how many eyes had been on us. At the time, our final was the UK's most-watched TV programme of 2022, and the UK's most-watched women's football match ever. The peak audience of 17.4 million, plus 5.9 million streams online, was way ahead of the 11.7 million who watched our 2019 World Cup semi-final. It was also the most-watched women's football game in Germany. We were breaking records left, right and centre. It's incredible to think.

But we wanted more. Sarina had always been eager for us to use the tournament to convey some sort of broader message about society. We knew we'd inspired a nation at the 2019 World Cup and we'd wanted to do the same this time, but we had to do something more permanent.

We wanted to build a legacy. And a lasting one. It was so, so important to us. This tournament couldn't just be something people would speak about for a summer before things went back to how they were.

We had started thinking of ideas weeks before the final. Throughout the tournament, we spoke often as a squad about what kind of message we'd like to put out and the best way to do it. Yes, we *could* just play football. Yes, we did want to take the profile of the game to new heights – that's a given. Yes, we wanted to inspire the younger generation. But how would we do it? How could we make it as easy as possible for young, aspiring Lionesses to play?

I was sitting with Leah and Lotte the day Lotte had her brainwave. We were both in instant agreement and encouraged her to present her idea to the team.

On the coach back from Trafalgar Square, Lotte outlined her vision. We should all write, and co-sign, an open letter to the Conservative Party leadership candidates – the two potential new prime ministers – asking for a minimum of two hours of PE for all girls. We wanted more support for female PE teachers and for them to receive the resources to provide girls' football sessions.

Everyone agreed that it was an incredible idea. We're ready to back her 100 per cent. We know of the power we have and we want to use it correctly.

'We have made incredible strides, but this generation of schoolgirls deserve more,' the letter said, when we all posted it to our Twitter accounts two days later. 'They deserve to play football at lunchtime, they deserve to play football in PE lessons and they deserve to believe they can one day play for England. We want their dreams to also come true.'

We took the bus back to Twickenham, where half the team got ready to leave. As we said goodbye to each other, and to our staff, it felt ruthlessly anti-climactic. We couldn't believe this was the end of the journey.

'Oh, right,' we said quietly to each other, deflating with each word as the realisation dawns. 'We're going home now.'

We'd organised a night out for that evening and we'd be glad for that – glad that it prolonged our time together for another couple of days. But by the end of the Trafalgar Square celebrations, some of us hadn't eaten for close to twenty-four hours. Leah and I decided to go to McDonald's.

'We've won the Euros,' we said to each other, as we pulled up to the drive-through. 'I think we deserve it.'

As we rolled down the window to pay, the staff realised straight away who they were serving.

'Let's just get this as quickly as possible and leave,' we laughed. Leah took a photo of me wearing a bucket hat and carrying two paper bags to post to Instagram with the caption: 'Couldn't be more deserved, could it?'

What does a Lioness order at McDonald's, you ask? A Big Mac, fries and a Coke.

19

Our New Reality

'What's the weirdest thing that's happened to you since the summer?'

It's the main talking point over lunch and breakfast at St George's Park at our first England camp back since winning the Euros. It's what Sarina Wiegman wants to know in the welcome meeting on night one.

Chloe says that her Manchester City teammates have been leaving sticky notes on her peg in the changing room. *Don't forget your shirt!* they read.

Ella Toone says the paparazzi caught her eating a pasty outside her local baker. Sarina, being Dutch, doesn't even know what a pasty is, so at some point Lotte Wubben-Moy has to explain it to her. Then Sarina teases: 'I've seen a picture of *you*, Beth.'

Everyone cheers and whistles. Earlier that day, I'd been on the cover of the *Sunday Times Magazine*, posing in a Prada sports bra and shorts, guarding the ball in designer shoes. Everyone has crazy things lined up, and I'm not the only one in the team who's been on a magazine cover over the past month. The mood is good; celebratory, buoyant. We're all eager to hear each other's stories, and still a little overwhelmed that this, for however long, is our new reality. It feels like I have a media or sponsorship commitment most days now.

We checked in to our rooms that afternoon to find the beds spilling over with boxes and gift bags – presents from major brands to congratulate us and wish us good luck for the next couple of games. There was a make-up hamper from Charlotte Tilbury and a card that said if we needed styling for an event, we only had to ask. Yorkshire Tea made us special Lionesses boxes. The best thing was my personalised pair of Nike Dunks: the lip says *Home* – because, of course, that's where we brought football – and the games and minutes of my goals are printed in silver inside the lining and across the Swoosh arcing across the upper. An artist designed special prints to commemorate our win and, of the 500 produced, he gave me number seven to go with my shirt number.

It was quite the welcome wagon. We knew what we achieved on 31 July 2022, sealing England's first senior trophy since 1966, and on home soil. We knew that nothing would ever be the same again, for the sport or for us as players. And we were ready to embrace it, even if it takes some getting used to.

It's funny, because in lots of ways, the final seems so long ago. In many more, it feels just like yesterday.

I got my first glimpse of our new world the day after the final. Once we'd recovered from events in Trafalgar Square, we hit the clubs, going to a venue called Cirque Le Soir in Soho. As we left, my head exploded in a whir of flashbulbs. White lights slashed across my vision and I could hear shutters snapping like cicadas. *Paparazzi*. Needless to say, none of us had ever experienced this before, and I half wondered if I was really ready for this. *Wow*, I thought. *This is what those A-list celebrities must feel like when they can't go anywhere.* But we had a good chuckle as a team when, the next morning, our goal-keeper Mary Earps appeared on all kinds of websites pictured with a man they called 'a male companion'. The newspapers thought she'd met a boy in the club, but it was actually one of our press officers, Callum, making sure we got to where we needed to be.

The next morning, with very little sleep, I was on ITV's *Lorraine*, a show I'd always watched with my mum. I took her and my dad along and we were both taken aback by how small the studio was. I could see Mum peeping out from behind the camera as I settled in the armchair with my Golden Boot and Player of the Tournament trophies either side of me.

Later that day, we were one of the lead items on *Loose Women*.

'I find it quite emotional,' said Ruth Langsford. 'It was girl power beyond belief. I looked at those young women and they were fit, they were healthy, they were sweaty, they were excited. That is a great image to young people to say it's not always about Instagram and perfection.'

'There has been this thing that, as women, we have to hide any competitiveness,' said Jane Moore, 'because it's not considered to be ladylike.'

My first thought when I heard about that was that it's a shame that young girls and women even think about what they look like in a gym or how other people might view them. We need to break that. It saddens me that one comment to someone could have such an impact on how they feel about themselves and how they act.

This group of women, and those who came before us, loved playing for our country. Most of all, we were true to ourselves. We blocked out the outside noise, and we had to. No woman in football would get anywhere if they let all the sexism they encountered or comments from other people hold them back. If there's one lesson people have taken from watching us this summer, I hope that it's that you have to be who you want to be. Don't care about anybody else. That's what I did all season as a footballer, and it's what we did at the Euros. We kicked as hard as we got kicked. That should be the norm for women and girls of all ages.

After my first TV appearance, I went on holiday. I'd booked to go to Zakynthos, in Greece, with Viv. To switch off after the tournament, we'd booked a secluded suite and a private pool for the daytime. As we flew out, I read online that I was partying in Ibiza with Leah Williamson and Ella Toone. *If the paparazzi don't know where I am,* I thought, *then that's great. This will all just be business as usual.*

Happily, I was wrong. Walking through the town square each evening, English tourists kept stopping me: 'We just watched you three nights ago in the final! We can't believe you're here!' It was the first time I'd heard people's stories about the matches and I started to get a handle on just how much the public had cared about us, how intensely they'd followed us over the past few weeks. 'I cried watching you,' one man said.

One night, a restaurant owner interrupted us to say that a family who had just left had paid for our meal. It was a silent gesture of appreciation, even more touching because it was so quiet.

I was always struck that people would apologise for bothering us, or for asking me for pictures and autographs. I understood where they were coming from – I was on holiday – but I was happy they had recognised me, and happy that they were recognising the other players. This is what I told them. We'd wanted this for the game all along. This was the level we had always hoped – and known, even if so many doubters didn't believe us – that women's football could reach.

Naïvely, I wondered if that was just the reaction of a handful of friendly tourists. I hadn't spent much time in England since the final and didn't know if the moment had fizzled out while

I'd been away, like a firework running its course – all the shine and fascination gone. Soon after touching down, I had a photoshoot outside the Emirates and it felt like the driver of every other car coming past wound down their window to shout their congratulations across the road. A dustbin wagon pulled over and its driver began chanting: 'Meado! Meado!' I've been at Arsenal for five years and done countless photoshoots, but that had never, ever happened before. That moment took me aback – people knew who I was.

I was by the pool when I learned that I'd been nominated for the Ballon d'Or. The notification pinged up on my phone. The Ballon d'Or Twitter account had tagged me in a photo.

'I'm so buzzing,' I said, shaking. 'Jonas said I could be a nominee at the start of the season and I didn't believe him at all. I can't believe this.' I scrolled down further. 'Viv! You've been nominated, too!'

I lowered my phone to find Viv staring at me impassively. 'Yes,' she said. 'It's my fifth time.'

Thanks so much, I thought. It was the norm for her, but I was so, so proud of myself. I watch the Ballon d'Or ceremony every year. It's a huge honour. But there's always someone waiting to bring me back down to earth. This time, it was Viv.

Back in England, my new level of fame had extended to Ben. At the pub in the village, a group of men went up to him.

'Are you Beth Mead's brother?'

He loves it when that happens, but his favourite thing is how many likes he can get on Instagram if I share one of his posts to my feed.

'Beth!' he'll say. 'I've got 37,000 likes. I've had to turn my notifications off!'

I know, though, as do all the players, that while the women's game is never going to be the same again, there won't be this kind of hype further down the line. That's why we've got to use this interest to push the sport forward. To build this kind of platform, so many people have given up more than the world ever sees. You won't always be liked, and you'll be on the end of opinions – good and bad – from every single person. But I never let those doubts define me, and that's why I have a gold medal.

There are probably more than a few similarities between my career and the wider rise of women's football.

For a long time, many of us in women's football – players included – have been grateful for training at the same training ground as the men or getting breakfast and lunch served to us at the club. Two or three years ago, we would have been happy with a subpar pitch. 'Thank you,' we'd have said. 'That's fine.'

Now, though, we will ask for better. Crucially, we're not scared to make demands. We're not happy to settle. We will fight for what we think we deserve – and we do deserve more. We are demanding more from the game because we want more *for* the game. We're delivering success and these things are vital for us to reach the next level.

We know what the men get, whether at Arsenal or at England. Throughout our careers, we've all had to fight for all kinds of things. Not so long ago at Arsenal, we had to wait until early evening to use the swimming pool because the men were on site, regardless of whether they even needed to go in the water. Our players were either sitting around and waiting or going home to then come back for an ice bath. Why couldn't we have our own time slot during the day? We were falling short when it came to winning major trophies and those are the kind of things – access to facilities – that make a difference.

We scheduled a meeting with Vinai Venkatesham, the Arsenal CEO, and he took our concerns on board, and committed to building the women's team our own area with our own ice baths and a bigger changing room. From now on, we will go with confidence to the decision-makers and outline what we need. That doesn't make us divas; just athletes who want the game to go in the right direction. We need things like our own chef cooking food tailored for us, instead of making do with the leftovers from the men's or youth teams or food that's been sitting there for a few hours.

We need more. The Women's Super League turned full time in 2018. That was a landmark moment, but I feel like it should have happened so much earlier. We saw Liverpool Women get relegated in the year the men's team won the Premier League. That's not right and it shouldn't have happened. Liverpool Women are back where they belong now, but they should have been able to expect more from one of the biggest clubs in the world.

You don't have to dig too far below the surface of women's football to find stories like that. I'm only twenty-seven, yet I've had teammates who've worked full-time jobs in addition to their playing career. Jill Scott is eight years older than me and she has some wild stories about what she did to build a football career. She used to borrow cars from her brother-in-law's garage to drive from her job as a football coach at Gateshead College to training at Everton in the evening. That's a three-hour journey each way, and she'd be eating meal deals at a service station on the way down. And there are lots of future Lionesses who will be driving hours just to be able to play in a local girls' team, or professional players now whose training facilities aren't up to scratch.

You can push for better standards while being decent people. One particular coach journey after an England game springs to mind quite strongly. It was an icy, frigid evening, in that period just before spring when the country hasn't quite shaken off the last of the winter. Our team operations manager had previously worked with men's teams, and I shuffled up the aisle of the coach towards him.

'Can you ask the driver to turn off the aircon?' I began.

The staff member was flustered.

'What's wrong?' I asked.

'I've never had a player come and ask for something themselves,' he said. 'They usually text from the back of the bus.'

Hearing that left me as stunned as I'd made him. What are those players' expectations? That people have to do everything for them? That they can't do anything for themselves? Why would they not walk halfway down a bus to ask a simple question?

The kitman at Arsenal asks us every day to put our boots in the box if we want him to wash them for us, but most of us don't bother. We can either wash them ourselves or cope with the dirt. We're not babies and we never have been. After all, we used to wash our own kit.

The male players have someone sat scrubbing their boots or they receive a new pair for every game. It always surprises fans to hear that I don't; they ask me for mine after matches and I have to tell them that I need them for the next game. I'm a Nike athlete, but I can't be wasteful – and who needs to break in a new pair of boots every game?

Everyone is a human being, and remembering that story about the coach reminded me that, as women, we're not being difficult or petulant for demanding what we deserve. We've fought so hard to make it to this level – and we'll never forget where we came from.

The reason I wanted to write this book is to show people that journeys aren't easy. There will be ups and downs, bumps in the road. Other people will have expectations and opinions.

But if you're doing something you love, your passion and joy will make it all worthwhile.

In the summer of 2022, we started a legacy. But we've always said it's just the beginning. I've had the pleasure of sharing my story, but so many other girls' stories are still to be written. I'm so excited about their futures.

20

Hardest Goodbyes

After the Euros, we had ten days off. Then it was straight back to business with the new domestic season. Our first league game was at home to Brighton, and I scored twice. In September, I was named PFA Fans' Player of the Month and Arsenal Player of the Month. In October, I scored two goals in our historic 5–1 win over the reigning Champions League winners, Lyon. I felt the same confidence from the Euros bubbling through me. Mentally, I felt wiped out from worrying about Mum, but football provided me with a break and there, at least, I was confident. On the field, I felt unstoppable. I wasn't.

I was away on camp with England in Spain when Dad called. Mum was deteriorating. I sat down with Sarina. Having lost her sister that summer, she knew what I was going through, and I knew that I could talk to her about my situation. The bottom line was we didn't know when Mum's time would be up. Mum didn't want me to come away from something I loved – I was due to earn my fiftieth England cap that camp – but I didn't want my family to be dealing with everything on their own. Together, Sarina and I worked out a plan.

'If it's at all possible,' I said to Sarina, 'I want to play our first game, against Japan, win that cap and go home to Mum the day after.'

After the England camp, I was back in Whitby. Mum knew she was dying, but she didn't want me to give up on my dreams. All through the Euros, the thought of making her happy and putting a smile on her face had pushed me to have the tournament of my life. That weekend, Arsenal were due to play Manchester United at the Emirates and the club had sold more than forty thousand tickets. Mum wanted me to be there. She wanted me to go back to London and play. And after the warm-up, I did. I'd felt mixed emotions that morning but trained well leading up to the game.

In the ninety-first minute, Alessia Russo made it 3–2 to United. We had expended so much energy getting back in the game after going 1–0 down and pulling ahead to 2–1. We gave away silly free-kicks and corners and it made for a chaotic finish in a game that would be important to the title race.

Out wide, I closed in on the United defender Hannah Blundell, who was watching the ball as it got ready to bounce out for a United throw. I've spent so many hours since wondering whether I would have chased that ball were we not losing, were it not so late in the game. I've done this movement a million times. I anticipated the nudge from Blundell to keep me off the ball.

The moment I planted my foot, I took the nudge. Instantly, pain flared in my knee. Time seemed to stall. I pitched forward and I felt as though someone had smacked the inside of my knee with a hammer. I crashed to the ground, both hands clasped to my knee.

My mind flicked to the letters all footballers fear: ACL. The anterior cruciate ligament is one of the key ligaments stabilising the knee. It's there to stop the tibia, or the shinbone, sliding forward or rotating beneath the femur, or the thighbone. The ACL controls rotation. It's what allows us to change direction or suddenly decelerate. As my foot had stuck in the ground, my bodyweight had kept shifting forward.

Teammates for club and country had told me of the popping sound they had heard when their ACLs tore, and of this sensation of their knee giving way. Sometimes the players near them had heard that snap, like a rifle shot. My knee reverberated with pain, but I didn't hear that snapping sound. Maybe, I told myself, this isn't what I think it is. But what if it is?

At that thought, I began to cry. I knew what was at stake. A World Cup was on the line. The rest of my season was on the line. ACL injuries used to be career-ending. Even now, they mean close to a year out, and months of learning to walk and run again. The memories of the past few months flashed through my mind. The truth slammed into me in one jolt. Could I really be about to lose it all?

The physios rushed onto the pitch.

'It feels OK,' I told them as the pain left me. 'I think it's wearing off.'

I was able to stand up, but my eyes glistening with tears as I walked off the pitch. I knew I had to get off quickly to give my teammates a chance to get back in the game. The club booked a scan for the following day. I tried to stay upbeat, but I couldn't shake the feeling that I'd never felt that movement, or that level of pain, in my knee before. At Arsenal, our medical staff always tell us to fear the worst so that any other outcome is better. En route to the scan, I tried to make it sink in.

I've done my ACL, I told myself. Anything else is a bonus. Telling yourself that is one thing. Believing it is another, and I don't think I did. I clung to the hope that it would be something else. Just twenty minutes after my scan, the physios called to say they had my results. I knew as soon as I saw the physio's face. Viv came into the room with me. She watched me nervously as the club doctor asked me to sit down. I heard him say the words no footballer wants to hear. And I don't know if I did hear them. Maybe I zoned out.

Complete rupture of the ACL.

My ACL had torn all the way through. That was the banging sensation inside my knee. I'd been chasing the ball down at such high speed and the nudge from Blundell had caused my knee to abruptly change direction against its will. I'd felt my knee wobbling, my ACL snapping because of the force going through it.

I learned why my pain vanished on the pitch that day. My knee gave way and partially dislocated. That initial flash of pain was from the semi-dislocation. Then my knee popped back in again. When ACL injuries are painful, it usually means something else has been torn. I'd been able to walk off without assistance.

I saw Viv becoming emotional. Then more of my teammates came in, and I started to cry. They were devastated for me because they knew what awaited me. As I looked at them, the truth rolled over me in waves. *I can't play with you for the rest of the season*, I thought. *I won't be at the World Cup. Even if I do make it, I won't be at my best. And football – my escape from the pain of watching Mum get sicker – is being taken from me.*

Knowing I would have to navigate whatever Mum's illness held without the happiness of playing for Arsenal was so tough to take.

I went to an appointment with Sam Church, a consultant orthopaedic surgeon. He brought up my scan pictures. Where my ACL should have been, there was a complete mess. My ACL was attached but it had sprung apart in the middle. As soon as an ACL ruptures, it loses its blood supply, shrivels up and dies. You can't stitch an ACL back together, but you can reconstruct it, making a new one out of something else. In football, the most common donor sites are either the patella tendon or the hamstring. The first is the tendon running from the patella (the kneecap) to the tibia (the shinbone). The hamstrings are two strong bands of tissue at the backs of the thigh.

Sam assessed my style as a footballer to help me determine the kind of graft I should have. A hamstring graft would give my new knee a more normal feel and full range of movement, but he warned that it might have a slightly higher re-rupture rate. Using the patella tendon would be a more intrusive surgery and leave a bigger scar, but it would be stiffer and more robust. I wanted the strongest knee possible. I chose the patella tendon. Sam ran me through the procedure. He would drill up through the shinbone, creating a tunnel that would come out where the ACL attached to my thighbone. Then he would drill another hole through the femur. He would pull the whole graft through those two tunnels, along the line of my original ACL. Over nine months, it would heal in that position.

We scheduled my appointment for 8 December. I arrived at the hospital at 6am, waking up from the surgery four hours later. They tested my mobility right after surgery and I was back home for 2pm, Viv keeping me fuelled on cheese and crackers while I drifted in and out of sleep.For the next week, the Arsenal physios visited and we worked on bending and extending my knee. Between their visits, I sat on the sofa battling the constant pain in my knee. It was relentless. I tried strong painkillers like tramadol but the pain continued to reverberate through my leg. That was the first and last time I cried about my knee. It felt like the pain was never going to end and I got myself stressed and upset. Once I'd let the emotions out, I could accept it wouldn't last for ever.

When Viv was out at the club, I'd lift my leg on the table, trying to bend it. The pain was close to unbearable, but I had to push through to give myself the best chance of recovering. When Viv came home, she often brought our teammates with us, and they filled every chair and every bit of floor space while I sat in the corner. Kim Little brought me jigsaws. Others came with coffee and banana bread from the café. Kim and Jordan Nobbs opened up on their own recoveries and what had worked for them.

I was getting used to watching Arsenal from the sidelines when one day I watched Viv go down in a Champions League game against Lyon. I was in the directors' box with Jodie Taylor and I didn't even see what Viv had done as she was a few passes behind the ball. Then the physios ran on. I saw the gestures: *Viv needs to come off.* My heart quickened. I hobbled to the lift on my crutches, cut through the tunnel and stood on the side of the pitch. What's happened? What's going on? Viv passed me on a stretcher and I followed her into the changing room.

'I've done my ACL,' she said breathlessly. 'It was exactly what you explained to me. I felt it. I heard it pop.'

This can't be happening, I thought. You expect a big injury maybe once a season. That was mine. I was the one. It was me. I took that hit for the rest of the team. There weren't supposed to be any others. I had barely even processed my own injury, and now the person I love and live with, who had shared all the horrors of my early recovery with me, had done the exact same thing?

'I can't take you home for Christmas,' Viv said. 'You can't drive down either because you've done your knee.' In that moment, she got more upset about that than what was to come for her.

We realised, too, just how emotionally exhausted we were. We'd both received bad news in the days leading up to our injuries. Days before mine, I'd left an England camp to be with Mum. The night before hers, Viv had received some further bad news about my mum. She'd had to pass that information to the coaches before kick-off. She had barely slept. We had both felt fine to play, but had our emotions affected our decision-making? Had we been so eager to play because that was our way of escaping everything else?

When the girls came to us after the game, half the team broke down alongside us. I was physically and mentally sapped. Everyone knew how unwell my mum was, and that I would lose her at some point during my recovery period. All those emotions just slammed together. Our teammates cried for us. The amount of sadness in that room was hard for anybody to process.

At home, I set my crutches at the side of our bed. I swung myself up and rested alongside Viv. I look at my knee, bound in a Tubigrip compression bandage, touching Viv's, wrapped in a brace. Side by side, leg by leg, we wondered what we had done to deserve this. *Are we bad people?* I wondered. I laid there that night questioning everything.

The physios confirmed what Viv had known all along: she had ruptured her ACL and would be out of the World Cup. Because I was a few weeks ahead, I still had a chance of making it to Australia and New Zealand in 2023. An ACL injury is a forty-week rehab.

My motivation was to get myself as close as I could to getting there. The squad announcement was in May, seven months away, and the tournament itself started in nine. It was doable, just. Even if my rehab progressed without a hitch, I would be a big risk for Sarina, but I was very positive. If I could be ready at that point, I stood a chance of going. Once the pain had settled, I went home to Whitby. Most players, in the first few weeks after ACL surgery, will go straight to their clubs for the next stage of their rehab, but I wanted to spend what precious time I had left with Mum. I didn't go back to London for almost two months, and did what I could – the smaller, tedious exercises – while spending my mum's final weeks with her.

All along, I reminded myself that I had something I could come back from: my mum didn't. I saw so clearly the pain she was going through. Every time she put food in her body, she was sick. I couldn't sit there and feel sad over an injury. My parents were there to support me, and I wanted to do the same for them.

This injury must have happened for a reason, I thought. Mum would have pushed me to play games if I was fit. Now that's been taken away from me, I can make some final memories I wouldn't have been able to if I was still playing.

From one day to the next, we didn't know if it would be Mum's last. She'd go out in the car with my dad for an hour each day and they'd drive to all the places they had visited when she was younger: where they met, where they'd gone to dances. It was a nice trip down memory lane, but sad at the same time because it felt so final. In those last few months, that was the only way she'd get out of the house. Then she didn't have the energy to do any more.

Mum wasn't well enough to travel to Salford for the BBC Sports Personality of the Year ceremony in December. Once I'd been nominated, a film crew travelled to film interviews with Ben and Dad, and came to the boardroom at Arsenal to film an interview with me. Beneath the glare of the lights, I gave one of the hardest interviews of my career, reflecting on all our family had been through that year. Sometimes, speaking about things brings them to life. As they dismantled the lights and the cameras stopped rolling, I reflected on what I'd told the interviewer: that Mum wouldn't be around to share every new moment in my career.

'You cannot miss out on this,' Mum had said in the days before as I'd deliberated whether to go to the ceremony. 'It's a once in a lifetime experience.'

I went with Viv and Dad. An accident on the motorway turned our short drive there into one taking hours. It meant for a rushed check-in to the hotel and I flew through hair and make-up, meaning I didn't have too much time to dwell on all my emotions. Despite that, those feelings were never far from the surface and Mum was rarely out of my thoughts. It was surreal to think I'd even been nominated for such a prestigious award, but I wished I could be sharing it with her. I'd watched this ceremony with my parents for so many years. As Viv and I had our photos taken with our crutches on the red carpet (although I didn't need mine to walk at that point, I needed people to know I was recovering so that they didn't knock into me), I knew Mum would be watching at home with Ben.

'If you win, you need to go up this way,' said one of the directors, pointing to the stage, 'and give your speech, then they'll put some music on and you will stand there holding the trophy for an awkward amount of time.'

Their words passed over me in a haze because I never thought I was going to win. I didn't have to worry about it.

The lines were open for thirty minutes. Then they shut. All the nominees had cameras on them. I looked down at the floor as the former curler Eve Muirhead came in third. I had spoken to Eve that night: I'd always admired her resilience to keep coming back and win the gold medal she'd been chasing for so long. Ben Stokes was the runner-up. My thought then was that I hadn't placed. Ronnie O'Sullivan was on the list. He must have won. I kept my eyes fixed on the ground.

'The winner,' Tanni Grey-Thompson began, 'of the 2022 BBC Sports Personality of the Year is Beth Mead.'

I could feel them all with me: my family, friends, my teammates celebrating a few rows behind me. I could feel Mum sitting at home with Ben. I would have loved for her to have been with me, and that feeling was so strong. It is such a historic award for your baby to win. I struggled to then go up and speak about it – I broke down a little bit – but the crowd applauded as I tried to lift the trophy while only being able to lean on one knee. I was willing the England players to come up with me because it didn't feel right to win it without them. We had won the Euros as a team, and this was their trophy as much as mine. Eventually, Alex Scott came over to congratulate me.

'I was trying to make eye contact with you but you were looking at the floor!' she said.

'Alex,' I said, 'I had a camera in my face the whole time. I wasn't looking anywhere *but* at the floor!'

All I wanted to do was get home and show my mum. I just couldn't wait to get home to her and see how proud she was. I wanted her to see the trophy in real life, considering she would have been the first person I'd have taken there with me. Winning that trophy still hasn't sunk in, but my emotions were very much consumed by Mum.

After leaving the stage, the first thing I did was check my phone for a message from her. I still have it – the last text message she ever sent to me.

My beautiful baby girl. Beyond words. I'm in bits. You're amazing. I love you so much.

Those final days with Mum felt so long but she was amazing. Every night, she wanted to come down for a few hours and watch TV with us, and we watched nice films over Christmas.

One of the final films we watched together was *Matilda the Musical* – the original film had been one of our favourites growing up – but we all went to bed each night exhausted with the emotion of it all.

She slept lots, but we would still hear her pipe up from upstairs: 'I can hear you all! I'm listening!'

In her final week, I sat on her bed with her and went through every little detail of what she wanted for her funeral. I found it incredible how she was able to speak so calmly about what was happening and what she wanted to achieve. Around the same time, Mum and I decided on the tattoo I would get in memory of her. I was shocked when she came up with that idea. She'd hated the one I'd got after the Euros: the word HOME just above my elbow.

'What have you got that for?' she'd said. 'There was no need. You'd already won it.' I knew she'd got over that when she said: 'What tattoo are you getting for me?'

'Well, I wasn't planning on it,' I said, 'but I'm going to have to now, aren't I?'

We agreed on *Love you loads*, with three love hearts. That was the text we'd send each other at the end of every day.

Ben and I were in the room with her when she passed. I'd gone in to say goodnight to her at half past ten. She was so sleepy, and had the oxygen tank next to her bed.

'Love you lots,' I said. 'See you in the morning.' We always tried to keep things as normal as possible for her. That was what she wanted.

She suddenly sat bolt upright. 'Where are we going?'

'We're not going anywhere,' I said. 'We're just going to go to bed.'

At that point, she hadn't moved for the last two days. For her to jump up like that was strange. She couldn't breathe, and then she got back into bed panicking, telling us that she didn't feel right. We called the doctor from the village, who came to see her.

'It's quite close,' he said. 'It will happen within the night now.'

'I think I'm ready,' Mum said. 'I think I'm ready to go.'

She was struggling and in distress. He offered her a sedative so that she would be able to pass away peacefully. Still, she thrashed and fought in her sleep. Dad stepped out, and Ben and I called him in when it was time. We were all at her side.

I felt at peace knowing that she was at peace. I felt the peace of knowing that she was no longer in pain, that she was comfortable. I knew that she was somewhere better now, even though I physically didn't have her with me anymore.

Despite this feeling, it was difficult to look beyond the moment I was in, and I felt very, very empty. After her passing in the early hours, we sloped off to bed utterly drained. There was nothing we could do or say to each other. There is a big hole in my life that will never, ever be filled. I remember waking up the next morning, looking at Dad and Ben and thinking, what do you say?

We met my uncle, gran and granddad and went for a walk on Mum's favourite beach at Runswick Bay. In the weeks that followed, we got her a memorial bench there overlooking the sea. We walked across the beach, dodging the little streams that run into the sea from the cliffs. I went to help Gran cross one. As she stood in it, it gave way. Gran toppled over, and then it started. We all burst into laughter, and then tears.

'June probably did that!' we shouted to each other. 'She's playing tricks on us already!' I knew that Mum would be wetting herself. Mum wanted us to carry on and do things with our lives. We are all trying our best to do what would make her happy and proud. The world keeps spinning. We have a night time. We have a day time. Sometimes, that's a comfort. At other times, you have so much pain that it's hard to bear.

I feel differently every day.

I struggle on days when I just want to sit and chat with her. I used to speak to her every day, about anything and everything. Dad wouldn't believe that we could sit and talk to each other for so long. I want to tell her about things, but then I get upset because I can't do that anymore.

Mum's funeral song was 'Sweet Caroline'. It's played a lot at football matches, as a joyful song. That song has some amazing memories attached to it. On some days, though, I absolutely break down to it.

On Mother's Day, Dad gave me a teddy bear made out of Mum's clothes. Sometimes it's nice to look at. At other times, it reminds me she's not here. On good days, I think about her and enjoy the memories we made together. On sad days, I wish I was still able to make those memories with her. Some days, I cry talking about Mum. On other days, I can just about keep it together.

Sometimes, I just feel Mum, and know she's there. When I went to Windsor Castle to collect my MBE, a robin watched from a wall. Our family had always recited the well-known phrase: 'When robins appear, loved ones are near.' I couldn't look at Dad because I knew he would break down. He got upset, but for all of us, it was Mum saying she was there. She had said she would be, and she definitely was.

I'm so happy she got to see me winning. I'm happy she knew I was getting my MBE. Everyone who walked through the house once the letter arrived was told instantly. She'd have loved that day – she loved the royals, and took us on trips to Buckingham Palace when we were kids. She would have taken every photo possible up at Windsor Castle. We joked about it that day, when I travelled up with Viv, Dad and Ben. We saw signs reading: 'No photography'. Mum would have found a way.

Walking past certain places reminds me of who she was and what we did. Mum used to love going to Covent Garden: when she visited, we'd have an Aperol spritz together, go to a theatre show. At other times, I feel like I have lots of unanswered questions. If Mum had been older, I'd think that she'd had a full life, but my mum had so much more to do in her life. Losing Mum didn't feel fair. She was still young. She was only fifty-four. She still had so much to teach me and my brother.

I sometimes wonder what it's all about – we get up, we work, we eat, we sleep, we stress, we struggle, we fight. For what? What's there? Unfortunately, we'll never know until that day comes.

I do believe that time is a healer, but you still miss them no matter how much time has passed. The next year was tough for us in so many ways. Viv was a great support for me, even while she was contending with the physical pain of her ACL surgery. She came back home with me within three or four days of being injured and stayed with me until 2 January, when she went back to Arsenal for her ACL operation on 6 January. When Viv said goodbye to Mum, we didn't know whether it would be the last time they saw each other. Mum said to Viv: 'Just look after my baby girl.' Maybe Mum knew.

21

The Return

Going back to Arsenal meant throwing myself into full rehabilitation. My and Viv's rehab schedules were split into six-week blocks: five weeks of rehab followed by a week off.

Some days, I would lift weights in the gym and want to break down, my knee buckling, my body screaming for a rest. I was so tired, so fatigued. The weight would be heavy. I would feel my muscles jittering, begging me to drop it all, walk away and quit. I was putting myself through physical and mental torture six days a week, just to know that I was still months off being able to play football. Every day was the same: strength sessions, bike sessions, upper body circuits, upper body conditioning, uppers, lowers, agility, proprioception. Proprioception is about being aware of how you position and move your body: every day I'd stand on the balance cushion and withstand the wobbling to strengthen the areas I needed to. You're tested constantly, trying to hit the numbers you recorded before the injury. The words 'you've improved by a centimetre on this test' become the soundtrack to your days. There's no change of scenery.

No one is going to shake your hand and applaud you for doing what you're supposed to. I knew I was cheating myself if I didn't do everything in my power to get back to the player I was. We'd be well into our rehab programmes by the time the other girls came in to get ready to go out on the pitch. We'd watch them walk by knowing what we had ahead of us: a visit to the same gym to do the same sets of the same exercises, the same as every day. When players with new injuries joined us in the gym, we all knew they would be out before Viv and I.

Hard days were harder because I would think about my mum. I just wanted to talk nonsense with her, but the girls made sure I was rarely on my own so that I couldn't dwell on things. When Mum's birthday came around, they took me away for the weekend. My chatty personality sometimes masks the dark times I go through, but my teammates kept me standing.

Moving on to the next stage of rehab was always exciting and a chance to mark how far you had come, but I was very conscious of how Viv was feeling, knowing she was still behind me. I reassured her that she would be enjoying those feelings a month later.

It has not been an easy process, but thanks to the documentary about our recoveries, *Step By Step*, that we worked on with Arsenal's media team, people have been able to see all the things they'd otherwise have no idea about. I filmed myself washing Viv's feet. Our teammates came around to install a shower stool in our bathroom, and you can see me showing Viv how to bend her knee. We had to tape up our scars so that they didn't get wet in the shower. You can see us in the gym, learning to balance and cycle again. Viv and I had joked that the ten-month recovery period was like having a baby, except we'd be babying our knees. And it really was baby steps.

For the documentary, I had to watch a replay of my injury taking place. Thankfully I was able to see it without getting upset. It happens so quickly that unless you slow the footage down, it doesn't look that bad. I don't cringe at the physical aspect of it. The emotional aspect was the tough part. Watching it brings back the pain and heartbreak of knowing that I wouldn't be playing for months and that my World Cup was in doubt.

For an idea of how long and excruciating the ACL journey is, I was able to run again 143 days (or four and a half months) after surgery. At three months, I had been able to run on an anti-gravity machine that took my body weight, but I can't tell you how excited I was to get back on a pitch and run in a straight line. That feeling only lasted a week because then you have to move on to the next goals: running in an S-shape, and running with a ball, and changing direction, and accelerating and decelerating.

'Don't do anything stupid,' Viv said, as she filmed me on the sidelines.

We have all of those moments captured in an album on our phone: ACL. Two ACL injuries in one couple. We're putting this in a book, but you couldn't write it.

I would joke that I was the guinea pig for everybody else. When Viv was worried about something physical connected with her injury, I could reassure her that a feeling or sensation was normal. There were days when I'd make a joke about something and Viv would say to me: 'I really needed that.' On other days, she didn't want that humour, and I'd give her space. Sometimes we both had bad days, but 80 to 90 per cent of the time, she welcomed my positive attitude.

Viv's injury meant that I'd had to become the mobile one in the house very quickly. Out of the two of us, I couldn't be the one with the bad knee when Viv was a month behind me. I had to pick up the ice machine while she was sat on the sofa. A player wouldn't normally do that a month after injury.

Going into carer mode was another mental shift. Before my ACL injury, the longest I'd ever been out was three-and-a-half months. After being able to run again, it would still be another six months of work before I would be back in contact training. I went from winning the Golden Boot at a Euros to that – to being so happy to be able to walk without a limp and run on a machine. It's not easy to comprehend at all, but at some point, you have to commit to them otherwise you'll only make it harder for yourself.

I used my rehabilitation time to become an ambassador for Ovarian Cancer Action, the UK's leading ovarian cancer charity. Mum always wanted to raise awareness herself, and fortunately I'm in a position where people might listen.

Ovarian cancer is a silent killer. It's often diagnosed at a later stage when the odds of surviving are at their lowest. Only 33 per cent of women are diagnosed at the stage that would give them a 90 per cent chance of surviving for five years or more. The UK has one of the worst ovarian cancer survival rates in Europe.

In March, I asked my social media followers to sign up to Ovarian Cancer Action's Walk in Her Name, which set them the challenge of walking one hundred kilometres that month in memory and support of women lost to or fighting ovarian cancer. My rehab meant that I couldn't walk, but I asked fans to walk for me on behalf of Mum. It's about raising awareness as well as money. I've heard from women who, because of my mum, have got themselves checked and found their cancer is in its early stages or treatable. I've also heard from women who've been checked and found that everything is fine. All of that is for my mum. I feel like I owe it to her.

That month, I had my first face-to-face meeting with Sarina about my injury. We'd had phone calls every month throughout my rehab, but alongside an England doctor, she wanted to give me clarity on her thoughts and I needed to give her clarity, too. She came to one of the Arsenal games and we found a quiet room.

'We're not saying a billion per cent *no*,' Sarina said, 'but on the timescale and how things are working, it's not going to be likely. This isn't a definite no, but it will be very, very hard to be able to get into the squad.'

It was the first time I'd let the realisation sit on me – that I might not be going to a World Cup. It was the first time I'd viewed my situation with a little more realism. I was in a good place, but not a good enough place to go to a World Cup. It wasn't an easy conversation, but it felt like Sarina and I had made the decision together. She had been transparent with me, and it shows the respect we have for each other that she is willing to be like this even in the tougher conversations.

I agreed with her. I think that early on, Sarina knew that I probably wouldn't be able to go. Deep down, maybe I knew that as well. But I'm a very positive person, and my mindset was that if I was ready by the deadline, I stood a chance of going. If I was in a really good place, time-wise, I *possibly* could be ready. I didn't say that because it was what people wanted to hear – it was what I'd truly believed.

But I would have gone to the World Cup having not played in the league since the injury. Would I have been at my best level? Probably not. And I'd be playing in a tournament where there would be huge expectation for me to do well. That might not have been easy to deal with.

To have a World Cup taken from you through injury is a funny thing. With the Olympics, I wasn't picked because I wasn't good enough. I could then go into training, work hard and improve on all the things that weren't good enough for that manager. This, though, was all beyond my control. To this day, I still don't know what's worse – losing something because you're not good enough or losing something when you're playing the best football of your career. With no World Cup, my next motivation had to be coming back for the start of the season – a goal that *was* possible.

While I was recovering, the England captain Leah Williamson ruptured her ACL away at Manchester United and our teammate Laura Wienroither ruptured hers in the Champions League. When Viv and I watched Leah go down, we both felt physically sick. We'd put our injuries down to circumstance, and blamed stresses and pressures off the pitch. Watching Leah made us so sad and low. We desperately wanted to help them both. We knew what they had coming. But how can you make them feel better when they're out for nine, ten months? The emotional scars have lingered for Viv, who has said to me that she really hates playing with me now because since our injuries, she panics every time I go down. I've told her she'll have to get used to that because it will happen. It's part of being a forward.

That the World Cup was on the other side of the world helped when it eventually came around. Some games clashed with our training and rehab sessions, but I woke up early to sit and watch all the matches I could. Watching the tournament itself was fine. Watching your own team – England, or Viv watching the Netherlands – was tougher. I'd sit and think, *I wish I could help them. I wish I could have been there. I wish I could have been a part of that.*

Being at home did allow me to feel the buzz around the team. My social media feeds were all England and the Lionesses. It was a nice moment to see it from a different side, to see the perspective in England while they were all the way over in Australia.

We watched the final at Arsenal with the girls who were around for pre-season training. Watching was tough. I was so invested in the game and I felt every emotion possible, all while wanting to be a part of it so, so badly. I felt a little bit of envy and jealousy at not being able to play in a World Cup final, but at the same time, I was so, so proud of the team. I'd been in the middle of that kind of excitement just a year earlier, in the Euros, so I knew what went into reaching the final of a major tournament: the training hours, the analysis, the meetings, the culture. I'd been a part of everything that had culminated in the amazing moments of our 2–1 victory over Germany. I'd been playing the level of football I'd always dreamed of playing for my country. Now, I was watching the World Cup final wondering if I could have made a difference. Could I have done something? I was devastated for the girls when they fell short, losing to Spain 1–0. I'd done the same in 2019 when the United States beat us 2–1 in the semis: I know how it feels to put so much into something and for it to not be enough.

I did nine months of work in the gym before I was allowed back in team training. I had my eyes set on my comeback: our home game against Liverpool on Sunday, 2 October. The end was almost in sight. Then, four days before this game, I had a complication. Out of nowhere, my knee began to swell. That had never happened at any point in my rehab. The frustration slammed into me: I'd endured a nine-month recovery and felt ready to go, and then on the cusp of my comeback it was all pushed back again. I had to dig deep inside myself. Mum had always hoped I'd come back stronger.

Epilogue

Jonas called a meeting. 'We've got so many game-changers in our team, and we've just got one back,' he said. 'When we sit here and get upset about not playing, remember that this person has had ten months of not being able to play football at all.'

He congratulated me on making it back into the squad for our upcoming game against Aston Villa. I would be on the bench and the physios had cleared me to play for up to fifteen minutes.

'Get the game done early so I can come on!' I joked to the girls as they cheered around me.

Never in a million years did I think he would bring me on in the eighty-eighth minute when we were 1–0 down and there were twelve minutes of added time coming up and the stakes were so high.

As I stood on the touchline, ready to play my first match in 330 days, I couldn't look at the bench. I knew that the physios would be welling up. They'd been with me every step of the way: through every pained leg extension in those early days when painkillers would barely take the edge off the pain raking through my knee: through all those sessions in the gym when I just wanted to go home: through the first jogs on the grass when I had to learn to run in a straight line again. I knew all my emotions would come pouring out if I looked at them. I put my blinkers on until I stepped onto the pitch.

The noise of 35,000 people welcoming me back will stay with me for ever. It was spine-tingling. Goosebumps rippled up my arms. Four minutes after I came on, Katie McCabe scored, firing the ball into the roof of the net from close range to make it 1–1. She pumped her arms at the crowd. Game on.

From the bench, I'd watched the game unfold and could see what had been happening: we'd been shooting, but Villa had always put three or four players in front of us to deny us space inside the box. I knew that I needed to either make the space so I could shoot, or create an opening for somebody else.

When the ball came to me on the edge of the box, I pulled left with my second touch and cut the Villa defender, Rachel Corsie, adrift. I knew that I wasn't as fit as I had been and the game felt harder than it had been before. My touch was heavier than I wanted, but it meant that two more Villa players raced towards me to close me down. I got to the ball first, lunging in with my right leg – the same one I'd injured almost a year ago. I had opened up Alessia Russo to have a free shot on goal. I hooked the ball towards her. She met my pass and with one touch had the ball in the bottom corner.

I'd not been able to celebrate like that the whole time I was out injured. As the girls surrounded me and jumped all over me, chants of 'MEADO! MEADO!' rang out around the stadium. I'd not only created the winning goal, but I'd put my knee through the kind of movement that lots of athletes recovering from an ACL injury might have been fearful of. I hadn't even thought about it. I'd ticked off two milestones in one swoop.

As the whistle blew, the girls surrounded me again and many of them were crying. Viv was crying. So were the physios. That got me worked up too.

Then I looked for my dad in the crowd. It was the first time he'd seen me play live since the Euros final. That had also been Mum's last game. They hadn't come to any matches since then because she'd not been well enough. I was glad that Dad had had the pleasure of being there for my comeback game and seeing me get the assist, and I became very emotional, knowing just how much it would have meant to him. He had always loved watching me play, supporting me, but I knew he would have mixed emotions thinking about Mum.

At points in my recovery, I had pushed myself to my limits. I'd never, ever doubted that I would come back, but through all those days in the gym, I'd pushed again and again through so much physical and mental pain. On those days, the thrill of being back on the pitch and hearing the screaming of the crowd felt so far away. But that night, I knew all of that struggle had been worthwhile. I had pushed myself to be in the best possible condition when I was finally back on the pitch. I had wanted to do that for myself, for my team and for Mum.

I dedicated my first Arsenal goal since my injury to her. I scored our second and third goals in our 3–0 win over West Ham, the first after cutting inside beyond Hawa Cissoko and hitting it with my left foot. It was my first goal in 428 days so lots of emotions came out. Once my teammates pulled away, I kissed my fingers, raised my arms to the sky and looked up for Mum. All of the hard work that had gone into that moment was for her.

I made it back to the England squad for our final two Nations League games that December. We had a must-win game against the Netherlands at Wembley, then a match against Scotland a few days later. We had to win our group and reach the final, or finish third if Olympic hosts France made the final, for Team GB to qualify for the Olympics. I had grinned like a

Cheshire Cat all week at camp, and Sarina welcomed me back by joking that I'd scored those two goals to show off and get back in the squad. It was tough, though – the last time we'd played at Wembley, my mum was still here. That was difficult to think about, but I wanted to make her proud.

We were 2–0 down at half time. I hadn't expected to come on then, but Sarina respected that I'd trained well and come back as the best version of myself. Georgia Stanway, Lauren Hemp and Ella Toone pulled us back to 3–2, and I was really glad I'd been able to come on and help the team to get the win. I'd very much missed that feeling of playing for England in front of a big, big crowd, this one of 71,632.

I got my first England start and goal since the injury in that Scotland game. It felt like a lifetime since I'd had the chance to start for England, and when the team was announced to us on the eve of the game it marked another moment where I realised how hard I'd worked through my recovery. It felt extra special to have the chance to start again and I celebrated my goal as though I'd never scored in my life, but we had to run back to the centre circle quickly as we needed to get as many goals as possible. We had to better the Netherlands' score against Belgium by three goals to make the final four of the Nations League.

When Lucy Bronze made it 6–0 with the final touch of the game, we were top of the group with just minutes remaining in the Dutch match. We stood on the sidelines and in clusters and huddles, waiting for news. Then it came: the Netherlands had scored a second goal in injury time and won their game 4–0. I was devastated to miss out on the Olympics again.

We will keep coming back stronger.

Since my ACL injury, a lot of people tell me it's like I've never been away. That's nice to hear, but by my own standards,

I still think I'm nowhere near where I want to be. I'm not the player I used to be, but I've accepted that it will take time.

I know how hard I've worked to get back to playing for Arsenal and England. That hard work has to continue. Fans want to see me after matches to interact like we used to, and I want to see them, but I have to go straight down the tunnel to load my tendon. I have tendonitis now from the tendon graft used in my recovery, so at full time I have to go through exercises with 16-kilo dumbbells, flywheels and Nordics. If I don't, I'll struggle to play and train the following week. The next six to twelve months are important for my knee.

For now, I trust the process I've gone through. I've spent so much time in the gym, fine-tuning my knee, that I'm not going to start second-guessing myself now. It will never feel like my normal knee again – it's stiffer and tighter – but this is my new normal. Every day is learning to live with it.

The way I look at it now is that things happen for a reason. I hope I'm stronger for my injury, that I'm a stronger person, a stronger teammate, a stronger partner, a stronger sister, a stronger daughter. I'm a stronger new dog-mum, and I'm enjoying raising my puppy Myle Meadema with Viv. I feel lucky and blessed to have the support I do around me: in the past, maybe I've underestimated just how much I can rely on those people. And most of all, I'm proud of the journey I've been through and that I've come out on the other side.

AFTERWORD

When I was at Sunderland, there was a lot of talk about a girl called Beth Mead.

The talk came from the Sunderland press officer, Louise Wanless. 'There's this young girl in the women's team, and she's amazing,' she'd say, as I walked past her in the canteen each morning.

The talk came from the coaches. 'This Beth – she scores nearly every game. She's so quick.'

The talk came from the analysis staff. 'Look at this,' they'd say, pulling up clips of her goals. *Woah*, I'd think, admiring her pace and finishing as she darted across the screen.

It piqued my curiosity. Who was this girl everyone was talking about? I needed to find this Beth girl, Beth Mead. Who was this Beth Mead?

At that time, we shared the gym and the canteen with the women's team. We used to have breakfast with them, our teams spread over two tables. That's how I began to bond with Beth. I'm a good judge of character and Beth was – still is – a genuine person. She wanted to learn and it was immediately clear she had so much potential. I wanted to see how far she would go.

I've always felt it important to buy in to the culture of the clubs I signed for, and that included being interested in the women's team. As a young player, I'd benefited from the experience and wisdom of players like Ian Wright, Trevor Sinclair and Frank Lampard, and I wanted to give something back and be the person the women's or youth team players could talk to.

Beth and I spent hours in conversation about finishing, movement and goalscoring. I'd tell her that it wasn't just about what she did on the pitch, but the way she lived her life too. I introduced her to green tea and antioxidants. It makes me smile that she remembers how I'd have a green tea with my breakfast every morning and have one waiting for her.

I was delighted when she signed for Arsenal in 2017. She deserved that chance and I knew she would shine. She's confident, but most of all, she's a good person.

I'm not at all surprised that she's gone on to achieve what she has. Her success at the Euros made me so happy. I would message her before matches: 'Good luck! Give me a shout after the game!' so that she knew I was thinking of her. I wanted England to win, but I also wanted my friend Beth to do well. I was so nervous watching some of those games because I wanted so badly for her to win the Golden Boot.

So much pressure comes with playing for England. It's often hard for people to understand how it's so completely different to the pressure that comes with playing for your club. Wembley was packed for the final, but the players still managed to perform under all that expectation. Scoring goals on the world stage is not easy, but Beth was so consistent and clean with her finishing.

From start to finish, the tournament she was part of was amazing. The team spirit on show was unbelievable. I imagine what those players did that summer was probably way beyond any of their wildest dreams. They probably don't even realise now what they've achieved.

I said as much to Beth just a few days ago. When I was growing up, I'd only ever seen boys playing football in the park. I imagine that, over the years, there have been loads of girls who've wanted to join in but felt uncomfortable or reluctant – like football wasn't for them. Now, we will see a huge change. Girls will be in the park playing football with their mates and want to be footballers. I'd love to see the young girls in my family go on to play football. What the England team achieved this summer flew a flag for every single girl in this country to follow. It's only right that we give those girls the opportunities to play.

Seeing packed stadiums and everyone behind the team was a huge step forward. Now, the sky is the limit for women's football. What those England players have done, how hard they've worked and how many big figures in the game are pushing the sport is amazing.

Those players deserve as much as the men. Everything I've got over the years, the girls deserve the same. They're no different. They put in the same work. They train just as hard. The pressure is exactly the same, for club and country. For me, there's no difference. They deserve everything that will come their way, and more.

I visited Arsenal recently as part of my role in the Spurs Academy and I bumped into Beth. That was when she told me about being nominated for the Ballon d'Or, and it was such a nice feeling to know she is taking her game to another level. I've been lucky enough to see her progress from a teenager at Sunderland to becoming a superstar on the world stage – just like I always knew she would.

Jermain Defoe
Former Sunderland and England striker
September 2022

ACKNOWLEDGEMENTS

It has been an honour and a pleasure to be one of the first female footballers to share my story in this way, and not something I've undertaken lightly. I firmly believe that it's important for people to get a wider, more in-depth look into the women's game and the challenges that preceded our Euros success. It's not all sunshine and roses but this summer we came out smelling like them.

Hopefully my story can help inspire the next generation, and I'd like to extend a huge thank you to Katie Whyatt for the hard work and persistence in putting this book together with me. You've been incredible throughout the whole process, going that extra mile. I couldn't think of anyone better to help bring my footballing journey to life.

That journey, of course, is not mine alone, and I would like to thank those who have been on it with me.

To Mum and Dad, thank you so, so much for the commitment and support you've given me over the years. I know I was far from the easiest child, but I wholeheartedly know and understand that I wouldn't be the person I am today, or achieved all I have, without you. I feel lucky and blessed but most of all proud to be your daughter. I love you both so much.

To Ben Bobs, my not-so-little brother. Although you may have felt like you were in the shadows growing up, what you did never went unnoticed. We love to wind each other up – I wouldn't have you any other way – and you make me so proud each and every single day of the amazing man you are growing up to be. Love you, our kid.

To Rona Roo Roo, my baby sister, now favourite child. Without even trying, you bring so much joy and laughter into our family. Not that you'll see this, but never change, my perfect little puppy.

To Viv, mijn meisje. Although we've known each other for over five years, these past six months you've really seen the real me and understood me completely. You always know the right thing to do and say. I thank you for being a great teammate but an even better human and girlfriend. Keep making me better, GOAT. Ik hou van jou.

To Andy Cook, thank you for unselfishly pushing me to be better every single day but also for helping me to develop into the player I am today. I wouldn't be where I am without your contribution to my footballing journey.

To Mick Mulhern, thank you for believing in me beyond all my doubts and the critics. You pushed me from day one and saw the ability in me that I couldn't see myself. Those Sunderland days were a pleasure, mainly down to you.

To Sarina Wiegman, thank you for helping us bring it home! You are one of the best coaches I have had the pleasure of working under. You make things simple, you brought enjoyment back into my game and I will be for ever grateful.

To Jonas Eidevall, my fresh start, my confidence, the fire in my belly. You instilled all of that into me and believed in where my abilities could take me to.

To Mags Byrne, you persisted, you pushed, you believed in me. Our journey together has been interesting, but one I wouldn't change. You are my agent but you are an amazing human and I am proud to call you my friend. You showed me how powerful and unstoppable women can be, and you make me want to be better every day. Thank you for being you.

The First for Players team – Debbie, Liam, Anne-Marie, Luke and Olly – who are always there for me.

My literary agent David Luxton Associates, with a special mention to Nick Walters for his guidance and help throughout.

To Phil Neville, we had a love/hate relationship but I know you always wanted the best for me. You pushed me, you tested me and you always wanted a reaction from me. Thank you for pushing my limits and believing in me as a player. You gave me my first cap for England and for that I'll be for ever grateful.

To Leanne Hall, thank you for always believing in me and persisting when I had homesickness at youth camps for England. I know I do your head in on a daily basis, but you are still one of the most caring and best humans I have ever worked with. You don't get all the plaudits, but you do so much for me and all the girls without expecting anything back. You are one special person. Don't ever change.

To Joe Montemurro, AKA Mr Laidback. That approach suited me just fine. You brought me and my teammates the joy of winning a WSL title. I learnt so much in the time we had together. Thank you.

To Jordan Nobbs, Steph Catley and Jenny Beattie. My sushi crew, the people that have stuck by me through the good and bad. My rocks who kept me afloat in my darkest moments, and girls I can truly call my friends for life. Don't ever change. I love you.

To my teammates, club and country, thank you for creating memories that will last a lifetime.

I would also like to thank all of the medical team that helped me through my recovery.

Finally, I would like to thank Orion and the team for giving me the opportunity to a) write a book and b) open up about my life and my story in a way I never have before. In particular, I'd like to thank Vicky Eribo, Tom Noble and Alex Layt.

IMAGE CREDITS

p. 1   All images: author's personal collection

p. 2   All images: author's personal collection

p. 3   Top three images: author's personal collection; bottom left: Alamy/PA Images; bottom right: Shutterstock/Tgsphoto

p. 4   Top two images and middle left: Getty/David Price/Arsenal FC; middle right: Alamy/Action Foto Sport; bottom left: Alamy/PHC Images; bottom right: DPPI Media

p. 5   Top left: Getty/Nur Photo; top right: Alamy/PA Images; middle left: Alamy Action Foto Sport; middle right: Rachel O'Sullivan/GirlsontheBall; bottom left: Getty/David Price/Arsenal FC; bottom right: Shutterstock/Liam Asman/SPP

p. 6   Top left and top middle: author's personal collection; top right: Shutterstock/Paul Greenwood/Colorsport; middle left: Getty/Laurence Griffiths; middle right: Getty/Charlotte Wilson/Offside; bottom left: Shutterstock/Jon Super/AP; bottom right: Alamy/REUTERS

p. 7   Top: Alamy/SPP Sport Press Photo; middle left: Shutterstock/Anna Gowthorpe; middle right: Getty/Harriet Lander; bottom left: Shutterstock/John Patrick

Fletcher/Action Plus; bottom right: Alamy/Vuk Valcic/ SOPA Images via ZUMA Press Wire

p. 8   Top three images and bottom left: author's personal collection; bottom right: Getty/David Price/Arsenal FC

CREDITS

Beth Mead and Seven Dials would like to thank everyone at Orion who worked on the publication of *Lioness*.

Agent
Nick Walters

Editorial
Vicky Eribo
Tierney Witty

Copy-editor
Clare Wallis

Proofreader
Martin Bryant

Editorial Management
Clarissa Sutherland
Jane Hughes
Charlie Panayiotou
Tamara Morriss
Claire Boyle

Audio
Paul Stark
Jake Alderson
Georgina Cutler

Contracts
Anne Goddard
Ellie Bowker

Design
Nick Shah
Jess Hart
Joanna Ridley
Helen Ewing

Picture Research
Natalie Dawkins

Finance
Nick Gibson
Jasdip Nandra
Sue Baker
Tom Costello

Inventory
Jo Jacobs
Dan Stevens

Marketing
Tom Noble
Yadira Da Trindade

Production
Katie Horrocks

Publicity
Alex Layt

Sales
Jen Wilson
Victoria Laws
Esther Waters
Group Sales teams across
Digital, Field Sales,
International and Non-Trade

Operations
Group Sales Operations team

Rights
Rebecca Folland
Barney Duly
Ruth Blakemore
Flora McMichael
Ayesha Kinley
Marie Henckel